When The Walking Defeats You

PRAISE FOR
WHEN THE WALKING DEFEATS YOU

"Gripping and gleaming with insight. Ledio Cakaj leads the reader into the very heart of one of Africa's least-understood but most enduring rebel movements."

Matthew Green, author of *The Wizard of the Nile*

"A heartbreaking story, unmasking the everyday complexities of a most gruesome and sorrowful war. Absolutely remarkable!"

Sverker Finnström, author of *Living with Bad Surroundings: War, History, and Everyday Moments in Northern Uganda*

"A remarkable first-hand account of life in the LRA, providing a compelling and convincing perspective on what it was like to be a combatant."

Tim Allen, co-editor of *The Lord's Resistance Army: Myth and Reality*

"A gripping portrayal of a rebel fighter's harrowing journey in central Africa. Without pulling punches, Cakaj provides a human face to the notorious but often caricatured Lord's Resistance Army. An insightful tour-de-force by an author whose deep knowledge about this group shines through on almost every page."

Ronald R. Atkinson, author of *The Roots of Ethnicity* and editor of *The Raging Storm: A Reporter's Inside Account of the Northern Uganda War*

"Cakaj skilfully takes the reader inside the harrowing world of the LRA. Interspersed with stunning photography, and reflections of persons who survived LRA attacks, a multi-layered story comes to life, further unfolding the complexities of such a devastating war."

Erin Baines, author of *Buried in the Heart: Women, Complex Victimhood and the War in Northern Uganda*

"Brilliantly weaves the dramatic and often horrifying experience of one man into a gripping story of two decades of the LRA war. A product of vast knowledge of the conflict, *When The Walking Defeats You* is sure to become a classic in the literature on conflict in Africa."

Adam Branch, author of *Displacing Human Rights: War and Intervention in Northern Uganda*

ABOUT THE AUTHOR

Ledio Cakaj is a researcher and writer focused on armed groups, demobilization and reintegration of former combatants, both adults and children. He has worked for close to two decades in the Balkans and Central Africa. Cakaj spent eight years studying the Lord's Resistance Army, initially during a master's degree at Princeton University, and later working as a consultant for the World Bank, the Enough Project, Small Arms Survey and Resolve, among others.

Cakaj is a native Albanian, born in 1978. He left home at 16 years old, as Albania was plagued by violence and struggling to shed its communist past. He walked along with other unaccompanied minors to Greece where he worked odd jobs to survive. After four years without a legal status in Greece, Cakaj managed to migrate to England where he was able to return to school. Several years later, he completed high school and graduated with a degree in ancient and modern history from St. John's College, Oxford University, in 2005.

He now he lives in Washington DC with his wife and three young children.

When The Walking Defeats You

One Man's Journey as
Joseph Kony's Bodyguard

Ledio Cakaj

Foreword by Roméo Dallaire

ZED

Zed Books

LONDON

When the Walking Defeats You was first published in 2016
by Zed Books Ltd, The Foundry, 17 Oval Way, London SE11 5RR, UK.

www.zedbooks.net

Copyright © Ledio Cakaj 2016

The right of Ledio Cakaj to be identified as the author of this
work has been asserted by him in accordance with the
Copyright, Designs and Patents Act, 1988

Typeset in Book Antiqua by seagulls.net
Index by Ledio Cakaj
Cover design by David A. Gee
Cover photo © Hossein Fatemi/Panos

A catalogue record for this book is available from the British Library.

ISBN 978-1-78360-812-6 pb
ISBN 978-1-78360-813-3 hb
ISBN 978-1-78360-816-4 mobi
ISBN 978-1-78360-815-7 epub
ISBN 978-1-78360-814-0 pdf

MIX
Paper from
responsible sources
FSC® C020471

For Alexander, Olivia and Sebastian

Ju dua shumë!

CONTENTS

ACKNOWLEDGMENTS

Sincere thanks go to "George" for his time and willingness to talk to me and answer uncomfortable questions. Testimonies from hundreds of people formerly with the LRA, in Uganda, South Sudan, the Democratic Republic of Congo and the Central African Republic, have been crucial to the writing of this book.

Ron Atkinson, Bernard Harborne, Philip Lancaster, Nicholas Opiyo and Paul Ronan read the manuscript and provided invaluable advice and true friendship. David Burnett read, edited and helped me think through the entire structure of the manuscript. Ken Barlow at Zed Books was enthusiastic and patient throughout the whole time and Joan Dale Lace was immensely helpful in the copy-editing process. Jakob Horstmann was crucial in ensuring a smooth road to publication. Many thanks go to Julie Linchant for the wonderful maps and to Erin Baines and Mareike Schomerus for allowing me to use their photos.

I am also thankful to the following people for having helped in various ways: Angella Atim, Wendy Atkins, Tony Awany, Adonia Ayebare, Gary Bass, Christopher Batu, Graham Burnett, Betty Bigombe, Matthew Brubacher, Jane Bussmann, Sister Giovanna Calabria, Tatiana Carayannis, General Romeo Dallaire, Lisa Dougan,

Frederick Ehrenreich, Sverker Finnström, Tony Gambino, Jon Gandomi, Hesta Groenewald, Gerald Hagan, Laura Heaton, Steve Hege, Jehanne Henry, Colonel Tingira Irumba, Colonel Mike Kabango, Paul Keating, Erik Kennes, Paul Kerengbanga, Michael Kleinman, Father Mark Kumbonyaki, Guillaume Lacaille, Beatrice Lagedo, Pamella Lamunu, Sam Lawino, Jonah Leff, Jason Lewis-Berry, Sasha Lezhnev, Louisa Lombard, Joseph Lwasa, Charlotte Mararv, Erik Mararv, Philip Maughan, Alexis Mbolinani, Tristan McConnell, Genti Miho, Archbishop John Baptist Odama, Moses Odokonyero, Gabriel Oost-huizen, Mike Otim, Bishop Samuel Peni, Wilson Peni, Michael Poffenberger, Sean Poole, John Prendergast, Peter Quaranto, Ben Rawlence, Andrew Rice, Richard Ruati, John Ryle, Michelle Shephard, Jose Carlos Rodriguez Soto, Father Ernest Sugule, David Sullivan, Kristof Titeca, Koen Vlassenroot and Tanya Zayed. Përparim, Selime, Marsjana, Erion, Mirgena and Ethan Raphael Cakaj have been supportive and loving even from afar. I am forever grateful to David Burnett and Claire Gaudiani for being generous with their time and affection, helping take good care of my children, and for raising an amazing daughter of their own.

This book, as many other good things in my life, would have not been possible without Maria Burnett, the smartest and most loving person I know. She, Alexander Zalo Cakaj, Olivia Alison Cakaj and Sebastian David Cakaj are my absolute everything.

ABBREVIATIONS

ADC – *aide de camp* (personal assistant)

AK/AK47 – *Avtomat Kalashnikova* (semi-automatic or fully automatic assault rifle)

BBC – British Broadcasting Corporation

CAR – Central African Republic

DRC – Democratic Republic of Congo

EDF – Equatoria Defense Force

FN FAL – *Fabrique Nationale (de Herstal) Fusil Automatique Léger* (semi-automatic/selective fire assault rifle manufactured in Belgium)

G3 – a selective fire automatic weapon produced initially by German manufacturer Heckler & Koch

GOSS – Government of South Sudan

HAPPO/HPU – High Protection Unit

HSM – Holy Spirit Movement

HSMF – Holy Spirit Mobile Forces

ICC – International Criminal Court

IO – intelligence officer

LRA – Lord's Resistance Army

LRM – Lord's Resistance Movement

M16 – automatic battle rifle, US army standard issue

MONUC – Mission de l'Organisation des Nations Unies en République démocratique du Congo (UN mission in DRC)

NGO – non-governmental organization

NRA – National Resistance Army

OP – outpost

OLT – Operation Lightning Thunder

PK/PKM or PK 7 – *Pulemyot Kalashnikova* (Kalashnikov
   machine gun), a 7.62 mm general purpose machine
   gun

RPG – rocket-propelled grenade, also known as rocket
   launcher

RSM – Regimental Sergeant Major

RV – rendezvous

SAF – Sudanese Armed Forces

SAM 7/SA 7 – a type of Man Portable Air Defense
   System (MANPADS), also known as *Strela* in Russian
   (arrow). A shoulder-mounted surface-to-air missile
   system with an explosive warhead

SPG9 – Russian-made 73 mm recoilless gun, usually
   mounted on a tripod

SPLA – Sudan People's Liberation Army

UN – United Nations

UPDA – Uganda People's Democratic Army

UPDF – Uganda People's Defense Force

WBEG – Western Bahr El Ghazal

WES – Western Equatoria State

GLOSSARY

Unless specified all terms in italics are in Luo.

Acholi – Luo Nilotic population group found primarily in northern Uganda and parts of South Sudan

Advanced or A-Levels – the last two years of secondary school in Uganda

adwii – rebels

aka – coal

aligu/lalweny aligu – rebels, guerrilla, usually as people in northern Uganda referred to LRA fighters

baba – father

boo – green leafy vegetable

coy – small unit or a company of fighters comprised of twelve or more people

Dinka – ethnic group inhabiting parts of South Sudan, used by the LRA to refer to most people from South Sudan, particularly soldiers or armed men

Dwog Paco – Come Home

gamente – a corruption of the English term "government"

gwana – cassava, also known as manioc or yuca

holy (sing.), holies (plural) – used by LRA fighters to refer to themselves

jerrycan, *jerekan* – plastic container used to store liquids. Commonly known in French as *bidon*

jok (sing.), *jogi* (plural) – spirit or god

kado – salt

kadogo – (Swahili) small, used to refer to child soldiers

Kaibiles – Guatemalan Special Operation Forces specializing in jungle warfare

Kandoya (Luganda) – also known as a "three-piece suit," this is a particularly brutal way of immobilizing someone by tying the forearms behind the back just below the elbows

kurut – corruption of the English term "recruit," used by LRA fighters to refer to new (usually young, male) abductees

kwete – alcoholic beverage made from millet or cassava

kwon gwana – doughy bread made from cassava flour, similar to *posho* or *ugali* which is usually made with cornmeal

Ladit – Mr/Sir

lakwena – messenger, the embodiment of the Holy Spirit

lalweny aligu – guerrilla fighter

lapwony – teacher/commander

Lapwony Madit – the Big Teacher/Commander, referring solely to Joseph Kony

luceke – reed straw

lut – sticks

Luo – the language of the Acholi

mina kic – home of honey (referring to a tree with a beehive)

moo ya – shea-nut oil

mzungu/muzungu (Swahili) – usually referring to a foreigner, or a person with fair skin

oddo miyangweny – four hundred lashes

omel – mudfish

omera – brother

ot lum – small circular huts made with mud walls and thatched roof, similar to the Sudanese *tukul*

pala – river flotsam

panda gari (Swahili) – load the truck (the act of arresting people in northern Uganda)

rail – LRA term for walking in single file

rec – fish

shamba – likely a corruption of the word "chamber," meaning a small hut near a garden

standby – an assault or looting team often including women and children

tamam (Arabic or Turkish) – good, ok

ting-ting – prepubescent girls who ran chores in the households of LRA commanders. Many often ended up being "married" to LRA commanders

tongo-tongo – term used primarily in Pazande-speaking areas of the Democratic Republic of Congo, Central African Republic and South Sudan to refer to LRA members. *Oto-tong* (the cutters, the mutilators) used to be a term referring to the LRA fighters in northern Uganda early on in the conflict

wang oo – Acholi tradition of telling stories around the fire at night

wod – son

youngus/yanga – young fighters/child soldiers; also young boys running errands, the male equivalent to *ting-ting*

SELECTED KEY DATES

9 October 1962 – Uganda gains independence from
Britain, Milton Obote becomes Prime Minister.

January 1971 – Idi Amin overthrows Obote.

April 1979 – Tanzanian soldiers and Ugandan dissidents
oust Amin.

December 1980 – Obote wins elections.

July 1985 – Tito Okello Lutwa leads *coup d'état*, ends the
Obote II regime.

December 1985 – Lutwa and Yoweri Museveni sign a
peace deal.

January 1986 –Museveni and the National Resistance
Army storm Kampala.

August 1986 – Some Acholi soldiers form the Uganda's
People Democratic Army.

December 1986 – Alice Auma creates the Holy Spirit
Movement.

May 1987 – Joseph Kony cooperates with some UPDA
units.

October 1987 – Auma's forces are defeated in Jinja.

November/December 1987 – Joseph Kony creates the
Holy Spirit Movement II, later names it the Lord's
Resistance Army.

April 1988 – George is born.

1992-1994 – Betty Bigombe engages in talks with the LRA.

January 1994 – George enrolls in primary school.

February 1994 – Museveni issues ultimatum to Kony, LRA fighters retreat to the bush and eventually to Sudan.

20 April 1995 – An LRA group allegedly led by Vincent Otti carries out the Atiak massacre.

December 1999 – Kony orders the killing of his deputy, Otti Lagony.

January 2001 – George starts secondary school.

March 2002 – Ugandan forces enter Sudan to carry out Operation Iron Fist.

16 October 2002 – Ugandan soldiers from the Fourth Division storm Gulu central prison, "Yumbe" dies.

December 2003 – President Museveni refers the LRA conflict to the International Criminal Court.

February 2004 – An LRA group carries out the Barlonyo massacre.

2004-2005 – The so-called Bigombe II peace initiative takes place.

January 2005 – George starts A-levels.

July and September 2005 – ICC issues arrest warrants for five LRA commanders.

October 2005 – Otti moves to Garamba Park in Congo.

January 2006 – George is expelled from high school.

23 January 2006 – An LRA group clashes with Guatemalan peacekeepers in Garamba.

May 2006 – Riek Machar meets Kony, discusses peace talks between the LRA and the Ugandan government, which open formally in July 2006.

12 August 2006 – Ugandan soldiers kill Raska Lukwiya, an LRA commander indicted by the ICC.

April 2007 – George joins the LRA.

2 October 2007 – Kony orders the killing of Vincent Otti and his loyalists.

2008 – Continuous LRA attacks take place throughout the year in Congolese villages near Garamba Park.

March 2008 – Odhiambo and his fighters abduct people in and around Obo, CAR.

June 2008 – An LRA group attacks SPLA soldiers in Nabanga, South Sudan.

14 December 2008 – Operation Lightning Thunder uproots the entire LRA from Garamba Park.

15 March 2009 – The Ugandan army officially ends Operation Lightning Thunder.

May 2009 – Kony, his large group, and George, enter CAR.

June 2009 – Ugandan army soldiers set up a base in Obo, CAR.

August 2009 – Kony sends envoys to Darfur to make contact with Sudanese Armed Forces.

October/November 2009 – Kony's envoys meet with SAF personnel in Kafia Kingi.

October 2009 – LRA looting of Djemah is stopped by a Ugandan army unit, many LRA members are killed in the aftermath.

November 2009 – Kony's envoys return from Darfur, meeting Kony in Djemah, CAR.

13-20 December 2009 – LRA groups perpetrate attacks in the Congolese villages of Kapili and Makombo, leaving 320 dead.

December 2009 – Bok Abudema is shot dead by Ugandan soldiers near Djemah, the first top LRA commander to die since Kony had Vincent Otti killed in 2007.

March 2010 – George makes it to the Ugandan army base in Obo.

December 2010 – After spending six months in a safe house in Kampala, George returns to Gulu.

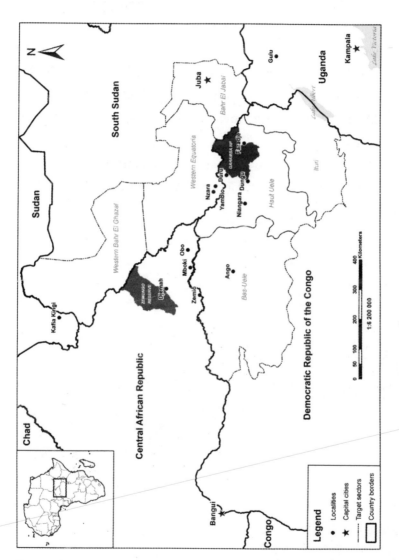

Region of LRA presence 1986–2016

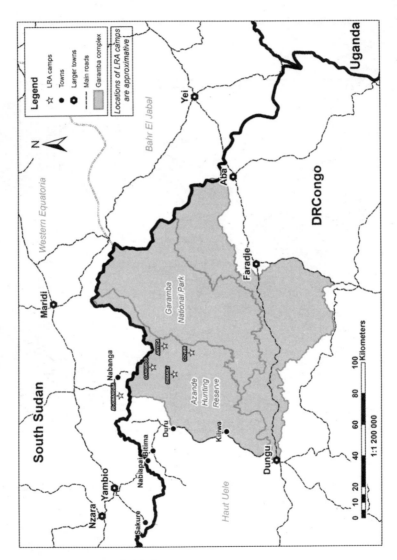

LRA camps in Garamba Park

Region of LRA presence in the early 2010s

Maps prepared by Julie Linchant. Data sources: www.esri.com, www.rgc.cd, African Parks, Google Earth.

FOREWORD

BY ROMÉO DALLAIRE

There are many books about war these days. Sadly, too many of them miss their mark as they try to make either heroes or villains out of ordinary people caught up in extraordinary times or distort the ugly realities of war by turning it into something worthy of a Hollywood blockbuster. This book does not fall into either category. Instead, the author, who knows much about what has happened in one of the most obscure conflicts of our time and has a visceral understanding of what it feels like to be lost and alone, takes us on a long journey into a hidden part of Central Africa. He shows us the inside of one of the most secretive and brutal armed groups in recent history. But not only does he show us, he makes us feel it.

George, the main character in the story, foolishly thinks he can find refuge from a difficult family situation and make a better life for himself by joining the Lord's Resistance Army. Using family contacts, he arranges to volunteer and soon finds himself a personal body-guard to Joseph Kony, the Army's charismatic, ruthless leader. Initially, he is led into thinking that the LRA is serious about trying to get justice for the Acholi people of northern Uganda. As the days and many, many miles pass, George slowly comes to realize that he has become part of something very dark and very ugly. He learns to participate in attacks, to punish captive children who are enslaved or forced to fight and to loot and pillage at every opportunity. He also learns what it means to survive in the unforgiving landscape in which the tale is set. He sees friends die and is reduced to fighting for his small share of food and water. After some time, the fighting loses all meaning and George sets his mind on escape. Unfortunately for him, it is much more difficult to get out of the LRA than it was to get in. He carries disillusionment on his back like a stone until finally he is able to flee.

The story is woven into a careful account of the history of the conflict that began in northern Uganda and there is an extensive discussion of how and why the LRA exists and survives. The author, who has devoted years to this research, often at considerable risk, uses George's tale to open a window through which we can try to understand events that seem incomprehensible. Rarely are we given such an opportunity to see history from the perspective of one of the foot soldiers that helped make it. As the author explains in his introduction, George's story is – aside from a few details altered to protect his identity – true.

I recommend this book for what it tells us about the plight of the many tens of thousands of children who have disappeared into the maws of the Lord's Resistance Army or other savage armed groups that recruit and enslave children. Young adults will enjoy the gritty reality of George's adventures and learn something about the exhausting boredom of military life. I also recommend it to scholars who want to learn something about a phenomenon that gets too little serious attention.

Far too many people have viewed the protection of children and the prevention of the use of child soldiers as something that should be relegated to the confines of child protection agencies. However, this has proven to be ineffective, and I have come to recognize that long-term systemic change is required for meaningful adherence to child protection. The LRA has proven that short-term quick fixes will never suffice as its campaign has outlived many of these ad hoc approaches. What is required is long-term, systemic change – doctrinal change as well as change in training structures, leading to changes in attitudes, behaviors and policy that prevent the "thought of the use of children as soldiers" as an option. The aim should not be to reinvent the wheel, but to fill key gaps that may exist in the holistic approach to preventing the use of child soldiers.

Today, after nearly 30 years of savage bush fighting, despite the rush of interest following Invisible Children's film, *Kony 2012*, Joseph Kony is still in action. An international intervention force jointly led by the United States and the African Union has failed to stop him. The LRA is still capturing children and terrorizing parts of southern Central African Republic, northern Democratic Republic of Congo and South Sudan. I recommend this book as we must continue to strive for new solutions to intractable problems that hit at the very core of the future of humanity.

Roméo Dallaire,
founder of The Roméo Dallaire Child Soldiers Initiative
May 2016

INTRODUCTION

I first met George (not his real name) in 2011, less than a year after he had left the Lord's Resistance Army (LRA) and a few weeks after he had returned home to Gulu in northern Uganda. At that point I had spent about three years talking to defectors and communities affected by the long conflict in Uganda, Central African Republic, Democratic Republic of Congo and South Sudan. My interviews with George continued whenever I visited Gulu until the summer of 2015, just as this manuscript was finalized.

George is one of over 500 former LRA members I have interviewed over the years. Our first talk stuck with me because of his keen intellect. He would often want to debate the works of local and international authors and demonstrated a very careful eye for detail. I also believe there are at least some parallels between his life and mine. Having dropped out of high school at 16 in my native Albania, where I felt hopeless and trapped, I could understand George's hard decision to leave his home in search of a better life.

"We never stopped walking," George said in one of our first meetings. "Walking is the biggest enemy. It can defeat you easier than the bullets." It reminded me immediately of the time I walked for days from Albania to

Greece worrying more about falling into crevasses than the bullets of the Greek border guards. The reference started a long conversation between us, and provided the inspiration for the title of this book.

While both George and I, like countless youth throughout the world who feel trapped in their countries, desired brighter futures, my options were not as stark as his. I did not have to join a rebel group, though guns were as easily available in Albania as they were in Uganda, and criminal enterprise became a focus for many of my class-mates. I rather immigrated illegally to Greece, worked odd jobs to survive, tried to go to school and eventually made it to England where, at long last, I graduated from high school and college many years later. Throughout my unlikely journey I was fortunate to receive help from many people who believed in good things for me even when I wasn't as confident. Sadly, the same wasn't true for George. As he sought to right what he saw as the historical grievances of his people, he chose to join the LRA and found the support of Joseph Kony, the infamous LRA leader known for ordering abductions and killings of thousands.

Kony was quick to recognize George's intelligence, making him one of his closest bodyguards. That allowed George intimate access to the boss and brought many related privileges. It also earned him the hostility of almost everyone else. Unlike George, the majority of the fighters in the LRA had been abducted. They were also often forced to kill early on in their captivity, making them feel full of shame and fear, and discouraging attempts to flee. George had experienced neither and was seen by his fellow fighters as spoiled and naïve. How dare he, a free man, join voluntarily when everyone else had not been afforded that choice?

Despite some unique characteristics, George's story contains many similarities to the accounts of hundreds of other former Ugandan LRA members I have interviewed. George shares with them the same sense of injustices committed against their families by Uganda's leaders. Like others in the LRA, George learned to fight and survive, as well as try to cope with the countless moral dilemmas that survival in the bush with the LRA presented. George readily admits that he found it hard to justify the breathtaking violence, perpetrated both within the LRA and against outsiders. He eventually, like almost all others, accepted violence as a normal aspect of daily life. "It is what soldiers do," he heard Kony say – a line George and other young men often repeated to me. But George was also fully aware than while the beatings and killings allowed the fighters to survive another day, violence was a tool of control for Kony and the other top commanders.

George was hesitant to talk openly with me about the violence he had perpetrated. It was a difficult topic between us, and one that I approached cautiously, aware of the possible danger of re-traumatization while also trying to maintain frank and open lines of communication between us. Over the course of our interviews, and as we grew closer, George opened up about some of the brutality he had experienced, as well as some he had carried out. I believe there is a lot more he has kept to himself, partly because of shame, I imagine, but mostly because of fear. He dreaded being regarded as a bad person, often telling me, "people don't understand what it is like in the bush." He also feared incurring the wrath of former members of the LRA, who "don't want to be reminded of what they had to do in the bush."

George was eager to tell me his story, but at his insistence I have agreed to protect his real identity by altering some identifying features while maintaining the truthfulness of events and locations. At times when I felt George's account lacked important context, I used information from my interviews with other former LRA members. I have also relied on testimony from people living in communities affected by LRA violence, at times providing an account of the event from the view of both the perpetrator and that of the victim. In some cases I have reproduced parts or almost entire interviews I carried out in the last few years. I also interviewed members of the Ugandan army and other regional military officials to corroborate locations of specific attacks and their movements in pursuit of the LRA.

While my intent has been to keep myself out of this account as much as possible, I feel that without historical background and context on the complex conflict between the Ugandan government and the Lord's Resistance Army, George's story would be incomplete and ultimately hard to comprehend. As with the interviews, the historical and contextual information comes from my own desk and field research over many years. In order to distinguish it from George's story, I have used italics for my own commentary, including some interviews with other sources.

My primary reason for writing this book has been to try to better understand this long conflict, and to add to our collective understanding of the complexities of war, particularly where the lines between victim and perpetrator are so deeply blurred. Much as I dislike the term, this is indeed an effort to "humanize" the LRA. It is a response to the caricature version of rebels such as LRA fighters, often described as savages, psychopaths, impossible to understand and engage, or as victims of savages, lost causes too inflexible and too far gone to engage.

George challenges the stereotype of the young fighter. He is compassionate and empathetic in a world where such feelings are often perceived as weaknesses. He exercises agency to survive and succeed or fail and recover to start again anew. He yearns for acceptance, companionship, love and respect but he is also reflective and self-critical, proud and timid, not unlike millions of youth around the world. But for the geographical accident of birth, George could have easily been me, or you.

Ledio Cakaj
Washington DC
December 2015.

PART ONE

HOLDING THE LION'S TAIL

CHAPTER 1

THE BLESSED LAND OF PEACE AND REST: PART ONE

Alone. The thought terrified George. He feared Ochan had been killed. Maybe the soldiers had captured him. George was not sure how it all happened. He remembered Ochan firing from the top of the hill, forcing the soldiers to take cover so that George could escape inside the forest. George wanted to return the favor but the advancing soldiers forced him to run deeper into the woods. He hoped Ochan had made it out alive and would join him at "Position Lunch," the place where they had eaten earlier that day. Night fell but Ochan did not appear. George was now alone and scared in the dark forest.

Throughout his years as a fighter in the Lord's Resistance Army, or the LRA as it was widely known, George had never been alone. "How long will it be," he thought, "before I am killed by the Ugandan soldiers or Congolese hunters or devoured by wild animals?" He tried to calm down and remind himself he knew how to survive the jungle. He was, after all, *lalweny aligu*, a guerrilla fighter, a real warrior, no longer a "lazy town kid," as LRA leader Joseph Kony had once described him. George was now a veteran "holy," as the LRA fighters proudly called themselves.

George sat down and thought about how to find his comrades. Earlier that day he had heard gunshots ringing in the northeast. He figured that the shots must have been fired by Ugandan soldiers attacking Colonel Opiyo Sam's group, his old unit. George determined to head northeast.

He had dropped his backpack when he ran away from the soldiers, only holding on to his gun, an old AK47. In that backpack were roasted cassava and peanuts as well as two blankets he used as bedding. He had to sleep without food, water, or warmth. He was so cold that he had to get up often and walk a few steps to warm his legs.

He managed to sleep for a couple of hours inside a large tree trunk but strange dreams made his sleep uneasy. He dreamed of cartoon animals, dogs and cats, chasing each other in an endless circle. A fast melody played as the cartoon characters ran frantically getting nowhere. He woke up early in the morning feeling embarrassed by his childish dreams. "Definitely not the time for Mickey Mouse," he thought. "Move soldier!" he said out loud, imitating Obwoya, his unit commander from Kony's security detail.

George was adamant about finding his group; no other options crossed his mind. "I am a real guerrilla now," he thought, "a bodyguard for Joseph Kony, one of the most feared men in the world. I don't surrender, I don't give up." He decided to start early in the morning but first he needed to find food. He was so hungry that he feared his body would refuse to obey his brain. He needed to find *kic*, honey, the best energy the forest could offer. Fortunately he had a lighter in the pocket of his trousers which he had never used, saving it for a day like this. He was proud that like a true jungle fighter he still possessed the two most important things needed to survive, his gun and fire.

George, skinny and haggard, moved carefully in the vast open space looking for a particular tree the holies called *mina kic*, "the home of honey." It was a short tree with a hollow trunk where the wild bees liked to build their hives. In lush areas such as the one he was in the bees only made their hives in trees but when the land was barren or the grass burned the bees made their homes in holes in the ground or in anthills. It was easy to get the honey from the ground, as the bees were not fierce. All you needed to do was to dig and the combs full of delicious honey were there for the taking.

But the tree hives were different, not easy to harvest. George prayed to God for assistance, that he find a beehive which had been opened before. He did not know how to extract honey from a new hive although he had often seen others do it, mostly when on a mission to find it for Kony. Honey was the boss's favorite food. It was good for many things, he always said. As food, medicine for coughing and soothing balm. The holies also used honey during ceremonial rites, mixed with ash and used to bless the new LRA arrivals. Honey was truly divine.

Luckily, God was on George's side. An hour into his walk he found what he was looking for, a beehive that had already been broken into months before, perhaps by Congolese hunters or other holies. There was no need to cut through the tree, inviting the bees' wrath. He was relieved and said a quick "thank you" looking up to the heavens.

He took off one of his shirts and tied it around his head, leaving only a small space around his right eye. He grabbed a few handfuls of dry grass and bunched them into small bundles. He lit the bundles, keeping them in front of the hive while gently blowing the smoke into the hive. He had witnessed this method before. "You want the bees to get disoriented like drunkards," he remembered someone saying when collecting honey for Kony. He was not sure how long he was supposed to blow smoke before the bees were lost but with the grass burning quickly and his stomach grumbling, he put his hands inside the beehive and searched around for the viscous honeycombs. The smoke quickly got into his mouth and nose, which made him cough and almost lose his balance. "I am now disoriented," he thought. "I am the one stumbling like a drunk."

Sharp stings prickled his hands but he was undeterred. Yanking out the translucent combs, he quickly threw them on the grass. He continued pulling out the combs until he could no longer stand the pain and fell to the ground screaming. He held his hands under his armpits, moving them only to lick his fingers. He gripped the honeycombs with his mouth – he could not even feel his hands – and ate them voraciously. Sitting on the grass with his hands under his armpits and his mouth full of honey, he thanked God for saving him from hunger and sure death.

Immediately he felt a desperate need for water, both to drink and to soothe his burning hands.

"Never eat honey if you don't know where water is," George had heard Kony saying. Finding water was the next problem that needed solving. He walked slowly, listening attentively for the welcome soft noise little streams and rivers made. It usually heralded the much needed rest stop for LRA groups on the move. He walked into a large forested area filled with the usual sounds: birds chirping to the tune of leaves rustling in the gentle midmorning breeze. Soon he found a small stream and drank for several minutes, carefully washing the sticky honey from his cheeks while licking his hands. He could not afford to waste any of the honey, the only thing he had eaten in the last twenty-four hours. He filled the small canteen he always carried around his neck and felt reinvigorated. "Time to find the fellows of my colors," he said.

He walked through the woods searching for signs of his group – broken twigs, gumboot tracks, discarded clothes and other items the holies used. He had to cut through dense brush using the rusty bayonet affixed on top of the AK. He wished he had held on to his machete but, like his bag, he had lost it when running from the soldiers. He used a stick to part the vegetation. It did not work well, as illustrated by the many cuts and grazes on his face and arms.

Before dark George found a small river; he thought its shore offered a nice place to spend the night. He drank some river water and washed his feet. He thought he should try to catch fish but gave up quickly when he could not figure out how to make a rod or even find bait. "I have never been a fisherman and that is not about to change now," he thought. He was feeling hungry but had no food. He drank a lot of river water to stop himself thinking about eating. He made a bed with leaves and twigs and rested while holding tight to his gun, safely tucked between his legs. "Lions and hyenas would find me a tough enemy if they attempted anything funny," he thought as he fell asleep.

* * *

It was the end of March 2009 when George found himself in the wilderness of a tiny corner of the northeastern Democratic Republic of Congo. The partially forested area was located in the Haut Uélé district, Province Orientale. It had been almost two years since George joined the LRA. He was an experienced fighter and was frequently deployed as a personal bodyguard to Joseph Kony, an honor afforded to few. At the end of March 2009 George was part of a group led by Lieutenant Colonel Opiyo Sam, a fierce commander loyal to Kony. Many such commanders led numerous LRA groups trying to evade the pursuing Ugandan soldiers and helicopters since the middle of December 2008. It was a Ugandan army attack in Congo's Garamba Park on 14 December 2008 that uprooted the holies from Garamba, the place they had called home since the end of 2005.

In the last week of March 2009, alongside his friend Ochan, and a third man they jokingly called Ladit ("Sir"), George formed a blocking unit – a small group of fighters whose job was to slow down or halt the pursuing Ugandan soldiers. A large group of soldiers had been chasing Sam's group for days so he ordered the three men to fall back and attack the soldiers. This well-practiced strategy allowed the main group to escape unharmed but the risk to the blocking unit was considerable. Sure enough, in the aftermath of ambushing the soldiers, Ladit was killed and Ochan went missing.

As George wandered alone in the bush, Kony's group started walking from Congo's Haut Uélé district toward the adjacent Central African Republic, heading north-west with the help of compasses and Global Positioning Systems. In the aftermath of a December 2008 Ugandan army offensive, LRA forces had dispersed, scattering throughout northeastern Congo and in border areas of South Sudan. The Ugandans deployed helicopters that located and bombed LRA groups on the ground, followed by infantry troops conducting sweeping operations. After three months of roving between Congo and the South Sudanese border, Kony decided that most groups would leave Congo and the Ugandan troops behind and relocate to Central African Republic. It meant a journey of about 300 miles, carried out mostly through paths they had to carve out of some of the world's densest forests.

* * *

George woke up in the morning still feeling the bee stings burning his hands. He knew he had to follow the routine of the previous day. Find food, drink water and walk. He had plenty of water but no food. There were no beehives in sight. He started foraging for wild berries and edible leaves. As he walked he found what he thought were the leaves of a particularly large type of yam he recognized from his days in Garamba National Park, where he had spent twenty months before the Ugandan army attack. He unearthed a few pinkish roots. These were indeed *ladidi*, the wild yams all holies credited for keeping them alive in the bush. "Hallelujah," he yelled. He continued to walk but could barely contain his excitement at the thought of the lunch break, when he could roast the yams.

Though alone, he obeyed LRA protocols, setting off early in the morning, stopping for lunch at around 1 or 2 pm and going to sleep around 8 pm, times he had learned to estimate by the position of the sun or the moon. "It is the sign of a disciplined solider to always behave as if his commander is watching," he told himself, unsure whether it was a saying he had heard or made up. "It sounded like something that Kony would say," he thought, smiling as he tried to imitate Kony's slight high-pitched voice. George liked the routine. It gave him purpose during his lonely walk. At lunchtime, he cooked the yams and ate a couple, saving the rest for dinner. "Too bad I don't have any *kado* (salt) to sprinkle on it," he thought. "Next time I will keep a small bag of salt and soap in my pockets right next to my lighter," he decided.

As the days passed, his initial fear of failing to survive gave way to the elation of self-confidence followed by eventual boredom. All the days were the same: the hunt for food and water, the walking, and then sleeping by some river, stream or marsh, hoping to find a sign of his people, any people, only to return to the lonely walking each day.

On the sixth day of walking, George came across what he thought were three distinctive footprints, still fresh in a muddy marshland. He studied them carefully, trying to work out whether they belonged to holies, Ugandan soldiers or Congolese villagers. After some internal deliberation, he determined the footprints belonged to holies and were fresh, made the day before. The group could not have gone far. Excited by his discovery George quickly followed the tracks, which soon joined a larger trail made by a sizable group. He followed it and found bits of dry maize and cassava, sure signs he was on the right path. It was exactly what the holies ate.

He prayed for the strength to catch up with the group. He knew how fast groups moved and had to push himself hard. He kept crossing rivers and streams without stopping for lunch, hoping to see his friends before nightfall, not wanting to spend another night alone. As the sun set he came to an abandoned hut where someone had recently uprooted a few cassava plants. He increased his pace, now almost sprinting. Minutes later he saw two men jump to the side of the path, guns at their sides ready to fire. George crouched into a defensive position, his AK by his side.

The two men must have had a hunch George was no enemy; otherwise they would have shot him. They were probably not sure. The rule was to always confirm the intruder was not an enemy in a holy disguise.

"Who are you?" they shouted in Luo.

"*Omel*," George yelled back, meaning "mudfish."The two men relaxed their stance and asked George to approach. Staying put, George asked them who they were. They both yelled "*rec*," meaning "fish" in Luo. These were passwords that George had learned during his time in the LRA. This particular combination was often used by messengers to pass communications to other groups or by fighters who were lost. In this case the password and counterpassword were simple, both *rec* and *omel* lived in water, therefore they were from the same home.

"If you are fish like me then come out," George said.

They walked slowly towards each other, all three squinting as they tried to make out who the other was. George quickly recognized the two, Patrick and Okello from Opiyo Sam's group, the very people he had been searching for throughout the week. They were quick to embrace him.

"Yankee!" Patrick yelled, referring to George's nickname. "What a lucky man you are! We thought you were shot in battle. How did you survive?"

George gave a short account of what had happened, fully aware he would have to provide a detailed report to Opiyo Sam later. "Well done," they said when he finished. They said they did not know what happened to Ochan but assumed he was captured or killed.

"It was not your fault that you separated," Patrick said. "There were very many soldiers coming for you," he continued, "because later we had a fierce battle with them."

"I heard the shots," said George, "that is why I took this direction until I finally found you."

"God must have been on your side," said Patrick. "But you have also become a truly skilled rebel."

Patrick and Okello, who were rearguards, directed him to where the main group rested. George walked the one mile to the base, making sure his clothes and hair were tidy. He expected to be brought in front of Sam the moment he arrived. Sure enough, the guards immediately brought him to the commander's tent. Sam, a tall, broad-shouldered man with a shaved head and a square jaw, was intimidating. He questioned George thoroughly. George replied carefully, making sure his answers were not contradictory. He knew that commanders were paranoid about Ugandan army infiltration. Also, those who separated and came back were often suspected of attempting to escape. Sam could have George shot if he harbored such suspicions.

When George finished recounting the story, Sam congratulated him for being brave enough to survive the bush alone and for rejoining the group. "You are free," Sam said. "Join your coy" (the small unit of about a dozen fighters). George was relieved. He had been thinking a lot about the moment when he would join his friends and after his lonely week he looked forward to spending the evening talking to people around the fire. He was warmly received by his coy mates and enjoyed their company, although he later had to sleep out in the cold without his blankets.

For the next few days George was told to rest while his comrades brought him food. Despite the group not having much, George ate more in a day – maize, cassava and goat meat the group had looted from a Congolese village – than he had had in the entire eight days he had been alone. After three days back in Sam's camp George thought he had regained all the lost weight. His *coy* mates also contributed all the basic necessities he had lost. One gave him matches, another salt and yet another soap. Two days after his arrival at camp, one of the men tore his blanket in half and gave one half to him. George was happy to have his supplies back and happier still to be warm at night.

Soon after, Kony and his large group appeared. Kony looked skinny and tired. He wore a grey long-sleeve shirt and military-style trousers stuffed inside black gumboots. He was his usual calm self, talking quietly to his guards and playing with his children. George was content to see the boss and his old friends from the security detail, but he felt happier with his new unit in Sam's group and hoped he would remain with them. Kony's plan, as George understood it, was for Commander Dominic Ongwen to gather the remaining commanders in Congo and bring them to Central African Republic where they would join Kony. In CAR everyone would live the same way they had in Garamba, farming and hunting wild animals. There, there would be peace.

On 15 April 2009, Kony gave a long speech. He said the day had come for his government, his preferred way to describe what the rest of the world knows as the Lord's Resistance Army, to move to CAR where they would not be harassed by the army but live a peaceful life instead. "We are not giving up on Uganda," he said, "the day will soon come when we will return home victorious. We need to be patient and have faith in the spirits whose guidance has kept us safe." After prayers, the holies set off for Central African Republic, their new home.

* * *

Kony divided the 800 men, women and children bound for CAR into four groups. Sam's group, which included George, traveled with Kony, often doubling as his security. George was happy to stay in Sam's unit but the walk was as terrible as ever. Perpetually tired, sore, hungry and thirsty, he thought of nothing but rest, food and water. The only distraction from the hunger was the intense ache of his shoulders sagging under the heavy weight of the goods he carried.

He was genuinely worried about staying alive as people around him dropped like flies. It was even worse for Congolese civilians, who were killed each time the fighters came across them during the journey. The usual excuse was that the Congolese could inform the army of the LRA's whereabouts if left alive, but George thought that it really made little difference what the Congolese would do if set free. Everyone in his group was too focused on their own survival to contemplate anything but walking and finding food and water. Killing seemed normal, another act in the struggle to stay alive.

It had been ten days since the group started walking to CAR and for the last forty-eight hours there had been no water in sight. Some women and children fainted from dehydration and beatings by the guards did not revive them. People's faces were dry and painfully wrinkled. Kony finally gave orders for all to stop and sent out water patrols. George was part of one of the patrols and he headed west with a group of twelve armed men and ten abductees carrying empty containers the Acholis call *jerekan*. After a few hours' walk the group heard the welcome sound of a stream nearby.

Approaching the river, George heard what he thought were human voices and motioned to the patrol to stop. Together with the armed fighters he slowly approached the stream, where he saw four Congolese men fishing with long spears and nets. The holies jumped out of the bush and caught the fishermen, who were terrified at the sight of the strange armed men. Without talking, one of the holies made a sign to the ten abductees to kill the fishermen. The abductees, who wielded machetes and sticks, bludgeoned the fishermen to death while George and the rest of the armed fighters drank water. George kept drinking, stopping only to breathe and stare at the bodies of the fishermen that twitched as life left them. The water tasted really good.

George said a quick prayer after the abductees drank and then filled their containers. "Thank you God for allowing us to find this water," he said, as everyone kneeled in prayer next to the battered bodies of the Congolese. After filling the jerrycans, the group quickly returned to the main position where the rest of the people waited. When news of the group's return with water spread, everyone started to run in the direction of the stream; "like bush pigs," George thought.

After people had filled their water containers the group resumed walking. A few days later they came across some large swamps. Walking across the muddy land was tough. People kept getting stuck in the sludge, their gumboots providing little protection. The combination of wetland and mosquitoes made people's feet sore and covered in blisters. Once on the other side of the swamp, Kony ordered a herb to be collected in the forest which his wives mixed with some secret ingredient, making a concoction that the holies were told to smear on their sore feet.

George put some of the mixture on his feet and felt better. He was impressed with Kony's knowledge of plants and remedies. Many believed Kony could even cure AIDS. Kony said that it was Lakwena, the Holy Spirit, who had told him the secrets of the medicinal plants. He also said that Lakwena would periodically instruct him to forbid the consumption of certain foods like cows, pigs, honey or yams. Those who disobeyed such orders and were caught faced the ultimate penalty of 500 strokes of the cane, which meant certain death. No one had survived 500 strokes but at the end of April, during the walk to CAR, one woman came close. As the group approached the border, people had woken up to realize that a woman was missing. Usually night camps were overseen by guards keeping watch to ensure no one escaped. But given the levels of exhaustion, it was no surprise the night guards had fallen asleep or were far from alert. Many thought the woman was probably hiding nearby, too tired to walk, waiting for the group to leave. Every escape attempt was treated seriously, particularly if it occurred in Kony's group, as he regarded defections as personal affronts. A number of armed men combed the area around the camp. Kony had already started walking early that morning – he never waited for anybody – and the other commanders called off the search soon after, wanting to catch up with the General. Kony set a terrifying pace when marching and was nearly impossible to catch once he had gone too far ahead.

As the fighters returned, a young girl screamed from inside the forest. It was another abductee who had gone to urinate when she felt someone grabbing her from behind the bush where she had squatted. The missing woman tried to make her stop yelling, begging her not to tell, but the terrified girl had already given her up. Fighters ran toward the two and dragged the woman in front of Otto Agweng, the chief security officer. What he lacked in physical stature, Agweng made up in brute force. With the exception of a few senior commanders, everyone feared Agweng and his penchant for ordering terrible beatings for the smallest of infractions.

Agweng questioned her for a while. She answered in broken Luo that she had wanted to escape as she was too tired to continue walking and feared she would die of exhaustion. She shook and asked for mercy, promising that she would never again try to leave. Her body was swollen from beatings by the men who first caught her and her hair and clothes were dusty from being dragged by her feet in front of Agweng. He said he would not kill her because she was just a stupid woman and ordered she be beaten. Four hundred strokes on her back, bottom and thighs. If she were to make a sound she would be shot. A fighter holding a loaded gun stood over her as two others beat her with sticks.

George witnessed how she absorbed the beating without crying or touching her back, a violent spectacle the likes of which he had rarely witnessed before. He did not know whether it was the level of brutality or her ability to withstand it without making a sound that made such an impression, but he was uncomfortable and angry. "It is one thing to make a mistake and pay for it," he thought, "but these experiences scar the heart and soul as well as the body."

After the 400 lashes were administered the woman could not lift herself off the ground. George helped her stand and walked her to the stream. She crawled into the water and washed herself. A few minutes later she walked slowly to the place she had spent the night, gathered her belongings and loaded up everything on her head. She walked at the back of the group, often falling to the ground but always getting up to continue walking. George was certain she would die from her wounds but she did not. Later that day she managed to keep pace with the group, walking in complete silence. Her resolve impressed the holies, who spoke about it for days. Ever since, the place where she was beaten was known to all as *oddo miyangweny*, the Luo term for 400 lashes.

* * *

The only thing that gave George a little joy during the seemingly endless march to CAR was Aimee. She was a young Congolese girl who worked as a *ting-ting*, a servant to Kony's family. She took care of Kony's children and cleaned and helped his wives cook. Aimee was the most beautiful girl George had ever seen. She was a Congolese Zande but spoke English well after a long spell as a refugee in South Sudan. She was probably fourteen years old but behaved like a mature woman, George thought. Her skin was dark brown and her eyes were large and beautiful. She kept her hair in many small little bunches, in the Congolese fashion that George thought suited her well.

He was happy to see her every day and try to talk to her once in a while. Everyone who saw Aimee admired her and George felt happy she always talked to him whenever he approached her. He knew that if he performed well, obeyed orders and fought hard, he could receive many rewards, particularly a wife and perhaps some young boys and girls to carry out chores. He dreamed that one day Kony would appreciate his deeds, maybe promote him to an officer rank and allow him to have Aimee as his wife. He was sure Aimee would be happy with that choice as well.

During the third week of the march to CAR, George heard rumors that Aimee was to become yet another wife to Kony. A deep sadness overcame him and he felt a burning desire to talk to Aimee. She must have heard the news too as she seemed distracted and was unusually silent. When he found a moment to talk to her, she said she did not want to be Kony's wife. "He had so many other wives already, why take another one?" She said she might reconsider if Kony was willing to leave all his other wives and only marry her. "One man and one woman, just like the pastor in my church said was proper in God's eyes." George remained silent, knowing all hope was lost.

Kony quickly found out about Aimee's opposition to his plans. George was certain that it was Kony who ordered his bodyguards to load Aimee with heavy luggage and to make her carry Lakot, Kony's three-year-old daughter. George witnessed how Aimee struggled to walk, falling often to the ground and barely making it to the rest stops. She was obviously exhausted and had no time to sleep or wash herself as the guards tormented her by sending her to fetch water early in the morning and collect firewood and clean late into the night. Her skirt became muddied and ripped exposing her skeletal, reeking body.

He did not laugh when his comrades made jokes about how flies buzzed around her because of her stinking body, and almost started a fight when they called her a moving latrine. But he was most of all angry with himself for not being able to rescue her. Aimee had stopped looking at him, let alone talking. She became skinny and frail. George fretted at nights that she would be dead by morning.

After a few days the bodyguards ceased ordering her around and Aimee was left with only Lakot to carry. Kony sent her two new dresses, probably looted from a Congolese or South Sudanese village. He knew her spirit was broken. It was no longer a secret; Kony had come to her rescue, ordering his guards to leave her alone. His wives brought her food and after two days Aimee began to look better. She had understood the message and every night when the group stopped for dinner Aimee sat near Kony's tent, smiling whenever he looked at her.

One evening George was on guard duty in Kony's yard. Alongside other bodyguards George set about preparing Kony's place of rest for the night. They warmed water over an open fire and filled an aluminum bathtub that abductees carried during the day, and dug a pit latrine – a hole in the dirt surrounded by a few tree branches – near Kony's tent. George waited for orders from Kony's ADC to bring a wife to spend the night with the boss.

He clenched his fists when the ADC asked him to fetch Aimee. Like all of his wives, Aimee was supposed to go to Kony's tent, prepare his bed and wait for him to come out of his bath. The two would be served dinner and left alone for the night. George went to where she stayed and asked her in a somber tone to follow him. She quickly understood and took a few minutes to wash herself. She paid no attention to him as she washed, exposing her body with little care. He tried to avoid staring at her, aware that she was now forever lost to him. George knew well that Kony did not take kindly to those stealing his "property."

He escorted Aimee to Kony's tent and left without saying a word. That night, her "wedding night," George did not sleep. He could not help thinking what she did minute by minute inside Kony's tent. What meal did he serve her? How did she react when he embraced her? He hoped that maybe she was unhappy, that maybe she hated every moment of being with the Big Teacher. He felt the tears coming down his cheeks and felt ashamed. "I am a soldier," he whispered to himself.

Early the following morning, when George started to pack the tent and Kony's possessions before the day's march, he saw Aimee, who seemed well rested. It was no wonder since she had slept on a mattress that night, not on the cold, hard dirt. She looked different, "shy but smiley," he thought. The other bodyguards also noticed. "*Ladit* made her happy," they joked. The team packed Kony's tent and started the day's journey. George tried his best to avoid staring at her throughout the day.

That evening George set up Kony's compound for the night. After orders were given to bring a wife to the tent two guards found that Aimee had already entered the tent to prepare Kony's bed. According to LRA rules it was a grave security breach for anyone to enter Kony's tent without permission and the guards immediately grabbed

her. They were about to bring her in front of Agweng
when Kony came out of his bath and asked what was
happening. When the guards told him, he laughed loudly.
"These Zande girls like us Acholi men too much," he said
and ordered her release.

So it was that without permission, Aimee spent a
second consecutive night with the Big Teacher. It was
rare for any woman to spend two consecutive nights with
Kony – throughout his time in the LRA, George had never
before witnessed such an event. Most wives who spent
a first night in Kony's tent were asked to join him again
only after weeks or even months passed. Some wives only
spent one night with him, never coming back to his tent
again. No one knew exactly how many wives Kony had;
some said forty, others said a hundred. George knew at
least seventeen. All the women Kony slept with, whether
once or many times, were considered part of his family
and were given preferential treatment – food, clothes and
other looted goods went first to them. They were also not
allowed to talk or interact with the other men. Aimee, as
Kony's wife, was gone, forever out of George's reach. He
knew he had no choice but to accept the reality. He hoped
there would be other women out there for him, just like
Aimee. All George needed to do was survive.

* * *

After almost a month of brutal hiking, the group finally
made it to CAR. George was happy and relieved. Like
everyone else, he hoped that the long marches accompa-

nied by helicopter gunship attacks would now end and that this was where Kony had promised there would be blessed peace and rest.

As they continued to walk deeper into the forest, the group came across a magnificent river that some Central African abductees said was called Mbomou. Everyone stopped to wash and fill their containers with the crisp, clean water of Mbomou. Many said prayers in the true LRA fashion, regarding rivers and other bodies of water as divine. The group slowly crossed the river by throwing a rope across a shallow area. They were now inside CAR. People sang religious hymns.

George thought CAR was beautiful. Wild animals grazed on the low plains. Small hills with flat tops dotted lush green areas. It reminded him of his home in northern Uganda, so green and fertile. Kony had figured out they were inside CAR by reading his GPS and gave an impromptu speech, announcing, "Here we will have respite from the endless attacks and harassment from the soldiers." Everyone clapped. People were happy and hopeful they could rest after the tiring journey. At night everyone stayed up late chatting happily around campfires.

Early in the morning the group walked deeper into CAR. Kony ordered that no killing, looting or other hostilities be directed at the local population. "We do not want to scare the people of Central Africa," he said. "We need to show them that we mean them no harm." "Ask for food nicely," he said before ordering a group to bring food from nearby villages. George was part of that group. The armed men did not kill and tried to do what Kony ordered but it was hard to ask for food nicely. The terrified villagers ran away. Those caught unaware in their huts nodded when asked if they would be willing to part with their food. "It is hard to argue with a man with a gun," thought George, "whether or not he says please."

They took as much food they could carry. They uprooted cassava and grabbed rice, peanuts, cooking oil, matches and soap as well as chickens and goats. On the way back to camp George saw that the guards had already caught a few fishermen and farmers who were taken to Agweng. On Kony's orders Agweng explained to them, as an abductee translated, that the holies were good people. "We are travelers on our way to a distant destination. Do not be afraid, we won't harm you," he said. "We are not people who kill others for no reason, but if anyone disturbs us, we shall retaliate fiercely. Pass this message to your government leaders," Agweng told the terrified villagers, who shook as they were escorted out of the camp.

After the rest of the 800 people traveling from Congo made it to the camp northeast of Obo, Kony called a large gathering. He asked them all to bare their chests and the fighters to remove the bullets from their guns, as signs of respect for the spirits. Everyone broke a branch of the tree the Acholis call *olwedo*, traditionally used in Acholi culture to bless warriors. They sat on the branches as Kony conducted prayers. When he finished, Kony asked people to join him in singing the verses so dear to him.

Pe tye gin maloyo Rubanga,
Lweny bene walwenyo I nyinge, hallelujah.
(There is nothing that defeats God,
Even this war, we fight in his name, hallelujah.)

After he signaled for the singing to stop, Kony spoke again. "The future of my government is bright," he said referring to the LRA, which he often called *gamente*, a corruption of the English term. "The spirits are on our side," he continued, promising a peaceful stay in CAR. He sprinkled water on all the assembled as a way of blessing them. "You are now cleansed of your sins," he said. He then smeared them with "camouflage," a mixture of *moo ya* (shea-nut oil) and ash. "You are the blessed ones who will inherit the peace of Central Africa," Kony said, smiling.

CHAPTER 2

THE SAVIOR OF ACHOLILAND

George Omona, the only son of Mary and Julius, was born on 23 April 1988 in western Acholiland, northern Uganda. He was named after his paternal grandfather, George Bongomin Abonga, a revered man, known for mediating conflicts throughout the north. "The old man's spirit was strong," a learned relative said, "and needed a new strong body to house it." George Omona was destined for great things.

George lived with his uncle, Quinto, his father's younger brother, a quiet and unassuming man. George's own father, Julius, had disappeared on Christmas Eve 1987. He was presumed dead, probably at the hands of National Resistance Army (NRA) soldiers or Karamojong cattle raiders from east of Acholiland, on the Kenyan border. Julius had a large herd of cattle. "He was probably killed by the cattle raiders," Mary told George when he was six and she thought he was old enough to understand.

Soon after George was born most of the family cattle had been stolen or slaughtered, and Quinto moved the entire family to Gulu, the largest town in northern

Uganda. He sold the cattle that had survived the raids and built a small house on the outskirts of Gulu, near the giant Pece stadium that the British had built in the 1950s in remembrance of World War II veterans. "It is the largest stadium in the country," Quinto would often say with pride. He opened a small store selling food and other goods he bought in the capital, Kampala, and brought to Gulu on the bus. Business was good enough to sustain his wife and two children as well as Mary and George, who lived in the same house.

Mary decided not to remarry after her husband's disappearance, and refused to become a mistress to rich men in town who could provide for her and her baby. She grew skinnier and sadder with the years, her eyes seemingly always moist. Quinto promised to take care of her and she agreed that it was better for George to stay in Gulu than to return to her poor family in a small village in a faraway corner of Acholiland. At least George could grow up and go to school in a town, away from the mud and hard toil of rural life.

Mary said little around others but told George everything. She held tight to her only child and, by her own admission, spoiled him. George ate candy before meals and had his mother's undivided attention. But he also learned to read and write in English as young as four years old. Mary had only managed to complete second grade at elementary school before her parents needed help working the land and taking care of her younger brothers and sisters. She took it upon herself to learn to read and write in English, which she did every night alongside George. They read children's books to one another and she sang him lullabies in Luo, the Acholi language, and English.

* * *

The late 1980s were difficult times in Uganda, and Acholiland in particular. Yoweri Museveni had stormed Kampala in January 1986 at the head of the NRA, his guerrilla force. In early 1988, Acholiland was considered a war zone, cut off from the rest of the country.

Museveni's rebels overthrew the interim government of Tito Okello Lutwa, an Acholi general. Lutwa had himself taken power in Kampala in July 1985 from Milton Obote. Born about sixty miles south of Gulu, Obote hailed from the Lango ethnic group. The Langi have a distinct history and many different cultural practices from the Acholi, but speak a similar version of Luo, the main language of the Acholi.

It was the second time Obote, postcolonial Uganda's first head of state, had become President. Idi Amin, the army commander from northwestern Uganda, ended Obote's first stint in power, from October 1962 to January 1971. One of Amin's first orders was to purge the army of Acholi and Lango soldiers perceived to be loyal to Obote. In February 1971 alone, hundreds of Lango and Acholi soldiers were killed, some bayonetted, shot or even dynamited and burned to death. Amin was also responsible for perpetrating atrocities against the Ugandan population at large, including many from West Nile, his birthplace, home to Lugbara, Alur, Madi and his own ethnic group, the Kakwa. After an ill-conceived attack on Tanzania in November 1978, a combination of Tanzanian soldiers and a collection of dissident Ugandan forces invaded Uganda, reaching Kampala hours after Amin fled to Libya in April 1979.

After Amin, a series of short-lived caretaker governments were formed prior to general elections scheduled for December 1980. As one of the leaders of the dissident groups that helped overthrow Amin, Museveni briefly held the post of Minister of Defense during this transition, but he returned to armed struggle after Obote won the December elections amidst violence and accusations of vote rigging. Discontent over the widely perceived fraudulent elections, combined with memories of the brutal manner in which Obote had ruled towards the end of his first stint in power, undermined the Obote II regime from the start. Rebel groups such as Museveni's NRA resisted Obote's new government, seeking regime change by waging a brutal bush war mostly centered in south-central Uganda.

As the bush war dragged on, there was discontent in the army as Acholi officers felt that Acholi soldiers bore the brunt of fighting while Obote promoted mainly from his own Lango ethnic group. Acholi generals Tito Okello Lutwa and Bazilio Olara Okello staged a coup in July 1985, ousting Obote, who fled to Zambia. The generals immediately entered peace negotiations with all rebel groups in the country. This included Museveni's NRA, beginning in August of that year in Nairobi, overseen by Kenyan President Daniel Arap Moi.

On 25 December 1985 Lutwa and Museveni signed final peace accords, which called, among many things, for the absorption of the NRA into the Ugandan national army and the inclusion of NRA leaders in the Ugandan government. Museveni participated in the talks and signed the final accords, while at the same time using the months during negotiations to reorganize his forces and prepare for a final assault on Kampala. The assault ended with an NRA victory and installation of Museveni as President on 26 January 1986. Museveni's duplicity was something many in the north would remember for a long time.

One man that never forgot was Joseph Kony, who in 1986 was in his early twenties. Kony often brought up the "Nairobi Peace Jokes" during various peace talks with the Ugandan government that eventually always failed. "The Munyankole cannot be trusted," Kony would say, referring to President Museveni's area of origin, Ankole, in western Uganda. Kony was also quick to take a page from his opponent's rulebook; on more than one occasion he used peace talks to reorganize and reinforce his troops, as Museveni had done during the Nairobi peace process.

The arrival of the NRA fighters in Acholiland a few months after they had stormed Kampala created fear and eventually hatred in the north, a mix that fueled various rebellions. As many of General Lutwa's soldiers retreated north, leaving Kampala to Museveni and his troops, there were concerns in Acholiland that the NRA would retaliate against the northern soldiers and civilians for a perceived domination of northerners over the country since Obote took over from the British in 1962. But as NRA troops entered Acholiland in March and April of 1986, the region was largely peaceful; many former soldiers had moved to Sudan with their commanders while a large number of troops had simply returned home and buried their weapons.

In April 1986, the new authorities in Gulu issued disarmament orders for all, and for the former soldiers to return to

Mbuya barracks in Kampala. Similar orders had been issued in 1971 and 1972 by Amin and had then led to mass executions of Acholi and Lango soldiers – historical lessons never forgotten in Acholiland and used as a reason to ignore the NRA edicts. In response, the NRA commenced a disarmament campaign associated with many instances of reported violence, usually involving looting, and harming or killing of civilians. Some said Acholi thugs were responsible for the violence while others blamed the NRA, particularly the hundreds of child soldiers in the first NRA units to enter Acholiland. Museveni himself blamed the violence, increasing as time went on, on undisciplined individuals.

By August 1986 a few thousand soldiers of the former regime re-entered Uganda from Sudan and a rebellion started to materialize, in part as a response to the NRA abuse of civilians. The soldiers called themselves the Uganda People's Democratic Army and claimed to fight for the rights of the Acholi. The UPDA split into groups and scattered in rural areas, a tactic that the LRA would later use to great success. But the new guerrilla-style fighting put the local population at greater risk of NRA retaliatory attacks. Indeed, NRA orders after August 1986 seemed to convey the message that local civilians were potential rebel collaborators. Tactics used to allegedly flush out the rebels and deny them local support included the mass rounding up of civilians in army trucks – the hated panda gari, *the term for "load the truck" – after which many were imprisoned, beaten or simply disappeared.*

In early 1987 the UPDA's modus operandi of operating in small groups without a strong central figure – unlike the LRA

*of later days when Kony was always its undisputed leader –
led to fragmentation and indiscipline. The UPDA could not
protect civilians from the NRA or even from UPDA splinter
groups that looted and harassed the locals. A new movement
called the Holy Spirit Movement formed in direct response to
the chaos and violence engulfing Acholiland. Formed in late
1986, the HSM was the brainchild of Alice Auma, a fishmonger
and traditional healer from Opit, a small village east of Gulu.
Emerging from a traditional patriarchal society, Alice's role at
the time was nothing short of revolutionary.*

*She claimed to have been possessed by many spirits, or jogi
in Luo. Chief among the spirits was a Christian holy spirit that
Alice identified as Lakwena, meaning "messenger." Alice came
to be known as Alice Lakwena after that spirit. Lakwena, or the
Holy Spirit, was the inspiration for Alice's insurgency, its name
and mission as well as its divine legitimacy. Many of Alice's
innovations and practices in the HSM continue to be used today,
with some alterations, by Kony in the LRA. It is no coincidence,
for instance, that the LRA fighters refer to themselves as holies,
a term first used as a self-identifier by Alice's followers.*

*Alice's message was initially one of healing, cleansing and
peace, which later transformed into a struggle against evil.
She created the Holy Spirit Mobile Forces to combat the NRA,
witches and other impurities created by the Devil. In a rare
interview with the media in October 1987, Alice told reporters
that the HSM fought to depose Museveni and unite all
Ugandan people. After initial successes against NRA fighters
in early 1987, Alice's reputation grew and her troops swelled to
about 10,000. The HSFM pushed the NRA south and started a*

long march toward Kampala, gathering popular support among most northern groups. At the end of October 1987, the HSM was defeated by combined NRA and local defense units in Jinja, about fifty miles east of Kampala. Alice fled to Kenya, where she died in a refugee camp twenty years later, in 2007.

Some surviving HSM members returned to northern Uganda, where Joseph Kony was making a name for himself as possessing spiritual powers on a par with Alice before the Holy Spirit abandoned her in Jinja. Aptly, Kony claimed to have been possessed by Lakwena and initially he called his movement the Holy Spirit Movement II. The HSMII later became the Lord's Salvation Army and by the early 1990s was known as the Lord's Resistance Army.

* * *

In 1991, soon after George turned four, Mary stopped receiving financial support from Quinto, who had taken on a second wife by then. To earn a living for herself and George, she sold *maka*, coal, in the central market every day, leaving early in the morning and returning after dark. She did not want to leave George all by himself and worried that he needed to continue learning so she enrolled him in kindergarten. It was two and a half miles away from home, and George walked for more than an hour to his kindergarten and an hour back. Sometimes a neighbor would walk with him but often he walked alone.

Other children took his food and called him a mummy's boy. Often he cried along with his mother, he due to the taunting and she from back pain after carrying heavy sacks of coal. She told him to be brave and continue with his schooling but did not tell him that Quinto's wives refused to take care of him during the day, and that the distant kindergarten was all she could afford. She had to pay for their food, his clothes and books – Quinto gave her nothing apart from letting them live rent-free in one of the rooms of the house. George often went crying to Quinto, complaining about the kindergarten, and Quinto promised he would take George to a good primary school and cover all expenses when he came of age.

Before George turned six, Quinto kept his promise and took him to the primary school in Gulu that everyone said was one of the best in the country. It was not close to home but George did not mind as long as he did not have to go to kindergarten. The rules of admission were tough, including tests in math and writing skills. When Quinto and George turned up for the admission interview just before Christmas in 1993, two school administrators said George was too young and could not take the tests. He needed to be six and his birthday was not for another four and a half months.

George cried so loudly in front of the administrators that they agreed to let him take the tests, thinking he would probably fail anyway. He completed the tests with tears in his eyes and trembling hands. He feared he would not do well and would have to keep going to the terrible kindergarten where his tormentors waited to take his food and pocket money. When the results came back a week later, George had scored in the top ten percent of the incoming class. Quinto was excited and promised to pay all his school fees. All George needed to do was study hard and be the best in his class.

"Someone from this family will go to university," Quinto said. He failed to mention that it was a boarding school until after George had already been admitted. George wept bitter tears thinking about being away from his mother. Mary was upset but repeated what Quinto said about George attending university. She urged him to be strong and go to the boarding school. "I would never be able to pay for as good a school," she said.

* * *

"My name is not really Yusuf," said the old man sitting under a large mango tree outside of his compound, in the outskirts of Gulu. It was a warm, sunny day in July 2011 and the man used his hand to shield his eyes from the bright sunlight. His white beard framed a big smile that made him resemble an elderly Nelson Mandela. "Yusuf is a Muslim name but I am not a Muslim. There are no Muslims in Acholiland because of all the fighting with the Arabs, who were not allowed to come down here. We are all Christians here.

The name Yusuf was given to me as a nickname by a friend, when "the Amins" were in power. The nickname was a way to avoid being killed by Amin's people, who were after me in 1974. Yusuf was the name of a prominent Amin soldier, his chief of staff or someone important, I can't remember. My friend thought that if I went by the name Yusuf, Amin's goons would not kill me, maybe confuse them into thinking I was a Muslim also.

After Amin chased away all the Asians who owned businesses in Uganda, I secured distribution rights from Nile Breweries for soft drinks for all of northern Uganda. It was in 1972, right after the Indian owners left. I had another business in textiles, also taken over from an Indian who left Gulu in 1972. Just like the soda business, I bought the textiles from the headquarters in Mbarara [western Uganda] and I was the only authorized agent to sell in Gulu and most of northern Uganda. But Amin's people did not want an Acholi man to own those kinds of businesses. They wanted their own people to be in charge.

By 1976, my businesses were taken from me, by people from West Nile who were connected to Amin, who was of course a Kakwa. The man who took the sodas, a Lugbara, hanged himself in 1979 when the Tanzanian army came to Uganda and Amin fled to Saudi Arabia. That man was connected to the regime and knew he would be in trouble with the new people who came in, so he killed himself. The man who took my textile deal, an Alur, stepped on a mine, so they both lost my businesses, ruined two really good deals. Too bad.

I returned to farming and taking care of my cows. I was spared after I willingly gave them my businesses. Maybe the name helped, who knows? But I saved enough money during four years to buy some cows and then worked hard to grow my herd. I had 285 cows in 1986 when Museveni took Kampala. His people came here and started taking our cattle. They took almost all of mine, slaughtered them all. I could not do a thing about it. Those people took all my cows and beat me up really badly. They were worse than Amin.

I had little left but I had a lot of anger and pain. Why did these people come to steal from us and kill us like that? We were not soldiers, we were civilians, Ugandans like everyone else. Museveni spoke of liberation but his NRA men came and killed us, like they were invading our country, not liberating it. We were not the enemy. They said, "you northerners have been killing us for many years, now it is our time to kill you." But we, the Acholi, did not kill them, we were ourselves treated badly by Amin. It was about greed in the end, like always. Everyone wanted to eat as much as possible, to get fat, it did not matter where you were born or what your name was.

There were many people like me who had nothing left and were angry. We organized ourselves. Some went with Alice Lakwena, some with former Okello soldiers, the UPDA. There was a group of former Okello soldiers; it was called the Black Battalion. They were part of the UPDA. They tried to fight the NRA whenever they could. They would attack barracks and then retreat to the bush or go across the border to Sudan.

I tried to help the Black Battalion and spoke to their commanders often. I met this young man in May 1987, Joseph Kony. He was very young and looked scared, fearful of the war. He said he was a spiritual man. He channeled spirits just like Alice. But he had tried to join Alice's Holy Spirit Movement and was rejected by her. "Because Alice is afraid of my powers," he told me.

Kony was not at all familiar with guns; he actually hated guns. He did not pick up guns, did not know what to do with them. Some of the old Okello soldiers made fun of him at first when he came to the Black Battalion. But Kony said he would help them win against the NRA using the spirits. All he needed was one jerrycan of paraffin, one jerrycan of diesel and pala. *Pala is the river flotsam that gathers on the river shores and sits on top of the water. People use it to varnish their mud pots.*

Kony also asked for white sheets to make robes, one rosary, one prayer book used by the Catholics and one prayer book used by the Protestants. But everything had to be new, not used. Kony specifically told me he needed all these things to be new for his powers to work. He also needed a new pot and a ring to hold the pot on top of the fire. I bought all these things and gave them to a friend who took them to Kony in the village where he hid together with most of the Black Battalion, about 200 people altogether. Kony was serious about what he said and seemed to know exactly what he was doing. The old soldiers started to believe in him and I thought it would not hurt to have his powers on our side. The NRA men were really well armed and numerous, we needed all the help we could get.

Soon after Kony received all the items he sent word to me that he wanted to test his powers so he chose forty members from the Black Battalion to attack the NRA garrison in Gulu, right next to where the UPDF barracks are now, in Kasubi. Kony said he wanted some clan elders to see him and give him their blessings. He assigned a meeting place and promised the elders they would not be attacked. He said the spirits would guarantee the elders' safe passage. The elders went to meet with him and they prayed together for many hours. They gave Kony their blessings and he decided to start a full-scale war with the NRA.

Kony later told me it was very important for him to get the elders' blessings, as it was a sign that the spirits were right in telling him to start a war. Usually in our culture the spirits are not violent, so Kony needed the elders' blessings to confirm that the spirits were right. Kony did not take the war lightly; he understood it was a serious affair.

I went to the top of a nearby hill to see the attack that Kony predicted was going to last thirty minutes. It was a Sunday and the forty men Kony chose attacked the NRA while Kony stayed away and prayed. The attack started at 6.30 am and ended exactly at 7 am. And as he had predicted too, only one UPDA soldier was injured. But many NRA soldiers were killed. When I went to meet the men afterwards outside Gulu, they were excited. "This really works," they said, and many were very happy with Kony. So the Black Battalion leader, a man called Okeno, decided to keep Kony with him. "To progress the attack," Okeno said.

Some UPDA leaders were jealous of Kony, particularly after Alice Lakwena was defeated and some of her followers wanted to join him. Some UPDA leaders did not want civilians. They said the UPDA was for soldiers only. I urged them to keep Kony and not ignore what he said. But Salza Lai, a political officer in the UPDA, did not like Kony. He said Kony was trouble and that the UPDA was an army, not a religious cult. When Odong Latek, an important officer under General Tito Okello, returned from Sudan and joined Okeno, Kony was ignored. They did not involve him, so Kony started to act independently.

Many of Alice's followers joined Kony. They were farmers and cattle herders like me, who had lost property or their families had been raped or killed by the NRA. The UPDA did not accept them so they joined Kony. Kony had spiritual powers, which people liked. They felt it was extra protection, which they needed since many did not have military training. Even some UPDA soldiers joined Kony after they heard about the attack on the NRA barracks. So the UPDA commanders decided to arrest him. He was splitting up the resistance and they did not want another problem like Alice, who led many people to their deaths in Jinja.

But the UPDA could not catch Kony. Soldiers sent to kill him reported that the bullets would not reach him. Kony was so bold and well protected by the spirits that he walked into the UPDA barracks, the same barracks the NRA held briefly right here in Kasubi, the same ones he helped the Black Battalion to attack, and freed this man, Lukoromoi, whom the UPDA had arrested. Lukoromoi told the UPDA he was also possessed by the spirits and wanted to pray for them to win, but the UPDA arrested him and put him in prison inside the barracks. Kony walked in and released him. He prayed together with Kony and they became good friends.

The UPDA and Kony started to fight one another; it was not good. They fought here but also in Sudan. Kony first learned about Sudan and its government during that time. But in 1988 the UPDA came out of the bush and surrendered to the NRA. They called it "a negotiation" but it was not. UPDA commanders took money from Museveni and abandoned the struggle, abandoned the Acholi people who suffered so much at the hands of the NRA. Only Odong Latek continued to fight. He later joined Kony but then Latek was killed in battle with the NRA. Latek was a good man, a good soldier; he taught Kony so many things about the military, how to fight like a soldier.

I believe in Kony's powers. He did many things that were impossible to do without the spirits or some other power. He fought the NRA and the UPDA, and he was never caught or killed even though so many men went after him. I was present one time when Okeno sent eighty-three men to capture or kill Kony; they came back and said they could not even get close to him, he was so powerful.

Kony predicted many things which came true, things that even I, as an older man, could not foresee. About the war and how people would turn on him and betray him. But he fought for the rights of our people. I met him in 1994 and again in 2006 and we spoke about the struggle. He believed in 1987 and he still believes he is fighting for us, for the simple people. He continues to believe he is chosen by the spirits to be our savior, to be the savior of Acholiland.

* * *

George's all-boys boarding school was run by Catholic priests, so religion took priority. Students attended mass twice a week, Wednesdays and Sundays, from 8.30 am to 10 am. There were religious classes every day, save Sunday. After compulsory showers at 4.30 pm, students prayed and sang the rosary for an hour. At dinner they prayed before eating. Following supper, which usually ended around 8 pm, there were more prayers, after which students were dismissed for the night. George found it hard to get used to the regimented and compulsory prayers. The heavily regulated praying in the LRA was not unlike Catholic school, he later thought.

Another aspect of the school George would later find replicated in the rebel life was the student leadership system. Student leadership roles were dedicated to rule enforcement rather than academic excellence. The head boy was the commander of all other boys in the school. He controlled personal assistants as well as a prefect for health, one for entertainment, and one per class. The prefects of health and entertainment had their representatives in each class and each class prefect, often called a captain, had two assistants. The head boy and all the prefects were chosen by a committee of teachers, solely, it seemed to George, on the basis of their large physiques – to command respect and compete in school sports – and their parents' bribes of food and money.

The main duty of each chosen boy was to punish students who broke the school rules or disobeyed the teachers. The head boy and prefects had free reign to punish others, which amounted to open bullying, mostly of the younger boys who were unable to defend themselves. As the youngest and smallest, George became an easy and frequent target.

Every first Sunday of the month was visiting day, and George looked forward to seeing his mother, who usually came alone and rarely with Quinto. In the beginning, his mother cried during each visit and George often did too. He was initially upset all day Sunday after Mary left but eventually learned to take it in stride. In his second month George became aware of the list of demands the prefects and head boys circulated among the young students. The list included food items the older boys wanted – candy, biscuits and sesame balls – as well as money. Mary did not have enough food or money to give George, and Quinto only paid his school fees. George never had food or money to appease the older boys so he was beaten constantly. It made him dread seeing his mother or uncle every first Sunday of the month, the time when most of the students received food and money from their families, parts of which went promptly to the older boys.

When he first enrolled George wet his bed most nights, which became a source of embarrassment for him and of constant harassment from the older boys. There were a few others like him, mostly first graders. Every morning, the health prefect would check for the bed-wetters and take them out of their beds, strip them naked and make them run around the laundry room yelling, "*Wan lulac Keken, eh, eh* – we piss in our beds," while other kids laughed and sprayed them with cold water.

Then the prefect beat the young offenders with a stick. On Monday it was ten strokes, on Tuesday twenty, Wednesday thirty and so on until Saturday, when it was sixty. Sunday was forgiven. The beating and humiliation took place in front of the night matron, an elderly woman whose job was to ensure the children were safe at night. She approved and even encouraged the prefect. "The drubbing teaches the kids to be responsible," she said.

The teachers also hit the kids, usually on their hands and wrists. The English teacher used a long ruler, ten strokes on each hand for poor handwriting and fifteen for not paying attention. Caning was as important an aspect of the school as studying. Even the school administrators had set the numbers of strokes for specific offenses. George would later be amazed to find that the rebels also had specific numbers of strokes for various offenses. The beating was delivered with branches of a fir tree that grew in front of the school and was decorated every Christmas. The students called the caning at the administrators' office "the Christmas tree" method and George was no stranger to it.

In his third year of primary school, called P3, he had had enough of the bullying and beatings and decided to leave. One night he climbed over the wall and out of the school, and walked home, despite fearing Quinto's wrath. Quinto had refused all of George's many pleas over the years to have him transferred to a day school. Mary had tried also to no avail. At midnight George reached home and tried to enter his mother's room undetected, but one of Quinto's children saw him and yelled in fear. Quinto came running and saw George hiding in a corner. Quinto yelled at him and called him stupid for leaving. "Don't you know you can be expelled?" Quinto had just paid the annual fee, which would not get reimbursed.

Quinto beat him with sticks his young children fetched. Mary threw herself over George but Quinto pushed her away and continued to beat him until all the sticks, and George, lay broken on the floor. Early in the morning Quinto took him back to school. Running after Quinto's bike George cried the whole time until they reached the school. He hoped he would be expelled but after a meeting with the school administrators, Quinto said George was forgiven, though the administrators would have to punish him, "as was their right."

In the administrators' office, George stood alongside two prefects and his class captain. One of the administrators asked the prefects to bring branches from the Christmas tree and hit George on his back and buttocks eight times, as was the rule. After the prefects beat George, the school administrators told the class captain to keep an eye on him. "George was an escapee," they said, "and would likely try to leave again." George was later shamed in front of the school assembly.

George was shocked by Quinto's viciousness. He was almost used to all the other beatings but the one from Quinto was hard to take, hard to believe. Witnessing his mother's powerlessness added to his pain of feeling abandoned. He did not want her or Quinto to visit him and blamed them for prolonging his personal hell. He did not enjoy spending time with them during holidays either and even looked forward to being back in the hated school. He dedicated most of his time to reading. He excelled, particularly in English and literature. It stood him in good stead with the older bullies, who copied his work and left him alone.

In P7, his final year in primary school, he bullied the younger children, demanding their money and food in return for protection. He did not much care for their food or candy and he did not like that he had become what he used to hate. The young kids, like him and many others before him, needed to learn to be tough. "Their parents will not always be there to help them in life, a lesson the kids need to learn sooner rather than later," he thought.

In the Primary Leaving Examinations, the final exams that determined his acceptance into a good secondary school, he came first in his class. He was the only one to receive four points – one distinction for each of the four main subjects: math, English, science and social studies – the highest mark possible. The good results meant he could choose any of the secondary schools he wanted, including the all-boys Catholic college in Gulu, one of the best countrywide. He did not hesitate and accepted their offer. Quinto was happy and vowed to pay all the fees. Another six years to endure in secondary school and George could finally become the first from his family to attend university. He could also become his own man.

* * *

In its early days, from late 1987 until the early 1990s, the rebel movement eventually known as the Lord's Resistance Army underwent many changes. Kony maintained a largely spiritual role although he learned a great deal from former UPDA soldiers in his group, such as Odong Latek. Latek had been unable to keep all the UPDA groups together and by 1988 the fragmented rebel army disintegrated as commanders signed peace deals with the government. Other UPDA officers, notably Nixman Oryang, aka "Tortoise," also joined Kony and later became the LRA's chief of training.

Just like Alice Lakwena, Kony's reliance on the spirits, particularly the Holy Spirit, was total, at least in the early days. The jogi, roughly translated as "spirits" or "gods," which Kony solely channeled, were in charge of everything, from military matters to personal behavior and hygiene. Kony conveyed orders as having emanated from a particular spirit and therefore not to be questioned by mere mortals. Some spirits were violent, while others were peaceful and taught people in the LRA about respecting nature, including water and animals. As chief priest and spirit medium, Kony claimed extraordinary powers, including foreseeing the future and controlling events.

Kony quickly learned to appropriate the military experience of the UPDA elements – after witnessing the large losses among Alice's HSM, whose members walked bare-chested and unarmed into battle – and incorporate it in his nascent organization. While Kony tried to combine the military ethos of the UPDA with the spiritual aspect of the HSM, throughout the 1990s Kony's role changed increasingly towards the militaristic and away from the spiritual. It was clearly better to be feared as a military man than loved and respected as a spirit medium.

The names Kony chose for his organization reflected the split nature of the movement between the militaristic and the spiritual, from the Holy Spirit Movement II, to the Uganda's People Liberation Army and the Uganda Christian Democratic Army to the Lord's Salvation Army and finally the Lord's Resistance Army, the latter being perhaps an accommodation of both martial and religious aspects inherent in the rebel movement.

The evolution of Kony and the LRA was made possible in large part by military and logistical support from the government of

Sudan, which changed the LRA from a disorganized group of rag-tag fighters to a highly disciplined and organized rebel outfit. Sudan's help with military gear and training also transformed and legitimized Kony's movement. Sudan's support offered Kony choices, particularly negotiating with Museveni, lessening the pressure on Kony to accept Museveni's demands, which were unhelpfully presented as ultimatums. Such was the case in late 1993 when the first serious rounds of negotiations between the LRA and the Ugandan government took place, in large part due to the efforts of Betty Bigombe, an Acholi politician appointed by President Museveni in 1988 as Minister of State for the Pacification of the North.

Bigombe initiated contact with rebel commanders in May 1992 and met Kony in late 1993 and in January 1994. The last few months of 1993 are still remembered by many in Acholiland as a time of peace. The rebels were allowed to mingle with the civilian population as the Ugandan army implemented a ceasefire allowing the peace talks to take place. Many genuinely believed the conflict was about to end, but in February 1994 Museveni claimed that Kony was using the talks to regroup in anticipation of support from Sudan. He gave the LRA an ultimatum of seven days to surrender – Kony had asked Bigombe for six months of consultations with Acholi elders in Uganda and the diaspora – which killed the talks. The LRA returned to the bush and the conflict escalated.

It is unclear if Museveni was right and Kony was replicating in 1994 what Museveni had done in 1985/86, or whether Kony was serious about the peace talks and Museveni's ultimatum drove him to Sudan. It is likely that, as he would do later on during the Juba talks of 2006–2008, Kony kept his options open; negotiating with Bigombe while maintaining a rapport with the Sudanese Army intelligence services to gauge which option would eventually suit him best.

In February 1994, as the peace talks between Kampala and the LRA stalled, a large LRA force of about 200 people led by LRA Commander John Odur crossed from northern Kitgum in Uganda to the south of Sudan's Eastern Equatoria, where they set up bases near Torit in Palataka and Aru. Kony and other groups joined them throughout 1994. The LRA was initially assisted by a Sudanese pro-government group, the Equatoria Defense Force. Like the EDF, the LRA fought the Sudan People's Liberation Army (SPLA), then rebels and now the national army of the Republic of South Sudan.

In response to Ugandan government support for the SPLA, the Khartoum regime, through its army, the Sudanese Armed Forces (SAF), provided training, weapons, ammunition and food to LRA forces, which at their peak in the late 1990s numbered between 3,000 and 4,000 people. SAF support was drastically reduced after September 2001 but continued sporadically at least until the signing of the Comprehensive Peace Agreement between the Khartoum government and the SPLA in 2005.

Training provided by SAF officers included daily military drills, attack and withdraw formations as well as hit and run, cordon and destroy, and ambush and anti-ambush tactics. Specialized training was provided in attacking and clearing out trenches, a tactic favored by SPLA soldiers who tried to capture territory and retain it, unlike the Ugandan soldiers who launched incursions into South Sudan to chase the LRA and then retreated to Uganda. Most LRA attacks at the time were directed against the SPLA and not the Ugandan army, indicating perhaps Kony's acceptance of his new role as a proxy fighter for Khartoum.

Training was conducted near Juba in South Sudan as well as in Khartoum. There were two LRA liaisons to the SAF, one based in Khartoum and another in Juba. The liaisons were in charge of organizing military training and medical care for wounded LRA fighters, who were usually taken to the military hospital in Juba, or to Khartoum in serious cases. Commander Caesar Achellam was based in Juba and traveled frequently to various LRA camps in South Sudan.

Military training was provided in handling guns of various calibers supplied to the LRA by the SAF. The AK47 (Russian-, Chinese- and Yugoslav-made) was and remains the weapon of choice for the LRA, although fighters are in possession today of Belgian-made FN FAL semi-automatics, G3s and M16s. The Sudanese supplied rocket-propelled grenades and squad-level support guns such as the Russian-made PK 7.62 mm general-purpose machine gun. Between 1998 and 2001, LRA fighters received training in using 12.7 mm anti-aircraft guns, Russian-made 82 mm illuminating mortars, SPG9 73 mm recoilless guns as well as SAM 7 missiles. These guns and appropriate ammunition were provided by the SAF.

In the late 1990s LRA fighters also received anti-personnel and anti-tank land mines and training on how to handle them. Mines were usually planted in secondary roads on the northern Ugandan border in Acholiland but also neighboring West Nile. It is unclear how many mines – which caused the death or dismemberment of many civilians – were planted by the LRA, as the Ugandan army also mined vast tracts of land to deter LRA movements from Sudan to Uganda. Selected LRA combatants also received training in communications, usually high frequency and two-way short frequency radios.

By the late 1990s, as the relationship with Khartoum blossomed, Kony transformed primarily into a military commander while still retaining his spiritual powers, displayed less prominently. In late 1999, soon after ordering the execution of his deputy, Otti Lagony, Kony told his top commanders that the spirits would only come to him in his dreams to inspire him. Lagony's killing on Kony's orders was a prime example of Kony's gradual transformation. In early 1999 the Ugandan parliament discussed a blanket amnesty for all rebels, in an effort to encourage LRA fighters to defect. Lagony, at the time Kony's deputy, was convinced that the amnesty was an honorable way to stop fighting and return home. Kony disagreed and had Lagony shot, then promoted himself to major general, the highest military rank in the LRA. He had come a long way from early 1987 when he was described as "a young man scared of guns."

The relationship between the SAF and the LRA gradually deteriorated as Khartoum sought to reach an agreement, first with Kampala as chief supporter of the SPLA, and eventually with the SPLA leadership. An agreement to cease support for rebels, made between Kampala and Khartoum in late 1999 and signed in Nairobi with the mediation of the Carter Center, provided the first serious crack in the LRA–SAF relationship. Despite the LRA not being mentioned, Kony took the agreement as proof of

President Bashir's duplicity even though SAF support for the LRA continued at least until the early 2000s.

In 2002 Bashir allowed the Ugandan army to enter Sudanese territory and attack the LRA. The Ugandan army carried out Operation Iron Fist, one of the bloodiest episodes of the LRA conflict, which resulted in many deaths on both sides and had the unintended consequence of pushing LRA groups inside Uganda, while Kony and a few fighters remained in Sudan. The toll on civilian life in northern Uganda was to be extremely heavy.

CHAPTER 3

KILLING RAMBO

George was happy in secondary school, which he started in January 2001. His relationship with Quinto was limited to a few brief interactions. He missed his mother but was used to being away from her. George was also adept at dealing with the bullying, which, compared to elementary school, was a piece of cake, he thought. He knew how to take care of himself and it showed. The older students did not harass him despite his relatively small size and his lack of friends. He turned to reading and excelled in all literature classes. He devoured the classics but he adored African literature.

His favorite author was the local writer Okot p'Bitek, an Acholi and one of the first Ugandans to have studied at Oxford University, often credited as a father of modern African literature. George read his works in Luo and English and hoped that one day he could become a notable writer just like p'Bitek. Throughout the first four years of secondary school, the so-called Ordinary Levels, George read extensively, including Ousmane Sembène's *God's Bits of Wood*, and all the works of Chinua Achebe and Ngugi Wa Thiong'o he could find.

He saw little of his mother as 2001 neared its end. She complained increasingly of migraines, which made her stay in bed for days at a time. In December, Quinto finally decided to have her see a doctor. George, Quinto and Mary boarded a rickety bus that had bullet holes in its sides – courtesy of a recent encounter with the LRA rebels – and made their way to Kampala. There, Quinto said, they would see the best Ugandan doctor on matters of head-aches. The doctor turned out to be a smiley young Kenyan in a large hospital, and his diagnosis was stark. Mary had cancer. It had already reached her brain. "There is nothing to do," said the smiley doctor, "it is now in God's hands."

Quinto ordered George to not utter a word about it to his mother, "no need to upset her any more." Quinto bought a pack of aspirins and asked Mary to take a pill daily. "Everything will be ok," he promised, as George bit his lower lip trying to stop it from quivering, and forced himself not to talk or shed tears. Mary felt better and held George's hand tightly throughout the ride back to Gulu. She spent the rest of December and all of January, the month George started his second year of secondary school, inside her room in total darkness. "It makes my head feel less heavy," she said to George.

One morning in February 2002, a few weeks after the trip to Kampala, the school's secretary took him out of his science class and brought him to Quinto, who was waiting outside the main gate in the rain. George knew his mother was gone. "You are a man now," Quinto berated him after he started to cry. He walked home with his books behind

Quinto, who pedaled slowly ahead. He felt truly alone, without anyone in the world. "I have become an orphan. What a terrible curse this is," he thought.

Mary's body was taken to her ancestral home, a small village west of Gulu, for burial. George sat at the back of a truck while his mother's body lay next to him covered in blankets. At her village George met his grandfather, whom he had rarely seen and barely knew, and a few uncles and aunts and their children. They all worked the land and lived in small circular huts without windows or electricity. Some of the villages around them were already abandoned for fear of LRA attacks, but their village had not been targeted, no one knew why. Everyone was scared it could happen and advised George to leave as soon as he could.

George promised to return and visit his relatives again and went back to school the same day. He was annoyed that Quinto had not even made it to the funeral. George also hated how Quinto had hurriedly cleared Mary's room and made it into a bedroom for two of his daughters. But he could not complain as Quinto assured him he would continue to pay his school fees. George could not imagine life without school and his books. He was sure he did not want to be a peasant tied to the land like his mother's family. He had bigger dreams.

* * *

Concerned, perhaps, about reports that Osama bin Laden had been based in Khartoum in the mid-1990s, President Bashir wanted to show that his government did not support terrorists in the aftermath of the terrorist attacks of 11 September 2001. As part of this newfound willingness to shed the image of a pariah state, Khartoum's regime continued to participate in peace negotiations with rebels in the south and decided to allow the Ugandan army to attack the LRA inside Sudanese territory. But movement restrictions placed on the Ugandan army, which could not operate north of the Juba–Torit road, allowed Kony and other top commanders to move beyond the reach of the offensive, and eventually return south of the Juba-Torit road and hide in the Imatong Mountains of Eastern Equatoria, not very far from the Ugandan border.

The Ugandan attack, codenamed Operation Iron Fist, came in March 2002, when an estimated 7,000 Ugandan soldiers, more than twice the number of LRA members, mounted an offensive against LRA bases in southern Sudan that involved intense artillery shelling, followed by infantry and air attacks from gunship helicopters. Kony, who was furious with the Sudanese government, went as far as offering to help the SPLA, Khartom's traditional enemy (and against whom the LRA had frequently fought since establishing bases in Sudan), to take on the SAF, Khartoum's army.

While the Ugandan operation aimed at crushing the LRA in southern Sudan, it had the unintended, yet entirely foreseeable consequence of pushing LRA fighters back into northern Uganda. Well-armed and trained by Khartoum's army, and angered by the Ugandan army attacks, LRA commanders ordered a bloody campaign of retaliation, targeting mainly northern Ugandan civilians to highlight the government's inability to protect them as well as to showcase LRA strength, which government propaganda claimed was low.

The period from 2002 to 2005 was a time when George, like many other Ugandans, heard almost daily about LRA attacks and their vicious acts of torturing, maiming and killing civilians. Abductions of young people including children soared; almost 7,500 cases of abduction were recorded in 2003, compared to just over 100 in 2002.

In February 2004, LRA fighters organized an especially brutal attack on Barlonyo, a camp for internally displaced people, southeast of Acholi, in neighboring Lango. Over 200 people were killed. By March of that year, Betty Bigombe, who had gone to work for the World Bank in Washington, DC, following the collapse of peace talks she had led in 1994, returned to Uganda and, with President Museveni's agreement, restarted negotiations with the LRA's top leadership.

The so-called Bigombe II talks created some hope for a peaceful resolution to conflict. Various ceasefires were agreed while Bigombe met with LRA commanders, including Kony and his top deputy Vincent Otti, in early 2005. But the surrender of the LRA chief negotiator, Sam Kolo, to Ugandan troops on 16 February 2005 caused anger in the LRA and further delays. Vincent Otti, however, told Bigombe on the phone that he was in charge of the peace talks, which were still not dead as far as the LRA was concerned.

Bigombe would later complain that while the talks suffered many setbacks, various statements from the International Criminal Court (ICC) announcing imminent indictments of LRA commanders for war crimes seemed to have killed any hope of the peace talks succeeding. President Museveni referred the conflict in the north to the ICC in December 2003 and ICC investigators carried out research into LRA crimes throughout 2004. The ICC issued arrest warrants for five LRA commanders in July and September 2005. Kony and Otti, as the two main leaders, knew by July that they would be indicted. Considering that the peace talks had failed, they made new plans.

Otti was to walk to Garamba National Park in Congo in charge of an advance party, which would ensure that the forest was safe and suitable for Kony and the rest to settle. Otti left South Sudan's Eastern Equatoria for northeastern Congo at the beginning of September 2005, needing to overcome numerous obstacles including the White Nile. He succeeded in establishing a base in Garamba which would later house all groups, including Kony's, relocating from Uganda and South Sudan. Just when the world thought the LRA leader had run out of places to hide, Kony managed, once more, to survive and fight another day.

* * *

A few months after he lost his mother, life became harder for George when Quinto was arrested. It was mid-September in 2002, when George was two months off finishing his second year of secondary school. Quinto's older daughter, a few months younger than George, called the school's main office and asked to talk to him. She explained how soldiers had stormed their home at midnight and taken her father. He was in Gulu prison that morning but word was he was to be taken to Kampala. Quinto was accused of being a rebel collaborator and was likely to be charged with treason, an extremely serious offence.

George was stunned. He knew Quinto was sympathetic to the LRA and that he had had a personal relationship with Kony. George remembered well when Quinto brought him to a meeting he held with Kony in early 1994 during the peace talks with Minister Bigombe, a time when the rebels moved freely in town and everyone thought the war would soon end. But while Quinto was one of many elders who knew Kony well, George thought, he certainly did not approve of the rebels' tactics and did not do anything to support them directly or materially.

It had been a difficult six months in northern Uganda, which probably explained the government's behavior, George reasoned. The rebels had moved back to Uganda only weeks after the much trumpeted Operation Iron Fist was supposed to have dealt with Kony and his men for good. Instead, the rebels returned to Uganda and started killing indiscriminately. The government responded by arresting many people in the north, accusing them of aiding the rebels.

Human rights activists said that the government was using its inability to deal with the rebels to silence voices of dissent, particularly members of established opposition parties such as the Democratic Party and Uganda People's Congress. A law passed that year by the Ugandan parliament called the Anti-Terrorism Act considered all opponents of the state, and of President Museveni and his party, as terrorists.

George later learned that Quinto was only one of many people in northern Uganda, particularly Acholiland, arrested towards the end of 2002. Supposed sympathizers of the Democratic Party were seized by the army and imprisoned in Gulu central prison, accused of treason and collaborating with the rebels. More than two dozen people were arrested at the same time as Quinto but twenty-two remained in Gulu, awaiting charges.

On 16 October 2002 soldiers from the Fourth Division of the Ugandan army stormed the prison, with the intention of taking the twenty-two prisoners to the nearby army barracks. It was for the prisoners' own protection, the soldiers claimed, as LRA commander Thomas Kwoyelo was about to attack the prison. During the violent transfer the soldiers shot one of the prisoners, Peter Oloya, a young official of the Democratic Party, at point blank range.

News of Oloya's death spread rapidly throughout Gulu and terrified George. He feared Quinto would be in prison for a long time or even be executed, as treason charges carried the death penalty. He met with relatives and clan elders trying to help Quinto, who had already been transferred to Kampala's Luzira prison. They found a lawyer who took on the case and hoped for a quick resolution. "It is going to take a long time," Quinto said, so George should continue to focus on his studies, for which Quinto had already paid.

The start of 2003 and his third year in secondary school brought more hardship for George. Some of his teachers who had lost family members at the hands of the rebels accused him of being an LRA collaborator after news of Quinto's arrest became public. George became really worried when he was summoned to meet with the school finance officer who asked why his fees were late. George tried to explain the situation with Quinto but was told that he would be expelled if no money was forthcoming. Eventually the money was paid by one of Quinto's business associates, but all the worries – about money, Quinto and his mother's passing – weighed heavily on George's mind. His grades suffered as a result.

Quinto was released a year later, in September 2004, after the government dropped the charges. He most likely paid a bribe and signed a letter saying he renounced violence, even though he was never part of the rebel movement nor had ever partaken in any form of violent conduct. "I could not stay in Luzira any longer," he told George, who was happy to see him. At least he needn't worry about school payments anymore. He did not mention his school performance to Quinto but vowed to try and do better now that at least some degree of normalcy had returned.

Things were relatively calm for the remainder of 2004, and George managed to pass his O-level exams with high enough marks to be accepted into the final two years of secondary school, called Advanced or A-levels. So, too, was most of 2005. Quinto was not harassed by government officials and he managed to pay George's fees in full. By the end of 2005 Quinto had secured a few photos from the peace talks between Bigombe and Kolo. George saw the pictures when at home during a half-term break and took a few copies that he later showed to some of his classmates. They feared and admired the rebels for being tough and taking on the army. They joked how badly they would fare as rebels and celebrated the end of the year by drinking little sachets of gin they had smuggled into the dormitory.

When George returned for his sixth and final year of high school in January 2006, he was in trouble. Someone told a teacher about his LRA photos and soon the school directors were involved. They informed a local official who in turn called a security officer to question George. Quinto was arrested again but later released once it became clear that the pictures were from the government-approved peace talks with Sam Kolo. Yet the school board refused to allow George to return. Quinto tried to have him read-mitted but the administrators did not budge. They could not allow a rebel collaborator, as they referred to George, in the school and did not want the security services keeping tabs on their students and the school. So it was that by mid-January 2006 George was thrown out of high school, only a few months before graduation.

* * *

As dawn broke in Garamba National Park in northeastern Congo on 23 January 2006, a young Ugandan known to his friends as Mugabe thought he heard whispers in the bush followed by steps in the distance. Mugabe signaled to a second man hidden in a tree above him, on the lookout for enemies, pointing in the direction of the noise. The scout perched atop the tree spent a few minutes trying to work out whether the people walking towards them were local hunters or Congolese soldiers. Quickly realizing it was the latter, the scout came down and readied his weapon. Without hesitation both men unleashed a barrage of bullets in the direction of the oncoming soldiers. Then they turned around and walked hastily deeper into the forest.

The two were members of an LRA group led by Vincent Otti. The group, about 160 people, had relocated from southern Sudan to northeastern Congo at the end of 2005. Otti had arrived in Congo to find an appropriate place where Kony and the rest of the LRA could be based. South Sudan was no longer hospitable, particularly since the county was being divided into two, and the army of the north, the LRA's previous backer, was returning home, leaving the south to the SPLA. The soldiers of the south, the SPLA – or the Dinkas as the LRA called them – were sworn enemies and the two groups could not live in peace after almost ten years of fighting one another.

On the morning of the 23rd the two young men, who were tasked with guarding the western side of the camp, did precisely as instructed. They fired shots to discourage the enemy from advancing on their camp and to warn their comrades of the threat. When the two arrived at the camp a few minutes later, men, women and children were already awake and ready to move. Otti stood at the center of the camp surrounded by his personal bodyguards. Two lines of twelve fighters had already taken up defensive positions on the outskirts of the camp when the scouts made their entrance. The two men walked directly to Otti and told him they had seen a large number of soldiers coming towards them.

Otti ordered the evacuation of the camp. The group was to return to a base Otti had set up earlier when he first entered Garamba. He instructed the defensive line to engage the incoming force for a brief period and assess their numerical strength and weapons capability. "Meet me at the little stream in an hour," Otti ordered the commander of the defensive force. Ten minutes later and now incorporated into Otti's security detail walking briskly behind his commander, Mugabe heard shots coming from behind. He could tell the first shots came from the PKM, a heavy machine gun manned by Kenneth, his friend who had stayed behind to fight. The distinctive staccato noise of the PKM and the accompanying cacophony of many Kalashnikovs continued for at least a quarter of an hour, after which the firing became sporadic and eventually died down.

An hour later Otti met with the commander of the defensive line. A battle-hardened fighter, he told Otti that the soldiers were not Congolese or Ugandan soldiers. They were dressed in brand-new camouflage uniforms with blue berets and were manning guns he had never seen before. There were probably 100 of them. "But are they Dinka or Congolese?" asked Otti. "No," came the reply, "they are not Africans; they are white. I think they are Americans."

Otti was stunned. Sensing fear was gripping his fighters, he quickly responded: "Let them come, God will help us deal with them just like everyone else." He turned around and put a hand on the shoulder of Bogi Taban, who was standing by him. An experienced fighter, Taban was Otti's most trusted aide and chief bodyguard. "Take a standby and go after them," Otti said. Taban chose eleven men while Otti and the rest continued to walk further away from the Americans.

Taban ordered his fighters to load up with ammunition. He pulled aside a man called Ujumbe and told him to be ready to fire when ordered. Ujumbe means "message" in Swahili, an appropriate name for the fighter who carried a grenade launcher. "Here is my message to you," Ujumbe would yell while firing, a permanent source of jokes in his group. The standby, a common term used by the holies to refer to an assault team, started toward the soldiers.

The group moved slowly. Two scouts went ahead, tasked with finding the enemy's position. Taban had a simple plan. He wanted to encircle the soldiers, attacking them from the rear, where they least expected it. It took the holies more than two hours of slow walking in the forest before one of the scouts reported that the enemy was close. The scout reported that the group was between fifty and eighty people, all well-armed. Taban gathered his men and explained that the success of their mission depended on their attack being unexpected. "This is a hit-and-run mission," he said. "Shoot, kill, take what you can and retreat." "One more thing," he added. "Take their guns, if you can. They would make a nice present for the General" – referring to Kony, who was still in South Sudan making his way to Garamba.

The dozen scattered in offensive positions, crawling until they had a good view of the enemy. It was clear the American soldiers were not expecting them. They were sitting on the ground, fiddling and looking bored. They were not black soldiers but white with painted black faces. They wore green uniforms and had blue berets. Taban stood next to Ujumbe and pointed to where a group of four soldiers were talking on a radio with a long antenna. Taban made a hand signal to the rest to hold their fire until Ujumbe shot first then tapped him on the shoulder.

The piercing sound of the RPG7 started the assault and took the enemy by surprise. The missile hit the four men directly, sending their body parts flying through the air. A chorus of eleven assault rifles ensued. More white soldiers were hit; some lay on the ground dead or injured while others ran away, and then dug in and returned fire.

Taban fought standing up. He shot one soldier near him and went to take his gun, a large black sub-machine gun no one among the holies had seen before. He grabbed the gun and the slain soldier's blue cap and yelled, "Retreat," moving back into the forest. As he made his way back to the group, he was shot in the back and fell. His personal bodyguard tried to help him but he was also shot and dropped next to Taban screaming in pain. They both died quickly as the soldiers, now established in defensive positions, shot furiously, riddling their bodies with hundreds of bullets.

Ujumbe managed to grab the gun and the beret from Taban's dead body. He joined the remaining nine men, who ran into the forest. Other holies had grabbed two more guns and some bullets. A few were injured but were able to walk. They continued without stopping until they reached Otti's camp. Breathless, Ujumbe told Otti what had happened. He told him about Taban and his escort, he recounted how he killed four enemies with one hit and how the soldiers were white with painted black faces, like the American actors they had seen in the movies. Elated, he yelled, "I killed Rambo."

Otti smiled, patted him on the back and said that pending Kony's approval, he and his team members were to be promoted, for bravery in battle. Otti then placed a call to Kony on his long frequency radio, explaining what had happened. "The Holy Spirit is with you," Kony said via his signaler, the person who handled his communications. Kony approved all promotions for the team but asked Otti to save him a gun and a cap from the dead soldiers. "Of course General," replied Otti and signed off.

Otti sat thinking for a while. He was worried about the future now that foreign soldiers were after him. It was one thing to fight the Ugandan army and the South Sudanese rebels – the LRA had plenty of experience with them – but the American army was a different proposition. He reached for his satellite phone and placed a call to a prominent Ugandan politician who had often asked him to convince Kony to agree to peace talks. "I am happy to hear from you Vincent," he heard from the other side of the line. Otti explained what had taken place.

"The Americans came here and thought they could just kill us by simply showing up. But these people are fools and God is great. We showed them. They are dead now and we have their guns and hats to show for our victory." The politician seemed surprised and said that even President Museveni did not know about it. "We had nothing to do with this Vincent, I am sure." After a pause, Otti said, "Tell Museveni we are ready to talk peace."

* * *

President Museveni was not informed ahead of time about the attempt on the LRA group in Garamba. In a speech at Pece stadium in Gulu on 25 January 2006, two days after the clash in Garamba, Museveni said that the soldiers were Uruguayan Special Forces from the UN peacekeeping force in Congo. "We told the UN you cannot fight Kony," Museveni said, "but do you think they listened? They did not listen, so they got those poor characters from Uruguay. How can somebody from Uruguay come to the African bush and deal with those characters?" But after an aide approached him mid- speech and whispered something in the presidential ear, Museveni said, "Apparently they were not Uruguayans but Guatemalans."

The soldiers were not American or Uruguayan, they were indeed part of a US-trained special force from Guatemala, called Kaibiles, deployed as peacekeepers in Congo for the UN mission, called MONUC, for Mission de l'Organisation des Nations Unies en République démocratique du Congo. UN officials sent the eighty Kaibiles to contain and perhaps arrest Otti, who was indicted by the International Criminal Court for crimes against humanity. At least eight Kaibiles were killed in the attack and more than a dozen were injured. The UN never made public exactly what happened but one thing was made clear: the LRA was not a rag-tag bunch as Ugandan army officials liked to describe them. Kony's group was capable of taking on any army, even specialized commando units such as the Kaibiles.

* * *

George was at Pece Stadium with Quinto to hear Museveni's speech. On the way home that day, George was surprised to hear Quinto talk openly about Kony and the LRA. "They are strong," he said. "There are rumors peace talks are starting again," Quinto continued, "but this time they are going to be big, involving foreigners, both black and white." Turning abruptly toward George, Quinto asked, "What do you think about joining the rebels?"

George did not say anything. He knew Quinto was thinking out loud and not really asking anyway. George wanted to say no, of course not, and he was annoyed that Quinto was already making plans to get rid of him, barely two weeks after he was expelled from school. George did not want to be part of the group that had brought so much suffering in Acholiland. He did not want to join the same rebels whose photos had got him expelled and ruined his life. He blamed himself for being stupid enough to show the photos around school and he knew that Quinto blamed him also. Quinto was furious with him, not only for stealing the photos and bringing them to school, but also for his nearly failing grades. He said George did not deserve his hard-earned money.

It was clear that Quinto was not going to enroll George in another school come January 2007. He said it was difficult to find the money to pay for George and his own children, particularly his oldest daughter who was doing really well in secondary school and had a good chance of going to medical school in Kampala. "There is not enough money to go around," Quinto said. He had spent most of his savings trying to get out of jail. George needed to find a job and figure out how to finish the last year of high school. He was welcome to stay at their home, Quinto often told him, but other than that, George was on his own.

It took George a few weeks to fully comprehend his newfound position. He had been certain a solution would be found, he was after all only two terms off graduating from high school. But when Quinto told him he needed to get a job, he realized there was no one coming to his rescue. He started to consume alcohol and got into fights with Quinto's wives and children, who lived in the same compound. He refused to even try to find a job. He knew he had no marketable skills and simply waited for Quinto to throw him out of the house. But Quinto appeared determined to have him join the LRA, especially after it became clear that the peace talks were being taken seriously by both Kony and Museveni.

Six months later, in July 2006, soon after Kony appeared in an interview with the British Broadcasting Corporation, Quinto floated the idea of George joining the LRA groups still present in Uganda but then dismissed it, saying it was too dangerous. He then said that he would try to find a way to have George join an LRA peace delegation. Quinto said Acholi representatives were already going to see Kony in the bush as part of the talks. George could perhaps join the delegation as an Acholi youth representative. Toward the end of 2006, Quinto told George to be ready. "You are going into the bush in Congo where the *aligu*, the rebels, are staying," he told George. George, who had never consented to joining, felt he did not have much choice. He did not have any other place to go and hoped that his stay with the rebels would be short. "You will soon come home and receive soldier's benefits like many others in the past," Quinto reassured him and asked him to be ready to leave at short notice.

* * *

Throughout early 2006, LRA envoys were in contact with the new semi-autonomous government of South Sudan. They reached out to Riek Machar, an old Kony acquaintance. Machar, an ethnic Nuer, was well known throughout the region for his shifting alliances in the North–South conflict. He was initially part of the SPLA, fighting against Khartoum's army, but changed sides in 1997 after falling out with the former SPLA leader John Garang. Machar signed an agreement with Khartoum's government and became an assistant to Sudanese President Omar el Bashir. It is likely that Machar met Kony back in 1997, facilitated by leaders of the Equatoria Defense Force. The EDF was composed of members from Central and Eastern Equatoria regions of South Sudan, including ethnic Acholi who became the point of contact for Kony. The EDF was supported by Khartoum and fought – alongside the LRA – against the SPLA.

In 2002, Machar rejoined the SPLA and, after the death of John Garang in July 2005, he was brought into the new, semi-autonomous Government of South Sudan (GoSS) in September 2005 as deputy to new President Salva Kiir. Having signed a peace agreement with the North in January 2005, which ended the fighting, the government of the South, based in Juba, had to deal with the pressing concerns of foreign fighters on its soil. The LRA remained a major threat, with many other groups previously affiliated with Khartoum having been brought into the fold of the new government. Machar used his old connections to reach out to Kony, making contact with the LRA as early as November 2005 and offering to mediate peace talks between the LRA and the Ugandan government.

Machar reportedly met Otti in April 2006, and a month later met Kony on the border between South Sudan and Congo. In a grainy video that appeared a few weeks later, Machar is seen handing Kony an envelope full of cash – apparently $20,000 – and is heard saying that the money was from President Salva Kiir, to buy food but not arms and ammunition. The video confirmed that the new government of South Sudan was in formal talks with the LRA's top leadership, something that President Kiir passed on to President Museveni in May 2006 while attending Museveni's swearing-in ceremony following his victory in the February presidential elections, which was also a celebration of Museveni's twenty years in power.

The talks opened formally in July 2006, mediated by the Government of South Sudan and held in the GoSS capital, Juba. The Ugandan government sent a delegation led by a senior diplomat while the LRA delegation – reportedly chosen by Kony – was composed mainly of Acholi diaspora members led by Martin Ojul, an Acholi who had spent most of his life in Kampala working for the Uganda Water and Sewage Corporation. There were no active LRA commanders in the delegation; they refused to travel to Juba, fearing for their safety. The lack of combatants in the delegation necessitated the need for consultations and therefore frequent trips to Garamba Park in Congo, where Kony and most of the LRA were located.

There were many issues with the Juba talks, which started and stalled often. Agreeing to and respecting a ceasefire between the Ugandan government and the LRA proved difficult. During August 2006 the LRA continued to attack civilians in northern Uganda and Sudan while the Ugandan army also fought the rebels, killing Raska Lukwiya, a top commander and International Criminal Court (ICC) indictee, on 12 August 2006. On 28 August, however, both parties agreed to a comprehensive ceasefire agreement that allowed the talks to continue normally and enabled the last LRA groups based in northern Uganda to move to Congo's Garamba Park via South Sudan.

The talks continued until the end of the year, but one major issue relating to justice for past crimes was neglected. The Ugandan government spoke of an amnesty for the LRA leaders, which did not sit well with the prosecutor of the ICC. The ICC had indicted Kony, Vincent Otti, Okot Odhiambo, Raska Lukwiya and Dominic Ongwen in 2005 for war crimes, and the government of Uganda and that of South Sudan were legally obliged to hand over Kony and other commanders to the ICC. Kony himself

Top LRA leadership Garamba Park, 2006. From right to left, sitting: Vincent Otti, Joseph Kony, Okot Odhiambo, Nixman Opuk. Photo courtesy of Erin Baines.

appears not to have fully understood the role of the ICC and was perhaps wrongly advised by members of the LRA delegation to ignore it. The ICC warrants were later mentioned by both parties as key barriers to successfully completing the peace talks.

In early 2007 the talks stalled again, this time in response to comments from President Bashir, Kony's old backer. In a speech on 9 January 2007 commemorating the second anniversary of the Comprehensive Peace Agreement with the South, President Bashir, alongside President Kiir, said that both Sudans were ready to constitute a joint force to deal with the LRA if Kony refused to agree to peace. The LRA peace delegation refused to return to the negotiation table in Juba and the talks were put on hold.

From 31 March to 7 April 2007 an international NGO convinced key leaders of the LRA peace delegation to meet in Mombasa, Kenya, with Ugandan government officials in an effort to break the deadlock. The leader of the Ugandan delegation was not the recognized diplomat who headed the delegation in Juba but Salim Saleh, President Museveni's brother. The Ugandan pro-government daily paper hailed Saleh as having saved the peace talks but what went on during the Mombasa meetings was not made public. Rumors circulated that Saleh, a former rebel and a retired general in the Ugandan army specializing in covert operations, came in to create dissent among the LRA leadership. Kony would later accuse Otti, his top commander and key liaison in the peace talks, of having received money from Saleh via an LRA delegation member present at the Mombasa meetings. Rather than saving the Juba talks, the Mombasa meeting signaled perhaps the beginning of the talks' end.

By mid-April 2007 the peace talks had resumed once more, partly due to the Mombasa meetings and partly because of the involvement of Joachim Chissano, the former President of Mozambique, who was appointed as United Nations Special Envoy to the Juba talks. There was renewed optimism in northern Uganda that the talks were finally going to succeed and that the war would end and the rebels would return home. This was made clear, many thought, by the LRA commanders' wish to have their relatives visit them in the bush, in Congo and South Sudan, in anticipation of their return home. Many relatives of LRA commanders boarded planes for Juba and then Garamba Park, where they joined the rebels.

CHAPTER 4

KONY'S JUNGLE HOME

George waited anxiously in Gulu for months. He hoped Quinto would change his mind but his uncle was adamant he would not pay for George's schooling or support him financially. George thought joining the LRA was a terrible idea but hoped it would be a risk that would pay off handsomely. He told himself that he had little choice in the matter, secretly wishing for an adventure similar to those experienced by some of the heroes in Achebe's stories that he loved.

It was a strange time to even consider joining the feared group that had sown chaos for decades. The last remaining fighters had finally left Uganda. The near-constant stream of news depicting all the horrors that the rebels inflicted on the locals gradually dried up. Kony was holed up in Congo's forests, seemingly interested in the Juba talks, which had brought a semblance of peace to the country. As a popular Acholi song went, people were "smelling peace."

His uncle told George that Kony had lost touch with the common man in Acholiland. He needed someone like George to advise him on how things had changed in Uganda in the last ten years, the decade that the LRA leader had spent mostly in Sudan and Congo. According to Quinto, George was to become Kony's personal secretary. The General needed someone smart who could engage him in conversation and note down his thoughts for posterity. Kony needed George to help him talk in a way that young Acholi, who were not even born when the rebellion started, could understand. "People need to know this war was fought for a reason," Quinto said.

Since 1987 Kony had been portrayed in the Ugandan and foreign press as a lunatic, leading a cult without any real objectives. In the eyes of many, particularly the younger generations, Kony was a monster, an anachronism of days long gone. To them, Kony seemed as old as slavery and colonialism, a warlord who wreaked havoc through his army of abducted children.

And yet, as Kony himself often claimed on worn cassette tapes that circulated secretly in the northern towns, he had been defeated in the war of propaganda that President Museveni waged against him. "The Acholi have forgotten or never knew the brutality that Museveni brought onto us," Kony lamented, "which then forced me to respond. The Acholi elders blessed my war against the army but then they abandoned me. I was left holding the lion's tail."

"Kony needed people to explain his side of the truth," Quinto told his nephew. "You can be helpful to him."

Whether Kony really needed George to supply knowledge of modern northern Uganda was never clear to George. It was certain, however, that Quinto wanted him to join the LRA because he hoped the peace talks would succeed and that George would benefit as a former fighter, bringing honor to the entire family, particularly his uncle. George, while knowing full well that Quinto also wanted to get rid of him, hoped for some of the benefits a demobilization package could bring. Money, a job perhaps, and some recognition of his personal sacrifice.

The hope for some form of rehabilitation was shared by many involved in the peace talks, including Vincent Otti, who sent for one of his sons and a nephew to join him in the LRA bases in Congo, which they did. Other commanders also had friends and family members join them in Garamba, about thirty people in total.

By early 2007 word came from Kony that George was to leave on the next flight. One spring day, George boarded a United Nations airplane together with relatives and friends of senior commanders. George's visit was justified on the basis that he needed traditional medicine to cure a chronic stomach pain, a medicine that only healers in the LRA possessed. Many believed that Kony was well versed in traditional remedies, which helped to keep his fighters alive in the bush, lacking modern medicine. Those who came out often told stories of how Kony would prescribe certain herbs or roots to alleviate pain, claiming that the Holy Spirit instructed him. Invariably, these cures worked, according to the stories.

The flight was overbooked. A man in blue overalls told George an important local politician had to take his seat. But an Acholi elder, also going to meet Kony, said it was wise to ask Kony about the change of plans. The elder placed a call to Otti on his satellite phone. Otti, who received orders directly from Kony and often spoke in his name, was curt. "If the boy is not on the plane, no one should come at all." Kony's orders were not up for discussion even when they involved United Nations resources.

The local politician was left behind, causing many to speculate about George's identity. Some wondered aloud whether he was one of Kony's many sons. George did not engage, feeling apprehensive about what lay ahead. He was sad, having had to say goodbye to his friends. It was the first time he had traveled alone, the first time he had left home. He had no idea when, and perhaps even if, he would ever return.

During the two-hour plane ride to Juba, George was anxious. It was his first time on a plane and he was terrified it was going to plunge to the ground. He was also afraid of meeting Kony. Having grown up with horror stories of LRA fighters mutilating and killing civilians, George had no idea what to expect. He hoped he was going to be received well and treated like an important person, someone who would have Kony's trust and the loyalty of his fighters. If only his mother had been alive to see him be part of this important delegation. She would have been proud.

The plane finally landed in Juba, the dusty capital of South Sudan where more people waited to be flown to Rikwangba, a straight line to the west, on the way to the Congolese border. A few hours later a large party, including George, boarded a white United Nations helicopter bound for Rikwangba. George braced himself for yet another nauseous air ride. Later, when he was part of LRA groups wandering in the bush staring at helicopters circling above, he often thought of the time he boarded the helicopter from Juba and was always happy that his feet, sore from all the walking, were firmly planted on the ground.

Upon arriving near Rikwangba, and after a short walk, four armed men dressed in mixed civilian and military garb took George and the family members and brought them in front of a short man with grey hair. George immediately recognized Otti from the pictures he had seen in the papers on Gulu's newspapers stands. He was known in Uganda well before the start of the Juba talks. Ugandan government and army officials had often charged Otti with having overseen a massacre of civilians in the small town of Atiak, his birthplace.

Annoyed that the village had created a Local Defensive Unit – poorly armed civilians organized to protect their communities from LRA attacks – Otti accused the people of Atiak of siding with the government and openly challenging the LRA. He entered the village with many fighters and ordered that all males of thirteen years or older be shot in front of their mothers and wives. About 300 people were killed, the government soldiers arriving only after Otti had returned to the bush, taking many women who were forced to carry food looted in the Atiak market. When some of the women returned, they recounted the horror they had experienced. "Vincent Otti wanted to teach us a lesson," they cried.

Since the Atiak massacre people were afraid of Otti, often saying that he was the man really responsible for the LRA violence, Kony being but a figurehead. But people also said other commanders were responsible for attacks and that Kony was not aware of what was happening in the killing fields. George did not know whom to believe and his first meeting with Otti left him even more confused. Otti was a short man with grey hair and a round wrinkled face, almost grandfatherly looking. He was sitting in a wooden chair drawing on a piece of paper the LRA coat of arms – a crane bird, Uganda's national symbol, and palm leaves symbolizing the Christian aspect of the organization. George was amazed at Otti's ability to draw beautifully, his hands resembling those of a teacher.

Otti welcomed George and the rest of the group and said they would meet Kony in the next few days. George would later find out that no one in the LRA spoke freely about Kony's schedule or his location. Being vague was a safety measure. Otti gave orders for the guests to be fed and shown to their lodgings, low huts made of branches and dry grass. It was then that George had a chance to meet and talk to some LRA combatants. There were many of them surrounding Otti's compound. These were the feared *adwii*, the rebels that had committed so many killings, the terrifying *lulweny pa Kony*, Kony's fighters. They just stared ahead and were reluctant to talk, unsure about George's identity and his role in the LRA.

George was amazed at the sight of the emaciated teenagers wearing dirty clothes and unkempt hair who carried large guns they could barely hold. He was surprised and a little underwhelmed. Having expected to see the scary fighters who had terrorized the people for decades, he found instead young boys, who, he thought, were pretending to be real soldiers. There were even small children around, no older than ten. They were unarmed and dressed in ragged clothes. George thought they were the offspring of LRA commanders who had been born and raised in the bush, and could not help but feel sorry for them. "They could not have known anything else but living in the forest like wild animals," he thought.

The next day, Kony emerged unannounced from the surrounding forest together with a group of sixty armed men and a few women and children. He wore a military uniform with black army boots. Men with big guns walked in front of him and many more followed behind. He was flanked by two unarmed men in civilian clothes. George felt nervous. He was about to meet one of the most famous and feared men in Uganda and possibly the world. Kony's arrival was greeted with great commotion in the camp. A group of heavily armed fighters ran into the large clearing and took up positions in a long circular line. Then a group of people in single file slowly snaked into the clearing with Kony and his personal bodyguards at the head.

At a prayer ceremony Kony thanked the Holy Spirit for the safe arrival of the people from Uganda. He assured the newly arrived that they were going to be treated well and that the LRA base in the forest was their new home. He said that they were free, a remark that George thought out of place in a gathering of many who were abducted from their homes. It was the first of many statements that George found defied logic during his time with the rebels. But he quickly learned to keep quiet and discuss such issues in silent monologues.

Kony said they should not be afraid. They were now with the mighty Lord's Army and that the spirits were looking after them. He then asked the guests about life in Uganda. They discussed politics, food and the weather. Kony asked after his mother, Nora, who was ill. He said he wished he could see her again – she had visited him in November 2006 – before she died but was not sure if it would be possible. He said he hoped that the peace talks would succeed.

After two days in Rikwangba, George prepared to join Kony and his men for the journey to northeastern Congo. Kony was happy that the peace process was moving forward but he wanted to return to his base. "I don't like all the Ugandan spooks around here staring at me and thinking of ways to kill me," he said with a slight smile. The people in Kony's group were loaded with heavy bags of food, mostly maize, sugar and cooking oil destined for the base in the Garamba National Park. George felt uneasy at the sight of eight- and nine-year-olds loaded with heavy sacks of food. He was annoyed at the commanders who did not carry a thing apart from their own weapons, forcing the children to do the heavy lifting. "A place of war should not be a home for a child," he thought.

* * *

By late April 2007, when George completed his maiden voyage into the world of the LRA, there were two bases in Garamba National Park, situated in northeastern Congo, adjacent to the borders with Central African Republic and South Sudan. The bases, home to a thousand people, were known as Angula (an Acholi name) and Gangboo, the Luo term for "home of boo," *boo* being a type of bitter leafy green. Gangboo was the same base Otti had settled when he first entered Congo at the end of 2005. Gangboo was about three days' walk south of Rikwangba, with Angula on the same route, midway between Rikwangba and Gangboo. Kony and Otti resided in Gangboo but a large number of fighters stayed in Angula to act as a blocking force for anyone attempting to get to Gangboo without permission.

When George arrived in Gangboo, he heard that unidentified helicopters had been sighted above the LRA bases in the previous weeks. Kony was afraid that the Ugandan army and the United Nations were scouting LRA camps for an eventual attack. He ordered the building of another camp, later named Anyica (Darkness), a day's walk south of Gangboo. The base was called Darkness because it was intentionally built inside a large forested area, and was barely visible from above.

During June and July of 2007 Kony ordered the establishment of a fourth base, half a day's walk southeast of Anyica. It was also built in thick forest and was named Cover. Later that year Kony scouted the area west of Cover and ordered the building of a large base he later named Swahili. He chose the name because of his own orders at the time to all LRA members to learn Swahili, the *lingua franca* of most of eastern Africa, also widely used by Ugandan and Congolese soldiers.

Anyica, Cover and Swahili were approximately fifteen miles apart and formed an isosceles triangle with Anyica to the north, Cover to the east and Swahili to the west. Swahili would eventually become Kony's main base but he had houses in each base in Garamba, complete with wives, children and domestic workers. All five bases were located in the northwestern part of Garamba, in the so-called Azande Hunting Reserve, close to the border of South Sudan.

In early 2008, as the peace talks stalled, an additional base was created outside of Garamba, about thirty miles west of Swahili, on the road to the Congolese village of Bitima. A small encampment five miles east of Swahili served as a sick bay where injured or sick fighters were treated with medicinal herbs and medicine stolen from village clinics in South Sudan and Congo. A company of twenty combatants was in charge of security and providing food for the sick bay patients, with a former male nurse as the overall commander.

When the first groups moved to Congo in the fall of 2005 they were under strict orders from Kony not to attack Congolese civilians or loot their food. Otti deemed it necessary therefore to hunt inside Garamba as well as tend the land. By the time George arrived, the LRA was cultivating a combined fifteen square miles of *boo*, cassava, millet, maize and beans. There were gardens everywhere, in between huts and outside each camp. The two years between 2006 and 2008 was a time when "the holy became a farmer," as a former fighter later said. Commanders, including Kony, seemed content with the pace of life in Garamba, where they hunted and ate vegetables from farms manned by young fighters and abductees from South Sudan and Congo.

The Garamba bases reminded George of the traditional Acholi villages. "Kony's own large village, his own little world," George thought. Groups of low huts lay at a short distance from one another. Kony's residence was invariably centrally located in each camp, complete with pit latrines, a prayer yard, food stores and small generators or car batteries and solar panels. Kony and his families lived inside the circular huts the Acholis call *ot lum*, made with sticks and mud and covered with thatched roofs. Harvested food such as dried peanuts and cassava was also stored in small *ot lum*. Kony used military tents when on hunting or reconnaissance trips in the forest.

A few important offices were located right next to Kony's compound. The secretary to the Lakwena, the Holy Spirit, who noted what Kony said, Kony's personal doctor, his chief bodyguard and his signaler, who handled all phone and radio communications, lived close to the boss. In addition, the so-called Operation Room headed by the chief security officer was also nearby. Each commander had an operation room, which did not consist of a physical room but referred to the act of debriefing, interrogating or otherwise extracting information, which was then transmitted to Kony or the appropriate senior officer.

Kony's *ot lum* was easily identifiable for each base. They were always found at the intersection of other huts which, when seen from above, formed a crucifix. The other huts housed Kony's wives and children. Kony had many wives, at least seventeen by the time George arrived in Garamba, women abducted from Uganda, South Sudan and Congo. George heard that Kony had had more than sixty wives over the last twenty-five years but many had died or returned home. He also had many children, over a hundred, as Kony himself would boast. Apart from wives and children, Kony also had many prepubescent girls referred to as *ting-ting*, cleaners, cooks and babysitters in his compound. Upon reaching puberty most of the *ting-ting* would eventually end up as Kony's wives, although there were cases when he would give some of them as wives to commanders, rewarding them for their loyalty.

At least a dozen bodyguards were deployed around Kony's compound to protect him and his families. The bodyguards stayed close enough to have a clear view of Kony's compound but not to infringe on his privacy, which usually meant a distance of thirty to fifty yards. Two armed bodyguards always stood guard outside Kony's door. They also acted as his messengers and errand boys within the base. No one, apart from the bodyguards, was allowed to enter Kony's tent armed. Guns had to be checked at the door. Senior commanders had to ask for permission in advance when they needed to see him.

In 2007, when George joined the LRA, Kony's personal security had evolved into a standalone unit, falling completely outside of the LRA command structure. Called Central Brigade, this unit's sole purpose was to provide security for Kony and his family and was composed of between 200 and 250 armed men. There were two groups within Central Brigade: Home Guard, responsible for the security of Kony's families, and High Protection Unit (HPU or HAPPO), responsible for the overall security of Kony's camp and Kony's wellbeing.

Within HPU there was an internal and external wing of up to about ninety fighters each. Each wing had three coys, small units of between twelve and thirty fighters, called Coy A, Coy B and Coy C, with a coy commander, called a coymaster, who usually held the rank of sergeant. George was placed in Coy A of the internal wing of the HPU. Kony's bodyguards, usually a dozen per weekly shift, were chosen by Otto Agweng, the head of HPU. The chief of bodyguards was also Kony's ADC, essentially his personal assistant.

The bodyguards, also referred to as escorts, were responsible for the security and wellbeing of Kony and his family, ensuring his compound was clean and tidy and carrying Kony's personal belongings. The most trusted bodyguards often cooked for Kony. They also carried his guns, when Kony traveled. He did not carry his own guns; two assault rifles, a Kalashnikov and a Galil, the latter taken from the slain Guatemalan forces in Garamba in early 2006. Kony only carried on him a 9 mm Beretta pistol people in the LRA called "Star." As far as George was aware no one had ever seen Kony fire a gun.

All bodyguards held the rank of private or sergeant while the chief bodyguard was a captain. Only the rank of junior officers and above could have wives, which meant bodyguards were responsible for cooking their own food and washing their own clothes. Those who were new, which usually meant the most recent abductees, were responsible for cooking and cleaning for their entire coy. The bodyguards were not allowed to live inside huts and always slept in the open. They often ate in groups of five but kept to their ranks, privates ate with privates and sergeants ate with sergeants.

Other commanders had arrangements similar to Kony's, including security rules, although on a smaller scale. Senior commanders stayed near Kony, also located near the middle to ensure maximum protection from external attacks. The more senior the commander, the more people he had to care for, including wives and children as well as security detail and a number of *ting-ting*. But like Kony, they often did not trust their wives to do the cooking. Otti, who was well known for his paranoia and fear of being poisoned, only ate the food his most trusted bodyguards prepared. He often made the cooks eat the same food, ostensibly to show his appreciation for them but as one of his former wives said, "to make sure that if Otti were to die from the food, he would take the bodyguards with him."

* * *

The large party of 100 people split into three groups and set off for Garamba in single file, called a rail. The group walked for most of the day with few stops. There was little respite for the children, teenagers and women who carried heavy loads of food, water, cooking oil and breastfeeding babies. George was amazed to see four- and five-year-old children walking faster than he did. Most of them said little, seemingly used to the difficult life.

Some of the children wore gumboots, as rubber boots were referred to, as did the majority of the people in the LRA, including Kony. George remembered how Ugandan officials made fun of the LRA people for wearing gumboots, calling them peasants, but he quickly learned about the importance of light and practical shoes in walking over long distances throughout forests, marshes and dry terrain.

At their first dinner in Rikwangba Kony had said he preferred walking at night as he moved faster when it was cooler, but the journey to Gangboo was done during the day, over three and a half days. At dusk, the groups stopped and prepared for the night. Kony's chief body-guard organized his tent and ensured there was food, water for a bath and a hastily built pit latrine. There was dancing and loud talking by the fire. Later in the evening, after they had all dined and the women and children had gone to sleep, Kony and some senior commanders listened to the radio, usually the BBC's World Service. Kony commented on the news while the commanders nodded silently. The mood only changed when Kony's name was mentioned. Kony would smile a broad toothy smile, his face beaming with pride.

The group reached Angula and continued further south. Upon arriving in Gangboo, Kony sent for George. George was impressed with Kony's compound. He thought it was "a really nice jungle home." The commander who escorted him asked George to button up his shirt and, "be presentable in front of the General." He patted George down for hidden guns and walked him to Kony, where, clicking his heels, he announced George's presence in a gentle voice. Kony asked for a chair to be placed next to him and invited George to sit down.

Having gone through the elaborate handover, George was nervous. He paused when Kony asked him what kind of drink he wanted. "A soda," he replied slowly, and was amazed to see that Ugandan soft drinks were quickly served, a Mirinda fruit juice for him and a Seven Up for Kony. "This place is full of surprises," he thought, from the pleasant jungle home in the middle of the forest to soft drinks he had rarely even had back at home.

Kony spoke to George softly and addressed him as *wod* (son), while George replied with "Yes sir," in English, as he had heard others do in Kony's presence. Eventually George would come to call Kony "Mister Chairman," since Kony was considered the chairman of the Lord's Resistance Movement (LRM), the political arm of the LRA. In this, Kony mimicked the Ugandan President Yoweri Museveni who came to power as the leader of the National Resistance Army. Once in power, the NRA became the National Resistance Movement, with Museveni as the chairman.

Keeping with the tradition where all commanders in the LRA were referred to as *lapwony* meaning "teacher" in Luo but used also as "commander," Kony was called *Lapwony Madit*, Big Teacher or Big Commander. Kony was also called General, after the title he bequeathed upon himself in the late 1990s. People also referred to him as *Baba* or Father, or Number One after his code name used during radio communications. George would in private refer to Kony as the King of the Jungle.

Kony called for two young boys and presented them as Salim and Ali, his sons. George looked at Salim and Ali, wondering quietly about their lives. They had never experienced anything other than living in the forests of Sudan and Congo, always on the run from soldiers. He asked after their mothers. Before answering, Kony sent the boys to fetch mangoes and then said that Ali's mother was fine but Salim's was burned alive in a fire in South Sudan when the Ugandan army bombed the LRA camp, setting it ablaze.

"Salim still cries for his mother at times," Kony said. "He blames me for her loss. I was not there," he continued. "Had I been there, she would be alive today. I would have saved her," he said in an almost apologetic tone that made George uncomfortable. He did not know what to say and kept silent. After a short pause, Kony said, "I am hoping that these kids will not stay in the bush for the rest of their lives. I want to send them to school in Nairobi when the war ends. I want them to be educated."

Kony then changed the topic and embarked on a long speech about Congo's rich nature. "We are blessed here with everything good God made," he said. As the daylight faded, Kony told George that he was happy to have him in their midst and that he would be treated well. "There are people who say we are monsters," Kony said, "that we torture and kill, but that is not true. Life here is not easy, but the life of a soldier, the life of a man is not easy. Our struggle is just and a hard life is worth living for a just cause."

Kony then said a short prayer, which George took to be the signal for him to leave. He walked out of the compound, making sure he did not turn his back on the Big Teacher. Upon exiting he was called by a man who introduced himself as Captain Justine, Lakwena's secretary. George would later learn that Justine was close to Kony, a position he did not wish to relinquish. Justine thought George was there to take his job, which did not bode well for George's future in the LRA. But fresh from his drinks with the feared Joseph Kony, George felt too giddy to fully understand.

* * *

Justine, a tall, dark man, was abducted in 2000 when he was in Senior 4, two years before he was to graduate high school. Given his level of education, Justine was groomed to become Kony's secretary. It was a much desired position which ensured many privileges associated with being close to Kony that even senior commanders did not enjoy, including good food, accommodation and influence. His proximity to the boss made Justine more powerful than his title of Secretary suggested. Justine's other function was that of deputy to Otto Agweng, the HPU commander. Justine commanded, in Agweng's absence, 160 loyal and ferocious fighters. He was also George's overall superior.

Despite being assigned to Justine's domain, George ended up under the care of a short, smiley man with curly brown hair and honey-colored skin, known as Dog's Knee, Kony's chief bodyguard, formally known as ADC. His proximity to Kony, shared only with Justine, also placed Dog's Knee on a collision course with Lakwena's secretary even though, technically, as deputy to Agweng, Justine was Dog's Knee's superior. But they shared the same rank and amount of time with the Big Teacher, which put them on a par in the ad hoc LRA hierarchy. It was clear they disliked each other, something George witnessed often. Justine spoke to Dog's Knee as if he were a child, while Dog's Knee often pretended Justine did not exist.

George did not ask Dog's Knee for his real name. He knew that the majority of people in the LRA gave false information to their abductors, afraid that if they escaped the holies would attack their villages and kill their families in retaliation. Many used nicknames to conceal their real identities from their comrades and government soldiers. Some holies carried the nicknames from home. Brigadier Opuk, *opuk* meaning tortoise, was a sixty-year-old commander who had joined in the late 1980s. Common nicknames referred to the fighter's area of origin, such as Atiak, Padibe and Adjumani; particular attributes, such as Murefu (tall in Swahili) or Hatari (danger in Swahili); or were humorous, such as Punu (pig), Ogwal (frog) or

Chong Gwok (Dog's Knee). The influence of foreign war movies had resulted in nicknames such as Rambo, Chuck Norris and Van Damme.

Justine assigned George to Coy A of the internal wing of Kony's security, which meant that George was supposed to lodge with his coy mates. Dog's Knee, however, told George to stay with him. He knew the Big Teacher would approve so he told George to ignore Justine. Dog's Knee lived in a small hut together with his wife, one of the perks of being an officer, unlike the rest of the bodyguards who had to share small open tents. Though George worried that Justine would not be happy with his choice, he much preferred to spend the nights inside Dog's Knee's warm hut than sleep in the open on the cold ground. No wonder all the bodyguards looked like beggars with guns, wearing dirty clothes and matted hair.

Dog's Knee was abducted at a young age and was curious to learn about life in Uganda. He asked many questions and even allowed George to listen to BBC World Service programs, asking him to translate into Luo. As a private, George was not allowed to possess or listen to a radio, a rule he initially found odd. "What is wrong with a little entertainment?" he thought. "It could be good for morale." He later understood that Kony did not want low-ranking soldiers to listen to messages encouraging them to defect, the so-called *Dwog Paco* (Come Home) programs.

The lack of access to radios and information about life outside of the LRA was designed to keep the fighters insulated in the LRA bubble, the alternative universe that Kony had created with its own unquestionable rules. George quickly realized that, like the radio programs, as an outsider he too was a novelty, a sought-after commodity that people like Dog's Knee liked and appreciated.

Most commanders regarded George's education and outsider status as threatening. His access to Kony created jealousy and outright animosity, which he felt keenly when Kony was absent. George was frequently shunned and verbally abused by some officers when the Big Teacher was in Rikwangba or on various hunting trips in Garamba. Many made fun of his schooling, mockingly calling him Professor and Big Teacher.

He was happy in the company of Dog's Knee. Concy, Dog's Knee's wife, took care of George, preparing food for him and washing his clothes and boots. She was in her early twenties, abducted at thirteen. She told George she was taken by a large group one evening when coming back from her family's garden with her father. A commander called Tabulay was in charge of the group who took them. Tabulay said they should not be out late, "didn't they know the dangerous rebels were about?" Then, laughing, he told her father Concy needed to join the movement of Ladit Kony. All Acholi families needed to contribute to the fight against the usurper Museveni. They let her father go but took her straight to a camp in Sudan.

Too young to be a wife, Concy became a *ting-ting* in Tabulay's home. She took care of the commander's kids and helped clean the compound she shared with four wives and three young girls. The wives beat her often and gave her little food. Tabulay was later killed in battle so Kony redistributed his wives and servants to other officers. He gave Concy to Dog's Knee as his first wife. "It was God's plan," Concy once told George. "I am happy with Dog's Knee, but not his name."

George and Dog's Knee spent a lot of time together, growing close. They talked about life in Uganda and taught each other English and Swahili. George often walked with Dog's Knee near Rikwangba to bring back food for Kony and his families from the secret reserves. The food was donated by international organizations in an effort to discourage LRA attacks against civilians while the peace talks were ongoing. Dog's Knee and his men hid most of the food, usually buried it in the ground, near Rikwangba on the Congolese side. George enjoyed these trips. He learned about the secrets of the forest and Dog's Knee never made him carry heavy loads.

Following Kony's orders, Justine spent a few days a month teaching George about the duties and responsibilities associated with being Lakwena's secretary. He showed George a large book he carried everywhere. It contained many notes in Luo, mostly of speeches and prophecies Kony had uttered. There was also a comprehensive list of all the spirits. George had not heard Kony talk about many of the spirits mentioned in the notebook but Justine told him that those spirits came to Kony in his sleep and gave him orders which he then shared with the people.

Justine frequently reminded George about the general rules in the LRA. No alcohol or cigarettes allowed and definitely no drugs."A holy should be pure just like the noble cause he pursues," he said, no doubt repeating what Kony often preached. "The LRA soldier is fighting for the rights of the Acholi people, rights that were trampled by Museveni and his ilk," Justine would say as George nodded silently, waiting patiently for the time when the lecturing would end so that he could rejoin Dog's Knee.

* * *

For the first few weeks of his LRA experience life was not bad for George. He learned a lot and felt safe, even cared for, in the company of Dog's Knee and Concy. There was progress in the talks and according to fighters who traveled to Rikwangba "peace was on the horizon." George was happy. He felt certain he would soon return home as a former fighter and receive government support, perhaps even a job. With his education and experience as a former holy he could join the national army and maybe make officer rank.

One morning, about a month into George's stay in Garamba, Dog's Knee took him aside and said that he was bored and that they ought to have fun. "Let's make wine," he proposed. George was surprised and initially worried that Dog's Knee was testing him. As Justine often said, those who were caught breaking the rules received severe beatings, without exception. But when Dog's Knee told him that he knew that many commanders drank it in secret, George thought that even in the LRA there were exceptions to the rules. It reminded him of Brother

Seraphin, the priest who taught in elementary school. Everyone knew that Brother Seraphin – who had taken a vow of celibacy – slept with one of the night matrons, the women who slept in the children's dorms. She even bore his child. Everyone knew about it but no one said a word publicly.

George agreed to make *kwete*, a type of alcohol made from millet or cassava. Dog's Knee had already boiled the cassava, which they later squeezed in a big pot over an old mosquito net they used as a sieve. They added sugar and placed the covered pot inside a hollowed tree stump, "to ferment and turn into delicious wine," as Dog's Knee said. Four days later a grinning Dog's Knee said it was time to enjoy the fruits of their labor. The two walked into the forest with their large pot of alcohol, which they drank with a long reed straw called a *luceke*.

They laughed loudly and rolled around in the grass, too drunk to notice a group of holies passing by, who reported them to Otto Agweng, head of Kony's security and Dog's Knee's superior. Agweng sent a coy led by Captain Otika from Central Brigade to fetch the two merry men. In the late afternoon George was startled to see fighters jumping out of the bushes, guns pointed at his and Dog's Knee's heads.

Otika's men brought George and Dog's Knee in front of Agweng, who was waiting in the open in front of Kony's compound. George was so scared he sobered up immediately. He had been told that few people came out unscathed after facing Agweng. Agweng was in charge of not only

Kony's security but of also instilling discipline in the troops and "keeping them honest," as Concy once told him. "You do not want to have anything to do with Agweng."

Dog's Knee was still drunk and continued to laugh loudly, repeating, "Nothing to report sir." Agweng and Otika discussed how many strokes they should each receive, having already decided the form of punishment. Hearing the commotion, Kony came out of his hut. Dog's Knee made a serious face when he saw Kony and tried to stand straight but stumbled and fell over. Terrified, George felt his knees tremble as Kony stared at him.

Kony told Agweng not to beat them. He made fun of Dog's Knee for being "Wobbly Knee," adding, "Many people drink secretly around here. I know everything that goes on even though I don't talk about it. Why should some commanders drink every night and never be in trouble but these young soldiers make a mistake and be whipped? It is not fair."

Kony then proceeded to talk to all the people assembled in the open that the rules, as passed on by Lakwena, were there for a reason. "If you disobey the rules you only harm yourself," he said. The Holy Spirit knows you are not pure of heart. The impure will be punished sooner or later. But we all make mistakes. It is important to show penitence and strive to be better next time. I am sure these fellows are already regretting their actions. I just hope that some of the people, who have been around for a long time and should know better, also regret their actions and follow the rules.

"Take them home," Kony ordered. George had no need to be helped. He grabbed Dog's Knee by the arm and walked hastily to the little *ot lum* where Concy waited, wearing an expression of relief and a slight smile. "You are lucky," she said to George. She let the two men inside the hut, brought them some water and let them sleep. "I am sleeping outside tonight," she said, "you two reek of bad wine."

The next morning George was summoned in front of Kony. This time he did not offer a seat but let him stand by the door. George apologized profusely while keeping his gaze firmly on the ground. Kony told him to be careful in the future as he could not always vouch for his safety. "I will need your help in Rikwangba," Kony said, referring to the peace process. George was happy he had not been beaten and happier still he could be part of Kony's negotiating team, maybe even as an adviser to the Big Man.

A week later during Sunday prayer, when all the people in the camps gathered by a stream to listen to Kony preach, the Big Teacher said he had a big announcement to make. The Holy Spirit had come to Kony during the night and instructed him to allow people to drink alcohol. "It is time for us to celebrate after the many years of suffering," Kony said. "We will be going home now that the war is ending and wine is a feature of civilian life." "Cheers," he said as hundreds of people clapped.

Dog's Knee looked at George and winked. George smiled and felt strangely proud. He thought his actions might have caused Kony's change of heart. Maybe the

Big Teacher saw George drunk and realized that some of the rules were nonsensical and needed changing. "I have been here for a few weeks only and I am already influencing things," he thought.

CHAPTER 5

YANKEE

George spent most of his time shadowing Dog's Knee. "You should be with Justine," Dog's Knee once told him. "I hope you are not after my job," he joked. George decided to keep away from Justine, who had grown hostile following the drunken incident. George thought he was safer staying with Dog's Knee, even if it meant being a simple bodyguard rather than trying to become Lakwena's secretary, Kony's wishes notwithstanding.

The Big Teacher spent little time in Gangboo. He often stayed two weeks of the month in the newly built Cover. When in Gangboo, Kony left for a few days a week, either to be in Rikwangba or to go hunting, no one knew for sure. Dog's Knee accompanied him at times, but not always. Kony had instructed him to provide enough food and security for his family in all LRA camps so Dog's Knee often stayed behind. Dog's Knee was annoyed any time he did not travel with the boss. "It is so boring here," he would say in English, rolling his Rs, which made George laugh.

George, conversely, was happy when Kony was away and Dog's Knee stayed behind. Other commanders did not bother with him or made fun of him. Justine usually accompanied Kony on his trips, another source of happiness for George. Often Dog's Knee turned on one of Kony's laptops powered by a car battery or solar panels. Kony's family members and George sat in the open watching foreign and Ugandan movies on the laptop placed high on a tall wooden bench.

George loved movie nights. He had to translate from English to Luo but he enjoyed the challenge. Members of the delegation from Uganda usually brought the movies from home together with Acholi music tapes. Kony placed orders in advance through his signaler, by calling from his satellite phone. He always asked for war movies, particularly American ones. "They are the best," he often said, "but the blacks always end up killed. This is the problem with America. There is a lot of racism towards black people."

One night Dog's Knee played a movie they had watched a few times already. He said he wanted to watch it again but wanted George to translate it slowly so that he could understand some the dialogue. "What did the soldiers talk about? I can never figure out what they are saying," he said, "you don't translate well." "It is not my fault," George replied, "these people talk fast." The movie was about captured American soldiers trying to escape a Japanese prison. A character called Yankee spoke a lot and George could barely keep up with translating. "Hey Yankee," Dog's Knee yelled at George, "What is he saying now?" Everyone laughed. George also laughed and did not think much about it until the day after when he heard people calling him Yankee. "That's it," Dog's Knee said.

"You are now Yankee. You speak like him and you are light-skinned like a *mzungu*" (the Swahili term for white, or foreign). From that day all holies called him Yankee.

* * *

One day in late July 2007 one of Kony's wives in Gangboo criticized Dog's Knee for not providing enough food. Kony overheard the conversation and summoned him. As Dog's Knee explained to George later, Kony accused him of having neglected his duties and letting his family member starve. Dog's Knee apologized and promised to immediately organize a team to bring back flour and sugar from the secret stores in Rikwangba. But Kony said he was to redeploy to Central Brigade and Otika was to take over his position and his hut. "Sorry Yankee," said Dog's Knee. "You will be fine, but you are not allowed to come with me. *Ladit* said you should stay here."

That afternoon Dog's Knee and Concy vacated the small *ot lum* and Otika moved in. Otika told George he had no business living with the chief bodyguard. "You should stay with the privates," he told George and reassigned him to Coy A. Otika repeated to him all the rules he needed to respect. George was supposed to listen to his immediate superior, the coymaster, Second Lieutenant Omony, and orders were not to be debated or disobeyed, or he risked a beating. George was not supposed to have a gun until he learned the ways of the LRA and became a true guerrilla. "You are a soldier of the LRA, a holy" he said, "and you have to learn to behave like one."

That night George slept in the open near Kony's compound where his coy mates camped. In the following days he learned about his new life. He had to cook, clean and deploy as a guard day or night, in what was called OP (outpost). This meant sitting still for hours on an anthill or in a tree on the outskirts of Gangboo. As a bodyguard, George was also to move with Kony but, since he did not have a gun, he mostly deployed as OP, a boring and hated task.

Despite his promised future as Kony's secretary, George became overnight the lowest in the pecking order. He was the last to receive food, which meant that he had almost nothing, and the first to be picked for patrols and guard duty. At first he thought that Justine instructed the men to pick on him. George was mocked openly, woken up at odd hours in the night, sent on every possible chore from collecting water to cleaning Kony's compound. He was even struck by officers when he stumbled or was too slow. Most such events took place when Kony was not present, but George knew better than to complain to the boss. At least three different HPUers, one from his own coy, threatened to kill him. Once, a lieutenant slapped him in the face when George, tired from being on a lookout post all night, hesitated to salute him. "Next time I will put a bullet in your head," he said.

As time passed and George began to know some of his coy mates he realized they did not like him because he had joined willingly. Unlike them, he had not been forcibly abducted from home or school. Unlike them, he had not been beaten almost to death to signify his entry into the hard world of the LRA. Unlike most of them, he had not been forced to kill or injure his family members or neighbors, as a way to seal his stay with the rebels with blood, since such actions made return home hard to even contemplate. Unlike them, he was not really a holy nor could he truly become one given his peaceful entry. This feeling was made obvious to George when on the nights he was off-duty, his coy mates sat around the fire – the Acholi tradition called *wang oo* – and lamented the way they were taken from their families, recounting their stories of abduction and violence.

Innocent, a sixteen-year-old sergeant who had a slight speech impediment, spoke first. He described how he had been taken from the Opit Internally Displaced People's camp in 2002 when he was eleven. Innocent always started talking in a low, steady voice, complaining how his family was so poor that he had to drop out of elementary school. They could not afford his school uniform and books. Innocent spoke of well-to-do Acholi who never experienced the kind of poverty or violence his family had to deal with and yet supported the rebels, all the while pretending to care for the poor.

Innocent spoke in short sentences, comparing his feelings at the time of his abduction with how he felt at that very moment. "I was scared when they first took me," he said, "but I am not scared now." "The commander did not give us any water and I was thirsty," Innocent said, "but I am not thirsty now. I was hungry then but I am not hungry now."

He then talked about his first beating ordered by Commander Odomi. Other boys were ordered to find *lut* (sticks) and beat Innocent so that he could learn to be a real soldier. "You are now going to become *lalweny aligu*," Odomi said – a real guerrilla. Odomi then ordered that Innocent receive fifty strokes on his back. "If you cry or touch your back, we will strike you harder and all over your body," Odomi said. "If you survive it means you are not weak and you are *lalweny aligu*."

Innocent cried when he was beaten and Odomi became so angry that he kicked him in the head. "These are the rules in this government," Innocent said. If you cried when beaten you were hurt more or even killed. "I cried then," Innocent said, "but I am not crying now."

Innocent then spoke about a woman in his group called Akello, who was killed after someone accused her of being a witch. They said she had urinated in a jerrycan of water for common consumption. Someone said she was a witch. People grew agitated and an officer ordered her execution. Three men took her away and killed her in the bushes. They hit her on the head with sticks.

He talked about how he did not see her being killed but heard the blows to her head. "When she was dying she made these noises," he said, "like noises that cows make." Innocent and three other boys were asked the next day to take her body near an anthill, so that the spirits would be appeased, as tradition required. It was the first time he had seen a dead body. He held one of her legs and tried not to look at her smashed head and naked body. "I was afraid she would haunt me," Innocent whispered, "but now I don't even remember her. I was sad then but I feel no sadness anymore."

These stories shocked George. He knew of people who had been abducted and beaten but he also thought that some joined willingly and their families lied to the authorities to avoid being seen as rebel collaborators. He thought he had been naïve in thinking that people in their right minds would join the rebels. He tried to assure himself, as he had done since the day Quinto had proposed he joined the rebels, that everything was going to be fine. But he now felt almost certain his move into Garamba was a terrible mistake. He wished he could get out immediately but he knew he could not. Attempting to escape was pointless. He had no idea how to navigate in the forest. He knew he would not survive in the bush alone and would most likely be caught and executed. Everyone knew the Big Teacher did not like deserters.

George felt trapped. He tried to think of a solution. If he went to Rikwangba again he might see his uncle or other Acholi elders involved in the peace talks. He would plead with the elders to take him home, away from this place where he was certain he would die. Maybe he could convince Kony he was not cut out for this type of life. He was no rebel. What was he thinking when he agreed to do this?

The Big Teacher, who seemed reasonable, would understand. Maybe Kony would be generous and let him return home. George decided he only needed to survive until he could return to Rikwangba and then home with the delegation of elders. After all, Quinto had told everyone George would only go to the bush for a short time. But until then, George knew that to survive he needed to work hard, cleaning the coy mates' boots, making their food and carrying the heaviest loads.

He set about working as hard as he could and life became slightly easier, but he always felt threatened by Justine. George stayed away from Kony's compound to appease Justine. He thought that being out of Kony's sight would also keep Justine away. George's coy mates remained unfriendly but they eventually stopped threating to harm or kill him. He started to sleep through the nights again. Maybe, just maybe, he was going to be fine.

* * *

Justine and Otika continued to treat George badly. George knew that Otika and Justine hated him for being promised a position close to Kony. But they also disliked each other, as each vied for Kony's attention, just as it had been with Justine and Dog's Knee. When the bullying continued even after George made it clear he was no longer interested in the secretary position, he started to fear that Justine and Otika were trying to push him to escape. They sensed George was weak and close to leaving but likely to be caught if he attempted escape.

One day toward the end of the fourth month of his stay in Garamba, Otika ordered George to accompany him to get food from the secret stores. George wished Otika would leave him alone and for the first time wished he was on OP duty instead. He could not refuse, however, and proceeded with the rest of Otika's group. On their return, having already brought a heavy sack of sugar for Kony, Otika said he had forgotten the Chairman needed soap and sent George back to fetch it. On his way back George became lost. Eventually he retraced his steps and made it back to Gangboo, four hours later than the rest of the group. Otika was looking for him, having already told others that George had escaped.

When George arrived at Kony's compound, Otika ran towards him and loudly accused him of having tried to leave and reveal LRA secrets to the Ugandan army, that he was a spy for the Ugandan government. A hostile group of fighters immediately surrounded George. They removed his shirt and shoes, a common procedure signifying he was under arrest. Justine appeared and started to fire questions at George, who was terrified and certain he was going to be killed especially since Kony was not in Gangboo that day. George knew that Justine would have no problem convincing Kony that George deserved death because of his attempt to escape, the gravest of sins.

But Otika and Justine disagreed on how to proceed. Otika was adamant George had tried to escape. He said George tried to leave but failed to cut a path through the bush. Justine disagreed, saying George was just lazy and took his time walking back. They both agreed George needed a beating, a task that Justine delegated to Omony. Omony sent two young fighters to collect *lut*, the dreaded sticks, and ordered them to hit George thirty times on the back while he was forced to the ground, spread-eagled on his stomach. As the rules dictated, he was not to make a sound. George clenched his teeth and kept silent as the blows on his back made his whole body tense, twitch and shake. He thought of the caning in elementary school and how he had survived then. He was sure he could survive this also.

After the beating, Justine told George he was not yet cleared of Otika's accusations and the issue would be taken up with Kony on his return. George breathed with difficulty. His back was sore and his chest burned. He feared his lungs were damaged. Later he felt that his back had become soft, as if filled with water. That night, his coy mates brought him food and water to bathe. They said little but acted in a way that made George think it was not the first time they had helped people in his condition.

It was as if the caning changed their behavior. George knew from listening to their stories that all the holies in the coy were beaten or mistreated when they were first abducted and on countless occasions after. He was beginning to understand what they had gone through. While his coy mates were not exactly friendly they did not shun him, the first time this had happened since Dog's Knee left. That night, as he lay on his side trying to forget about his painful back, George thought he experienced a fleeting sense of pride. "I made no sound during the beating but took it like a real guerrilla," he thought.

Justine and Otika briefed Kony when he returned a few days later. George was summoned in front of the Chairman and asked to explain. Suppressing emotions, George recounted how he was lost in the bush and never intended to escape. He wanted to protest his innocence and lament the way he was treated but decided that complaining to Kony was a bad idea. That sort of thing would definitely get him killed. George was not sure if Kony even cared. He was convinced that no one could help him but himself, not even the Big Teacher.

Kony listened and then said he agreed with Justine. "George is still a lazy town boy, not yet accustomed to the life of the bush." Kony agreed that the caning was the appropriate response and the charges of being a spy and attempted escape were to be dropped. With the tone and gravity of a judge Kony then said he considered the matter closed. He ordered everyone else to do the same.

A few days later, Omony appeared with a gun, an old G3, which he said was George's. He taught George how to disassemble, clean and put it back together. "We are not going to shoot it," he told George, "bullets are too important to be wasted on shooting practice. But you will get the chance to shoot when it matters." Omony also told George that the gun was not going to be his forever. George would need to earn his gun. He knew from having listened to the stories of his coy mates that earning the gun meant first killing the gun's owner, usually a government soldier. He was not sure he would ever be able to kill a person, but he nodded when Omony asked if he understood.

George continued to be deployed on OP but he now clasped his gun when on duty. He understood that losing the gun carried serious repercussions, so he learned to sleep with it clutched between his legs. He worried about shooting it accidentally and injuring himself or others, so he always tried to keep his finger away from the trigger even when the safety catch was engaged. "Without a gun, you are just like an abductee or worse, a woman," George had heard his coy mates say often. He felt proud when he walked around with the G3 on his shoulder, clad in the military fatigues Omony had also supplied.

In mid-September 2007, George was told to join a standby on a hunting trip. Troops in standbys were also deployed to attack soldiers or other hostiles and were regarded as the bravest. Most fighters vied to be in standbys as it meant finding food and other goods that, as George learned from his coy mates, "made one rich." But riches in the LRA were different to riches in the real world. Food, water and clothes were huge benefits in addition to having a good gun and many bullets. But the most important aspect of being in a standby was the prestige it gave the fighter, who was regarded as courageous and able to provide for the rest of the group. George knew it was yet another test he needed to pass.

His standby had orders to secure food for the celebration of Uganda's independence from the British on 9 October. Independence Day was always celebrated in the LRA: "the day that we Ugandans liberated ourselves, a day that should not be usurped by Museveni." We, the northerners fought and led Uganda from the start," Kony said, referring to Milton Obote, the first Ugandan Prime Minister, who came from Apac, just south of Acholiland.

The standby was ordered to bring back meat for the occasion. George's team leader chose a hunting spot near a small lake, two days' walk south of Gangboo. Garamba Park was blessed with many species of wild animals that the holies hunted as a major source of protein for their diets, consisting mostly of vegetables and roots like cassava the Acholis call *gwana*. Like many Ugandans, the holies ate cassava roasted, boiled or dried and pounded into a powdery form which when mixed with water made *kwon gwana*, a doughy bread similar to what is known as *posho* in Swahili or *ugali* in southern Uganda, usually made with corn flour. Meat was always sought after to combine with *kwon gwana* and edible plants. Big game animals were always prized as they offered plenty of meat. The holies shot buffalos, hippos, various antelopes and many species of monkey. The animals were usually shot, skinned and their meat chopped into small pieces, dried, and brought back to camp.

* * *

Garamba National Park is one of Africa's oldest parks, established before World War II by Belgian colonial authorities. Encompassing two thousand square miles, the park is home to elephants, giraffes, which risk extinction due to poaching, the park has a large variety of wild animals including elephants, giraffes, hippos, buffaloes, many species of antelope and monkeys as well as warthogs, bush pigs and leopards. The rare combination of grassland savannah with scattered trees in the park's south and the dense forests of the north, all crisscrossed by small rivers, creates an excellent environment for wild animals attracted by the abundance of water and food. It is also an appealing place for poachers and rebels.

The first LRA group to make it to Garamba, led by Otti, set up base to the northwest of the park, in the Azande Hunting Reserve. LRA fighters were already familiar with almost the entire park, having deployed prior reconnaissance missions to the park's east and south as well as looting parties to the small villages on its outskirts. Otti's group of about 150 people made the maiden trip to Garamba in September 2005 when Kony and the rest of the LRA fighters were still in Sudan's Eastern Equatoria state and northern Uganda.

Despite a decade-long residency in southern Sudan, the LRA leadership decided it could no longer stay in Sudan. Key to this decision was the final signing of a peace agreement between the Sudanese government based in Khartoum and the southern Sudanese rebels, the SPLA. The Comprehensive Peace Agreement, signed in the Kenyan town of Naivasha in January 2005, was the culmination of a series of power- and wealth-sharing agreements that started in the summer of 2002. This would eventually lead to the independence of South Sudan in 2011.

After months of deliberations among the LRA leaders, a decision was made to move to Congo. Otti proposed the move to Congo but Kony, as always, had the final say. Kony agreed but did not give up on reestablishing relations with the Sudanese Armed Forces. The SAF, or the Arabs as the holies referred to them, were in the process of retreating to the north of the agreed North–South Sudanese border. Kony hoped that LRA scouting parties moving northeast of Congo alongside the CAR–Sudan border could make contact with SAF officers in South Darfur, the SAF's new southernmost base.

Garamba was considered an ideal place to host over 1,000 people in relative secrecy but most importantly Kony believed that it was a good spot to receive airdrops. The government of Khartoum had supported other rebel groups in the past, such as the West Nile Bank Front, another northern Ugandan group, by dropping supplies in Garamba. Otti himself was to lead the reconnaissance team and colonize a corner of Garamba for Kony.

By the summer of 2005 plans for Otti's move to Congo were already in place. The journey, consisting of roughly 350 miles, presented many challenges, the biggest one being crossing undetected the expansive White Nile. Until the summer of 2005 LRA groups had operated mostly to the east of the White Nile, in Sudan's Central and Eastern Equatoria regions. Some commanders wanted to notify their contacts in the SAF and ask for inflatable boats that could carry the 150 people in Otti's group as well as the rest of the LRA troops that would eventually follow. There was however fear that SAF officers would sabotage their mission, pass information to the SPLA or the UPDF, and even try to capture Otti and Kony.

A combatant nicknamed the Technician, as he fixed radio and television sets before being abducted by the LRA in Uganda, came up with the idea of making canoes. The Technician presented the idea to Otti, who ordered his chief bodyguard, Bogi Taban, to help. After a few weeks of trial and error the

Technician's version of a floating craft was ready. It consisted of three dozen jerrycans, the ubiquitous containers that people in the LRA use to carry water, cooking oil, sugar, maize and every item imaginable, tied together with liana ropes to form a raft. Tree branches were inserted on three sides of the raft, creating a fairly stable structure that carried seven people at a time – five passengers and two rowers.

By the beginning of September 2005, Otti set off for Congo, crossing the White Nile near the town of Yei. Upon arriving on the eastern shore of the river, a narrow passage was identified where the water was relatively calm. At dusk seven fighters embarked on the raft; two rowed with oars made of teak, while the rest guarded against hostile forces appearing on the western side. They carried with them a large rope tied to trees on both sides of the river, a common practice. It took three nights for the entire group, including women and children, to cross to the other side. On 10 September the group proceeded towards Congo, attacking a few villages near the town of Yei on 13 September 2005 and making it to Garamba by the end of the month.

Upon arriving in Garamba, Otti ordered small reconnaissance teams to deploy and learn about the park, villages in its vicinity as well as all security forces. Otti also ordered the abduction of locals who were to be used as guides to help the fighters learn as much as possible about the terrain – a well-known strategy LRA groups continue to use today. One month later Otti had drawn up detailed maps of the park, particularly of the northwestern area, deemed suitable to host Kony. Otti ordered his fighters not to kill people in Congo, reportedly saying, "Be polite even when you are asking for people's stuff."

The general belief among some LRA combatants who were the first to reach Garamba was that Kony had the personal assurances of Congo's President that the LRA was welcome in his country. Many talk about a letter Otti possessed written by Laurent Kabila, the then Congolese President, authorizing Kony to enter Congo. It is not inconceivable that Laurent Kabila chose to support Kony in the late 1990s when President Museveni, a former ally, reportedly supported the Rally for Congolese Democracy, a rebellion against Kabila's government. But in October 2005 Laurent Kabila had been dead for three and a half years, killed by one of his bodyguards. He was succeeded by his son, Joseph Kabila, who had by then had something of a rapprochement with Museveni.

Otti requested a meeting with the Congolese army with the mediation of local chiefs, and he presented the so-called Kabila letter and a request from Kony asking for safe haven in Garamba. The meeting took place in November 2005 in Garamba. Congolese army representatives heard Otti's request and asked in turn that the LRA refrain from attacking civilians while waiting for a response from Kinshasa.

By the end of the year, Otti sent word back to Kony in Eastern Equatoria that he should make his way to Garamba. Kony and his large unit of 200 people were to come first, followed by the rest of the groups in South Sudan and Uganda. Otti ordered his men to clear the forest near his initial base and cultivate the land with seeds looted from Congolese villagers. The groups coming to Garamba from South Sudan were ordered to abduct young men and women who were to be used as slave labor for cultivating the land. Garamba was to become a new home to the holies as the struggle to overthrow the Ugandan regime of Museveni continued.

But by the end of January 2006, as Otti and the rest of his group awaited Kony's arrival, they encountered the group of fighters they initially thought were American soldiers. Having learned from the Congolese army of Otti's presence in Garamba, the MONUC Guatemalan Special Forces deployed to carry out reconnaissance in Garamba and reportedly to arrest Otti. The loss of eight of the peacekeepers' lives sent shockwaves through MONUC and the United Nations and is possibly the main reason why the Congo UN missions never further directly engaged LRA combatants. The Congolese army followed suit and all LRA groups were essentially allowed to live in Garamba hassle free.

News of Otti crossing the Nile, which became clear after his troops attacked near Yei in September 2005, shocked many in Uganda, including the Ugandan army and security service officers who had expected Kony and his troops to return to Uganda, as they had done after Operation Iron Fist of 2002, rather than move to Congo. By early October 2005, a battalion of the Ugandan army was sent to the vicinity of Yei to ensure Kony and the rest of the LRA forces remaining in South Sudan were stopped from crossing into Congo.

In the first week of February 2006, Ugandan secret services intercepted a radio exchange between Otti and Kony's signaler, Lieutenant Labalpinyi. Otti gave a detailed coded message of the route Kony should follow to join him in Congo. Ugandan and South Sudanese soldiers quickly deployed to all the areas they thought Kony would pass through but found no trace of him.

Kony's entire group, including his family and a large security detail crossed the Nile in the second week of February 2006 using the same rafts of jerrycans Otti had used.

Aware that Ugandan military intelligence was eavesdropping on LRA radio traffic, Kony came on air on 13 March 2006 via Otti's signaler, a clear sign he had made it to Congo. Through the signaler, Kony praised the Lord for his safe arrival in Garamba and asked other LRA commanders who were still in South Sudan and Uganda to follow suit. "Real soldiers never give up," he said in a none-too-subtle mocking note aimed at the eavesdropping Ugandan army. Despite the deployment of Ugandan and SPLA forces to thwart the relocation to Congo, all LRA groups made it to Garamba by the end of 2006. This included the last Uganda-based groups of Dominic Ongwen and Thomas Kwoyelo, who had to travel for over two months to reach Garamba via South Sudan.

* * *

George joined a large standby of eighty people, most of them fighters but also young boys and girls who were to carry most of the meat back to camp. The team, led by Captain Odong "Murefu," set off early in the morning, planning to spend a night in the bush and arrive at the lake in the evening of the second day. They planned to camp near the lake and start hunting the day after. Two holies in the standby told everyone to be careful; they knew from past experience that the lake attracted many hunters, some from Nabanga and Merida in South Sudan, and Congolese hunters from Dungu and Faradje.

After two tiring days of cutting their way through the dense bush, the team approached the hunting spot when they heard gunfire. Murefu called the group's IO (intelligence officer), a young lieutenant called Acaye. Acaye and five men, including George, were sent to check on the shooters. All six proceeded slowly until they reached high ground, from where they saw four hunters who had just shot a hippopotamus and were preparing the meat to dry. Acaye gave the order to surround them. "Shoot them if they have guns," Acaye whispered, which George thought was strange. They had just heard the shots so they knew the hunters had guns. He understood the hunters would die. Thinking he was about to participate in their killing made him uneasy but he could not do much about it and followed the group.

George inched towards the hunters' camp, his heart racing. He was not entirely clear how to fire his gun and was scared the hunters would shoot him first. He could hear them talking loudly and laughing as they cut the chunks of meat and placed them on wood stands over a small fire. He looked at the faces of his comrades. He thought they moved like leopards, slowly yet ready to pounce. He felt his throat drying and wanted to clear it but was too afraid to even think about coughing. He heard a loud yell and realized it was the cue for the attack. He heard shots, jumped and fired his gun but did not know where the bullets went.

Seconds later he stood near the bodies of the hunters, who were caught completely by surprise. They had no time to reach for their guns, two AK47s that lay next to a tree, a few steps away. George did not remember how he advanced from his squatting position to the bodies. He tried to avert his eyes from the bullet-riddled corpses and worried he would vomit. His heart pumping, he snatched some of the cured hippo meat and stuffed it in his bag. He was also quick to grab one of the AKs. Acaye took the other gun.

They took all the meat and returned to where the rest of the group waited. Acaye gave a quick report to Murefu. They discussed whether the people they had just killed were Congolese soldiers in civilian clothes since they had AKs. Most of the hunters the LRA fighters came across in Congo had homemade guns, what the Congolese called *zero zero*, able to shoot a single cartridge at a time. Murefu said they were most likely elephant poachers who had bought their weapons from Congolese soldiers. He congratulated Acaye and the rest for being good soldiers.

Murefu decided to let George keep the AK47 he already held on his shoulder next to his G3. He ordered George to give the G3 to a *kadogo* who was to carry it back to base. "This is now your best friend," Murefu told him, laughing and pointing to the AK, "a better friend than your dick, which sometimes does not do what you want." He called the gun a Yugo, which George understood was because the gun was made in the country called Yugoslavia. Some of the AKs were called China because they were made there. He later called his AK *mugupande*, a Luo term meaning "one-legged," after the gun's hollow butt. George smiled and felt content. He knew he had achieved a hard task; he had earned his gun even though he was not sure whether he deserved it. He clutched his new possession proudly and felt that he had taken the next important step in becoming a real rebel.

That night the group ate the meat from the hippo and planned for the next day's hunting mission. They hoped to find hippos, giraffes or the antelopes the Congolese called *okapi*. They set off early in the morning to approach the lake at the time the animals drank water, making it easier to shoot them. Upon reaching the lake they saw a family of hippos in the water and immediately opened fire. George ran close to a large hippo and shot it four times in the head. The hippo fell near the shore, bleeding heavily. Three men slaughtered and skinned the animal. One group needed help getting their hippo out of the bloodied water. They tied the gigantic hippo with ropes and twenty men pulled it out. The hippo was pregnant, carrying a fully formed fetus weighing thirty pounds, one of the bodyguards reported later.

Drying meat was something George had quickly learned when joining the LRA as an important survival skill. He knew how to make the four-cornered wooden stands with sticks on the ground the height of a chair seat. He knew to cut the meat into pieces just the right way, not too thick or too thin. He had learned how to make a nice small fire under the slabs of meat and to turn the pieces of meat over and over until they were ready. He knew never to use salt for curing meat. It was too important a commodity, to be used only sparingly for flavoring foods. He made sure to get as much of the meat from the hippo as he could. He knew people in his coy would appreciate all he could bring back and would thank him for it.

By the time the group started the journey back to Gangboo, George was so loaded with cured meat, water and his gun that he moved with difficulty. He thought he looked like one of those vans that came to Gulu from Kampala, full of goods spilling over the sides. He walked as fast as he could and did not complain when the weight made his shoulders and back ache. He never wanted to reach a place faster. He was going back to camp a changed man. He left a novice and was returning a real soldier with his own gun. He was going back as a provider, the most respected kind of holy. "I passed a test," he thought. Maybe he was capable of surviving in this hostile environment after all and did not need anyone to come to his rescue.

* * *

After the hunting trip, George was not deployed as an outpost guard for much longer. He started to spend a lot of time guarding Kony's compound. Noticing him more, Kony frequently invited George to sit near him, alongside Justine and some senior commanders. George listened to Kony talk about what was happening with the peace talks, events in Uganda and the world, particularly concerning the International Criminal Court. "This bad ICC wants me dead," he said. "It wants to hang me and for what? For no crimes I have committed but because Museveni said so. The evil ICC should hang Museveni for all the crimes committed against the Acholi."

Kony then spoke about history and religion. Worrying that this would be some sort of test George listened carefully. Kony spoke about the power of the spirits. He said that before white people came to Africa, it had a lot of riches but those riches were controlled by the spirits or gods of Africa (*jogi* in Luo), the God of Rain, God of Land, God of Expeditions and other gods that controlled each aspect of life.

In African culture, before anything was done, like an expedition or a hunt, rituals were performed to get blessings from the god in charge of that event. The people of Africa were informed of dangers and were protected when they praised the god by performing the appropriate rituals. These African gods descended on Kony and gave him the power to perform miracles and foresee events in the future. The gods came to Kony so that he would save the Acholi from Museveni's regime but the people of Acholiland were deceived by the Museveni government and rejected Kony and his movement.

"African gods did not tolerate foreigners in Africa," Kony offered, "because the gods were angry at the foreigners robbing the lands of Africa of their riches." This happened during the colonial times when the white colonialists robbed the continent they regarded as backward in culture but rich in minerals and natural resources. Kony would say that missionaries were first sent to soften the hearts of the Africans by preaching religious sermons Africans did not understand. Christianity had no meaning to Africans but it was used to turn Africans against one another, so that the whites could easily rob them of their riches.

Kony said that fake gospels spread from one corner of Africa to the other and, as stated in the bible, if an enemy slaps you on the cheek, you should turn the other cheek and give him a second chance to hit you. These concepts made it easy for white men to rule Africa through their own white principles while Africans were divided among themselves as their land was being split among the whites. While their lands' riches were swept away, a majority of Africans joined these foreign religions while neglecting their own African gods. The Africans were shamed by the white missionaries into not performing traditional rituals. They were told those rituals were wicked, sins against a God they never saw or received help from, unlike their own African gods.

"So it came to be," Kony said, "that the Africans were deceived and forgot their ways of praising their own gods." The African gods became angry as Africans praised a god that had been brought by the foreigners. The blessings the Africans used to receive from their gods turned instead to curses and thus war started.

Then the speech turned to northern Uganda and Kony's voice rose as he started to gesticulate excitedly. "Just as the Africans abandoned their own gods and supported a foreign one," he said, "the Acholi people were manipulated by Museveni, who turned them against me." The Acholi reported the ammunition and guns the LRA hid inside Uganda to the soldiers. He said some Acholis were stupid, deceived by Museveni, and that they deserved to be punished. But the Holy Spirit confided in Kony that the LRA would be victorious. Everyone needed to keep the faith and trust that with the help of the Holy Spirit they would return to Uganda and receive rich rewards for their part in the war.

* * *

In September 2007, Acholi traditional leaders arrived in Garamba for consultations with Kony and other commanders on the on-going peace process. George joined Kony's group of bodyguards who made it to Angula, coded Garamba One. Gangboo was known as Garamba Two. The elders, who were talking to Otti, stood as Kony approached and greeted him while George and the other bodyguards took over the security of the camp. George heard Kony start the meeting with a prayer. Kony called for patience to be bestowed on all the people who had suffered too long and for a positive outcome to the peace talks.

After the prayers, Kony spoke about the peace talks. He explained to those assembled that the LRA could win by talking as well as by fighting. "There is no shame in the peace talks," he said. "We are not surrendering, we are agreeing to something. But if Museveni does not want peace we will win by the power of the gun." When an elder asked Kony how he would do it since he had failed to win for the last twenty years, Kony said he would change tactics. "We will take a lot more people and build a huge army."

After his speech, everyone sat to eat while Kony's escorts distributed sodas. Ugandan music soon started to play, to the delight of a few children who began to dance. The guests, Kony and senior commanders sat watching and sipping tea. George looked at the group. Here were the infamous commanders who had ordered or carried out terrible attacks: Kony, Otti and Okot Odhiambo, the man people thought responsible for the massacre of Barlonyo near Lira in northern Uganda where more than 200 people were killed in 2004. George wished he could one day become respected like them. Maybe he did not need to leave after all. He could rise in influence now that he had finally figured out how this strange place functioned.

CHAPTER 6

A GENERAL WHO KILLS

The last days of September 2007 were tense. There was commotion in Kony's compound in Gangboo and various officers came and went in his tent late at night, which was highly unusual. Generally, Kony preferred to be alone or with his wives. George stood guard outside Kony's compound and thought that it had something to do with the peace talks. He hoped that a resolution could be found soon. He had done six months with the rebels, enough to be able to go home and show off to his friends, proving he was a real guerrilla.

On 30 September, Kony and a dozen bodyguards including George moved to the newly built Anyica, two hours' walk from Gangboo and home to Okot Odhiambo. The first day of October signaled the beginning of the operation that Kony and his security officers had feverishly planned. George was surprised to see Justine running towards Kony's compound bringing along all HPU troops available. Another 150 fighters from Independent brigade led by Major Charles Arop also deployed to Kony's compound, bringing the total number of guards to over 300, or about one-third of the entire LRA fighting force. George understood this was a high security alert and took his AK off his shoulder, released the safety, and crouched into a defensive position, following the lead of his coy mates.

Shots were heard inside Kony's tent and word quickly spread that Major Adjumani (Aimani) had been killed.* George did not know what had actually happened but the official story was that Aimani planned to kill Kony. One night in August, senior LRA commanders, part of the so-called Control Alter or what Kony called the LRA's Joint Chiefs of Staff, were watching a movie in Otti's compound. Otti's chief bodyguard, Colonel Ben Achellam, started to talk openly against Kony, saying Otti was the brains of the LRA, and that he had the support of the foreigners in the peace talks.

Achellam also said that Kony thought only about himself and that he refused to sign the peace talks, keeping everyone in the bush away from their families with little chance of returning home.

It was not the first time, George heard, that Achellam had been critical of Kony, once even suggesting Kony was a drunk and that he forbade other holies from drinking alcohol, while drinking secretly in his tent. When it

---

* Adjumani, whose real name was Swaib Aimani, was a Madi from Obongi in northwestern Uganda. The Madi live next to the Acholi in Uganda as well as in South Sudan and speak Madi-ti or Lugbar languages, distinct from Luo. Aimani was abducted as a young boy by Otti in 1989 and served as security to both Otti and Kony at various times. Because of their early relationship, Aimani was regarded as loyal to Otti, which proved fatal for Aimani that October.

became obvious he had a drinking problem Kony allowed everybody else to drink, to avoid embarrassment. That night, however, Achellam went as far as proposing to Aimani that they assassinate Kony. When Otti took over, Aimani would be appropriately rewarded. George heard that Aimani agreed to be the executioner since as a former escort to Kony he could get close to him armed and have a good chance of killing him.

Kony had his spies in Control Alter who infiltrated the group of conspirators and then promptly informed him of the plot. Kony responded immediately and planned to thwart the presumed mutiny. Loyal commanders brought Aimani to Kony's compound while Kony was out on the morning of 1 October. They told Aimani that Thomas Kwoyelo was to be arrested for planning to escape. Kwoyelo was called to Kony's tent where Aimani disarmed him. Aimani tied Kwoyelo but was surprised to find that other commanders in the tent aimed their guns at him. Aimani reached for his gun but the others shot him dead.

Rumors quickly spread that a group of officers planned to take over High Command and both Kwoyelo and Aimani were involved. George worried that open fighting was about to start and he could easily end up dead given his lack of experience. He made sure he spoke loudly of his loyalty to Kony to everyone he came across that tense day. It was as if everybody was being tested about their relationship with Otti and his followers. Some commanders were nowhere to be found. A senior officer, Lieutenant

Sitting from right to left: Captain Komakech (with hat), still in the LRA as of May 2016; Santo Alit, killed on the border with DRC and CAR in 2009; Ben Achellam and Otim Record (partial), killed on Kony's orders alongside Vincent Otti in 2007. Standing, front, from right to left: Okot Odhiambo (with beret), killed in 2013; Joseph Kony; Ochan Bunia (partial, with beret), died in 2012 in Congo possibly due to HIV. 28 June 2006, Nabanga, South Sudan.
Photo courtesy of Mareike Schomerus.

Colonel Opiyo Makasi who was the director of operations, disappeared that morning. Later, it became known that he had escaped. He had surrendered to a Congolese army garrison and eventually made it to Uganda with the help of the United Nations. Back in the camps Kony ordered everyone to be quiet and not discuss the events of the day. He worried that Otti would find out.

* * *

On the morning of 2 October, Otti, flanked by Ben Achellam and Captain Alfred Otim "Record," both Otti's protégées who hailed from Otti's birthplace of Atiak, turned up in Anyica. Over thirty of Otti's bodyguards and eleven of Achellam's bodyguards were also there. Otti had been in Rikwangba accompanying the delegation of Acholi elders who had just left, and knew something was wrong when Kony called from his satellite phone asking him personally to return to base. Kony rarely used satellite phones or high frequency radios himself but communicated via Justine or his signaler. Otti sounded reluctant on the phone, saying he needed to go to his house in Gangboo first but Kony convinced him to leave Rikwangba and make his way to Anyica.

Before Otti and his troops arrived at Kony's residence in Anyica, Kony left his compound and moved into the nearby home of Otto Agweng. It seemed that he wanted to avoid confrontation, leaving his loyal commanders to do his dirty work. Otti entered Kony's tent, where five senior commanders including Odhiambo waited. The HPU descended on Otti and Achellam's escorts, disarming them quickly. Others arrested Ben Achellam and Otim "Record," tying them up and bringing them inside Kony's compound. The officers in Kony's tent had already disarmed and tied up Otti. Kony followed the action from Agweng's tent but never appeared to talk or otherwise deal with the presumed mutineers. He spoke to Odhiambo on his walkie-talkie, yelling frantically that Otti, Achellam and Record be shot without delay.

Otti expressed indignation and demanded to talk to Kony, whom he referred to as baba *(father). He spoke to all the commanders, reminding them that he was their senior and their* lapwony. *Then, appearing resigned to his fate, he said that all that he had done was for the good of the movement. He had done nothing wrong but if that was to be his fate, he accepted it. As a witness to the executions of other commanders on Kony's orders, particularly Otti Lagony, the man he replaced in 1999, Otti must have known there was no hope left at that point.*

Ben Achellam yelled loudly that he wanted to talk. He said there were many things to discuss. However, two commanders, Odhiambo and Bok Abudema, ordered an execution squad of thirteen men, who took Otti, Achellam and Record next to a stream near Anyica and shot them. Two commanders shot Otti while the rest of the group shot Achellam and Record 100 yards away from where Otti fell. A fighter from the execution squad later told George that Otti asked, "What have I done?" before being sprayed with bullets. The same person also said that the orders from Kony were to bury Achellam and Record but to leave Otti's body in the bush for three days so as to appease the spirits, angered by Otti's duplicity. Kony was clearly making an example of Otti.

Fear spread in all camps when news of Otti's death broke. Many knew Otti well and respected him. Commanders like Makasi escaped as soon as they understood what was taking place, afraid that their affiliation to Otti, real or perceived, could cost them their lives. Officers seen as close to Otti, particularly those who came from Atiak, Otti's birthplace, were immediately arrested to preempt any potential confrontation. This included Otti's chief bodyguard Captain Pope and Major Okot "Atiak." Some commanders, maybe even Kony himself, thought Pope was still loyal to his former boss and had him shot. The same fate befell Otti's nephew, who had joined during the peace talks. Odhiambo accused him of possessing a secret satellite phone that was allegedly found when his tent was searched. Otti's son, who also joined during the Juba talks, escaped the same day Otti was executed.

Otti's compound in Gangboo was taken over by Odhiambo and his personal escort. Otti's six wives were distributed among six senior commanders, including Odhiambo, who became the de facto deputy to Kony. Three ting-ting were taken by Kony, one eventually becoming his wife. All the officers who took Otti's wives joked that the women were finally about to know real men, referring to Otti's supposed impotence. Otti's escorts were redistributed to other commanders too. In a matter of hours all physical signs of Vincent Otti's twenty-year presence in the LRA were wiped out.

On the afternoon of 2 October 2007 Kony called a meeting of all LRA officers from the rank of second lieutenant and above, around 200 commanders, at his headquarters in Gangboo. In a long speech barely a few hours after the executions were carried out, Kony said that Otti had made deals with foreigners to leave the movement and kill Kony, and that the Holy Spirit informed him of Otti's intentions. "No one is above the movement," said Kony, "but I am the father of this organization. You should not forget who is in charge and make sure that you obey my orders, or suffer his fate." To complete the total erasure, Kony ordered that nobody ever mention Otti's name again.

Kony said that everyone should know he did not hold the title of General for praying but because he could kill. "No one has ever heard of a general who did not kill," he said. He then pointed to Thomas Kwoyelo, who sat on the ground disarmed, shoeless and shirtless. A practice of Ugandan authorities that probably originated in colonial times, taking the shoes and shirt off someone were symbolic gestures of them being under arrest. "I am not going to talk about his misdeeds," Kony said, "but you, Kwoyelo, know full well what you did wrong." Kwoyelo said nothing, looking terrified. Kony then said that Kwoyelo was demoted to private and his gun and personal escorts were to be removed. He was left only with a wife and confined to his ot lum. He was not to leave his hut until further orders.

* * *

George was shocked by the events that had taken place. After Kony's speech, George's coy mates were told to take the evening off from guarding Kony's compound to prepare dinner and to deploy during the night around Gangboo. Kony gave strict orders that no one should leave the camp. He was worried that people would try to escape due to the executions and pervasive fear. Kony spared

Kwoyelo to avoid a mass exodus of officers who feared for their lives, particularly once it became obvious that such an influential commander as Makasi had already escaped.*

Despite feeling calmer that evening, George sensed that the tension created in the last couple of days would not dissipate for a long time. "This is not the end of this affair," he thought. He saw that his coy mates, as well as everyone else in the camps, behaved differently, more guarded and concerned about their safety. Everyone wanted to talk about what had happened but no one wanted to risk mentioning Otti's name and testing Kony's resolve.

George was scared but also a little relieved. He realized he could have been dead that evening had he been on the wrong side of the conflict. What if people thought he sympathized with Otti? After all, George was a man of books, more like Otti than Kony. Had he not been assigned to Kony's unit he could have been killed. In the panic that gripped the camps no one would have even questioned the reason, he would simply have been shot just like everyone else close to Otti. And what if the accusations against Otti were true and he and his people won

---

* Of the main characters involved in the Otti affair, Kwoyelo's role remains the murkiest. His perceived closeness to Otti made him a suspect but he most likely had little to do with any possible coup against Kony. Kwoyelo was shunned in the LRA until the Ugandan army offensive of December 2008. In the aftermath of the attack, he was given a gun and allowed to wander in the forest with his wife. In February 2009 he was injured by Ugandan soldiers in Garamba, where he was captured and brought to Uganda. Pressured to show results for their very expensive military operations in Congo, the Ugandan army paraded Kwoyelo with much fanfare as a top commander, third in charge after Kony, which was ironic given the events of October 2007.

the internal battle and succeeded in killing Kony? George would have been dead. Everyone thought he was close to Kony. While George was happy that his man won, he was shocked at his inability to understand how crazy this place was. A few days ago he had been convinced that he had figured it all out. Now he felt confused and vulnerable.

That night as he deployed as a camp guard, expected to shoot anyone attempting to escape, George realized that his life in the LRA, in the real LRA, had just begun. He became convinced that there was not going to be a swift and heroic return home. He was not even sure he would make it out alive. Otti's death was bad for the peace talks. By killing Otti, who was the main LRA interlocutor in the talks, Kony had essentially destroyed the peace process. "Nothing good can come out of Otti's death," George thought.

George knew that at this time of deep distrust among fighters he was already regarded with suspicion. As rumors about the so-called treason multiplied, one particularly popular theory held that the newly arrived were responsible for creating internal dissent and wanted Kony dead. Despite George's affiliation to the Big Man, no one was trusted and the young commanders did everything they could to showcase their loyalty by treating everyone as a suspect. George felt Justine's attention shifting onto him once again. He could not help think that this time Kony would have no problem signing off on his execution if Justine or Otika, who wanted to impress the boss, accused George of wanting to escape or being a spy. There was always a little hope that you could survive being caught trying to escape, but there was no coming back from accusations of treason, as Otti had learned.

* * *

It is unlikely that Otti planned to kill Kony but he did receive offers to leave the LRA alongside his loyal troops. As the Juba talks seemed to stall in late spring of 2007, there were reports of various entities offering Otti money to persuade him to leave. The leader of the LRA delegation, Martin Ojul, once hinted in an interview that he gave Otti money provided by the Ugandan government but that Otti refused to leave or betray Kony. It would not be surprising if the Ugandan government tried to persuade Otti to leave. His defection would have significantly damaged the LRA given his popularity and senior rank.

Otti was one of very few commanders who could debate orders from Kony and at times override him. He was responsible for deciding to move to Congo and eventually agreeing to the Juba talks to the dissatisfaction of Kony, who seemed more interested in reestablishing a connection with the Sudanese Armed Forces, not trusting that peace talks would work. Furthermore, Otti took charge of the Juba talks, again to Kony's annoyance. The previous top commander in charge of peace talks with the Ugandan government, Sam Kolo, defected in February 2005. Given his influence in the LRA, often publicly challenging Kony, it is surprising that Otti did not make a move against Kony sooner. If anything, it is remarkable that Otti remained loyal to Kony for twenty years.

Kony had eliminated those who threatened his status in the past. In 1999, in similar circumstances, Kony had ordered the execution of his then second in command Otti Lagony (no relation to Vincent Otti). Lagony was a former officer in the Ugandan army before Museveni's army took over in 1987. An Acholi, Lagony decided to join the Uganda People's Democratic Army (UPDA). As the UPDA disintegrated due to commanders cutting deals with the NRA, Lagony, like many former professional soldiers, decided to join Kony's nascent organization and continue the struggle. Lagony rose to power, becoming Kony's deputy in 1997; but in December 1999 Kony demoted him from brigadier to lieutenant.

A month after demoting him Kony had Lagony executed on charges of treason. Kony felt threatened by Lagony, who advocated for a peaceful return to Uganda under an amnesty deal the Ugandan parliament passed at the end of 1999. The Amnesty Act of 2000 allowed combatants to return home and not be prosecuted once they renounced violence. Kony worried that Lagony would leave with many fighters, so he had him killed and replaced by Vincent Otti. In a speech immediately after Lagony's execution, Kony said the Amnesty Act was an army trick to deceive the fighters so they could be executed. There would be no leaving the bush, he ordered.

CHAPTER 7

A PRISONER
OF THE SPIRITS

Uganda's Independence Day on 9 October 2007 was not the joyous occasion George had anticipated. The September expedition to secure meat for the celebration seemed a long time ago. Much had changed since his return to camp with his own gun and hippopotamus meat. George rarely saw Kony, who moved to other bases and kept out of sight. George was reassigned to OP station, the dreaded guard duty routine. Since Otti's death, Omony, George's coy commander, gave him hell, deploying him both day and night as a guard.

George thought about the preceding weeks and was convinced that many things he had seen or heard during that time were not accidental. There had been clear omens of Otti's bleak end. George remembered Kony's speeches, his allusions to the intruders, the whites who colonized Uganda and Africa, the priests who deceived the Africans and those who pitted the Africans against one another. He was now certain that Kony had been referring to Otti the whole time. The Big Teacher was alluding to the foreigners who convinced Otti to kill

Kony, like the priests who deceived the simple-minded Africans. Kony foretold Otti's fate when he spoke of the vengeance of the African gods, the curses they cast and how Kony was their messenger on earth, the executioner of their will. George vowed never to take lightly what Kony said.

On 9 October, George was happy to learn he was assigned to cooking duty. He yearned for the food he ate at home and hoped to celebrate Independence Day with traditional Acholi dishes. He joined the cooking team consisting of two other bodyguards and a young South Sudanese woman from Justine's family. George put himself in charge, deciding to cook two of his favorite dishes, *malakwang* with wild yams and *otwoya*. He loved *malakwang*, boiled leafy greens with peanut sauce. He boiled the yams and served them with *malakwang* while cooking *otwoya*, the most popular food in the camps.

Made with smoked meat, *otwoya* was a perfect way to use the remaining meat from the hippo George shot in the hunting trip. He boiled water and instructed the woman to make a paste from sesame seeds, or *simsim*, that George was permitted to take from Kony's granary. He put the remaining smoked hippo meat in the boiling water so that it would become moist, adding salt and eventually the *simsim* paste. It gave the meat a nice nutty taste.

Together with *malakwang*, the *otwoya* made what George thought was the perfect meal to celebrate Ugandan and Acholi culture. The food brought back memories of home and his mother.

As the food cooked, he was happy to see Dog's Knee sitting at Kony's table. He was looking forward to talking to his friend. Dog's Knee had brought a large pot of wine for the occasion. He had made it with honey, yeast and what the Arabs called *abukamira*, a tart fruit, a cross between an orange and a mango. Dog's Knee called the wine *mundo*, which he said was an Arabic word. The drink tasted sweet but it was potent. Dog's Knee told George to stay away from it after Kony took a liking to it. The boss claimed he knew about this concoction and discussed with Dog's Knee the exact proportions needed to make the best *mundo*. George listened in amazement to the LRA leader discussing how to make alcohol.

Feeling happy for the first time in a while, George served the food to his coy mates, who sat down to lunch with only a few men posted as guards. Small dishes were placed in a plastic baskets and brought to the guards, who were fewer in number than usual. Kony joked that the Ugandan soldiers were too busy getting drunk celebrating that day so the LRA could not be safer. Kony was cheerful, joking and talking to many of the people assembled. He even decided to drink some *mundo*, the first time George witnessed Kony drinking alcohol.

The food was a success with all the men, who said George was a great cook. A few did not miss the chance to tease him. "Great job, professor," joked one. "You make a poor soldier but someday you will make a man very happy as his wife." George was annoyed at the jokes but was happy to see his coy mates relaxed. In the afternoon, someone produced a tape player with Ugandan music and people started to dance. It seemed as if some normalcy had finally returned to the camp.

Deep into the night, after his wives and small children were sent to sleep, Kony called George to his table where a few commanders, including Dog's Knee, kept the boss company. Kony was cheerful. He spoke slowly and in a low voice, while taking small sips of *mundo*. He spoke of politics and the way Uganda was ruined by Museveni. Of how the Acholi were betrayed by the Banyankole, Museveni's tribe, and how Museveni himself was betrayed by his friend Paul Kagame, who worked for the Ugandan President but then abandoned him when he became President of Rwanda. "Kagame was the first to come to Gulu, with Museveni's rebels, but people said he was different. Kagame behaved better than the rest," Kony said. "But even he, even Kagame could not get close to me," Kony laughed.

"They can't," he continued. "They have tried many times but the Holy Spirit is always with me, always informing me in advance. Only once was I almost caught," said Kony. "I did not pay attention to the warning from the spirit and became careless. It was in the Imatong Mountains of Sudan, one day in the dry season of 2003. I had a bad dream the night before. I dreamt about a big ram losing his horns, they just dropped to the ground. It was a bad omen but I did not pay heed. That same morning we were surprised by soldiers who came out of nowhere. They passed our guards and came straight at me. *Min* [mother of] Ali was there," Kony said pointing to his young son sitting at his side. "We had just finished breakfast."

I ran as soon as I heard the shots right near me. The boys fought the soldiers and I just ran. But some soldiers came after me. I ran into a small forest and climbed up a tree. Most of them ran past and did not see me except one. He had a PK, the big gun, so he walked slowly behind the others. He saw me and shot at me from a short distance. I jumped down and ran into the bush. The soldier came after me, running slowly and yelling, Kony, *cung* (stop). *Cung* Kony, *cung*!

Kony laughed and said he hid inside a hollow tree in a dense part of the forest.

"He was afraid to come near. I could hear him telling the other soldiers, who returned after his shooting, he did not want to. So he just bullet sprayed the whole area. What a noise! One of the bullets hit me on the left calf, here is the mark," Kony said, rolling up his trousers and showing a faded scar. "Then he turned around and just left. I heard him telling the others I had vanished. No one came to check. I stayed hidden for a long time and then came out and dressed the wound, it was just a scratch," he said. "Kony *cung*," he imitated the soldier, laughing.

The Big Teacher spoke until the early hours of the morning. He was happy, almost affable, George thought. This was the Kony George knew, the Kony of the days before Otti's death. It was nice to see him act normal and happy again. Eventually Kony's speech became slow. He said he wanted to sleep and told the officers to leave. He asked George to accompany him inside his hut. George was surprised and hesitated for a while. He worried about Justine who stared as the two walked inside Kony's home. George helped the boss take off his pistol, which he put next to his mattress. He put water in a cup and put it within Kony's reach. He asked if he should call one of the wives.

"No, but stay," Kony said, asking, "How is your uncle?" "Fine," replied George, "I think. I have not seen him in a while." "He is well, I know," said Kony. "The other elders have informed me. How are you settling here?" George did not know what to say. He wanted to tell the Big Boss how badly he had been treated and that he deserved better, but at the last moment he decided against it, whispering a quick "*aber* (fine)." "You are a man of books, I know," said Kony. "I see you reading and I know about your good grades at school." "This is a good thing," he added. "You must be sitting there thinking about how bad this place is, how terrible I must be." "No, no," George said hastily in a low voice.

Kony continued, "You need to know that if I had a choice I would not be doing this, this life in the forest like animals. I wish I could be a schooled man, like you. I wish my children could go to school, just like you. It pains me that my kids are not going to school, I really want them to, I even spoke to some people in Kenya, some of our people there and they said maybe they can take Ali and Salim to school in Nairobi. Maybe even Candit, he is getting big now. That would be nice. Otherwise, what are they to do with their lives?

"But it is too late for me. I have all the wisdom in the world, thanks to the spirits who tell me everything. You surely know that, don't you? But you also need to know that I am myself a prisoner of the spirits. Yes, they help me and tell me everything but they also keep me hostage. I have no choice but to do all these things to keep the Movement going. I have no other way as I am in the service of the spirits and the Holy Spirit first and foremost. I was chosen to carry this burden." His voice slowed to a slur and then stopped. George stood as if frozen, amazed at what he had witnessed and terrified that everyone outside that tent hated him for the time he was spending with the leader. He walked out slowly and was relieved to find out that not many people had paid attention. Some were asleep while others, including the two bodyguards sitting outside Kony's tent, seemed too drunk to notice.

The next morning, after a long night of eating, drinking and dancing, George woke up to the sight of a distressed Omony kicking the still sleeping bodyguards. Yelling, Omony ordered them to fetch Justine, Otika and Agweng. They were to come at Kony's hut immediately. There was something wrong with the Chairman. "He is not waking up," Omony said, gesticulating wildly and looking concerned.

George felt a chill down his spine. "Here we go again," he thought. "Maybe someone still loyal to Otti poisoned him yesterday. Maybe they will think I did it when I was in his home last night." But as George started to contemplate ways to escape, one of the bodyguards still inside Kony's hut ran out saying, "*Ladit* is fine." As the group of bodyguards waited tensely outside, Kony walked out gingerly, looking hungover. He said he had just been a little tired. "Maybe I took too much wine last night," he later conceded, prompting nervous laughter from the mortified escorts.

* * *

George felt better after the Independence Day feast but life continued to be hard, even as a bodyguard to the Big Man. Often George and another nine or ten men would be deployed day and night for a whole week outside Kony's compound. If they were lucky, five or six of their coy mates would cook enough food and bring it to George and the rest of the guards twice a day. Sometimes there was only food served at dinner, the young boys bringing little portions in small baskets and reappearing later to take the empty dishes and wash them in the stream. There were days when there was not enough food or no one was organized to prepare it. George and the rest of the bodyguards on duty would have to eat whatever they had in their secret stashes, hidden deep in their backpacks.

When not on duty, he would wake up in the morning, eat a small breakfast and go to work in the garden assigned to his coy. He knew that the harvest would help sustain him and his friends and worked hard to care for the vegetables, as well as to show his coy mates and Justine and Otika that he was an able fighter, a good holy. He knew well that his books might not help him in the LRA, but growing healthy cassava and peanuts was crucial.

He could not understand why there was no help for the bodyguards, Kony's fierce warriors. George was confused by most of the tasks assigned to the bodyguards: preparing Kony's bath and bed, and serving his food. Expecting to see well-built, fearless men ready to put their lives at their boss's feet, George found the bodyguards to be little more than young servants. It pained him to accept that the version of a hero warrior he fancied becoming when assigned to Kony's bodyguard ranks could not be further from the truth. But he was still happy in his role. It could have been much worse; he could have been an escort to an insignificant commander, or worse, a *kurut* from Congo or South Sudan.

Palabek, a coy mate who had been a holy for a long time, once told George that in the past, particularly in the early days of their stay in Sudan, Kony's wives took care of the bodyguards, cooking and cleaning. "It was not like today where the wives only care for their husbands," he said. "Something changed, one day Mister Chairman forbade his wives to mingle with the rest of us," he added. "He said it was not proper for the wives to fraternize with the bodyguards, it was unprofessional. Some people said it was probably the Arabs who told Kony that it was not proper. Arab men don't really mix with their women; they even sit separated from one another."

It made sense to George. Kony worried his wives would cheat on him. This was the reason he was instructed never to talk to Kony's wives privately or why the wives always tried to be with one another. Also why they were not allowed to fetch water from the river, but had to send him or his coy mates instead even after a long day's march or work in the garden. It was why the bodyguards were not even allowed to shake the wives' hands.

Maybe it had already happened, George thought somewhat angrily. Someone had slept with his wife and now the Boss of the Jungle is still punishing us for it, even though we are supposed to give our lives for him. As he had done often in the past few months, George decided to let it go. "No use trying to figure out this confusion," he thought.

But he was unable to ignore the issue for too long. One day that November, Swahili camp was again a center of turmoil. That morning word spread that an intelligence officer had reported that Aciro, one of Kony's wives, was pregnant. George hated IOs, these so-called intelligence officers who were far from intelligent. Like the bodyguards who were primarily servants, IOs were more like spies. Kony used them to learn about life inside his organization rather than about external enemies. George had often heard from his coy mates that some of these IOs made stuff up just to get people in trouble. They abused their power, it was clear. George suspected that Otika, a former IO in Central Brigade, filled Kony's head with lies in order to get Dog's Knee fired, so that he could take his place.

Aciro was brought to Agweng's operation room, where Agweng and Otika conducted the interrogation. George could see Otika's men beating her, slapping her across the face and hitting her on the head with sticks. Apparently she was pregnant but Kony was sure she had not been in his tent for months. Agweng was trying to get the name of the guilty party, which quickly became known as Oloya, a bodyguard from Coy B. Oloya was also brought in front of Agweng and questioned alongside Aciro. The story later circulating among the bodyguards was that both Aciro and Oloya had confessed to having slept together a few months back when Kony had gone to inspect the new base called Cover.

George then witnessed a sight he could never erase. Agweng ordered the men to tie ropes to Aciro and Oloya's necks and drag them around the camp for everyone to see. The two struggled and seemed to suffocate but were still alive when they were taken to Kony's compound. When Kony came out, people saw he was livid. He looked even angrier than the time when Otti was killed. The old Kony, the man of the drunken night a few weeks before, had disappeared. Back was the angry, scary man, who screamed at his senior commanders to kill his own deputy and all his relatives.

Kony did not spend any time talking to the condemned. He yelled at Agweng, "What are you waiting for?" Kony took out his Beretta pistol and waving it in the air yelled, "Take them, kill them." George had never seen him take out his pistol before. But then again, George had never witnessed Kony so angry, almost disfigured.

Like all the bodyguards, George was scared. He tried to stay away from Kony and did not follow Otika's men, who took Aciro and Oloya into the forest. Kony went after them, waving his pistol and shouting. He returned only after the shots ended. Otika's men later said Kony stayed at a distance, yelling at them to finish off Aciro and Oloya quickly. "Leave their bodies to rot in the bush," he ordered.

When Kony returned to camp, he had all the bodyguards assemble in front of his hut. Yelling at them, he ordered that from that day on no one was allowed to even touch his wives. The bodyguards were not allowed to sleep in huts, not even the open ones. "You should all be sleeping outside," he yelled. "How can you protect me if you are sleeping inside huts?" Kony was incensed at some body-guards, whom he accused of building *ot lum* for themselves, even though George knew it was not true. "Probably a fabrication of these bastard IOs," George thought, but like everyone else he did not dare utter a word.

Kony repeated that he had been deceived by the same people who were supposed to protect him and that they all needed to be punished. He ordered Otika to organize a beating for all bodyguards present in Camp Swahili, about seventy men. For some reason, Otika and his personal escorts were spared, and instead put in charge of beating everyone else. George felt a little happy to see Justine was also to be beaten. Maybe it was because he was Oloya's supervisor or maybe because he had allowed the building of closed huts for the bodyguards. No one knew, but George could almost discern the joy in Otika's eyes.

Other IOs and their escorts started to appear at the main clearing carrying sticks. Lukwang was there together with other people from Otim Ferry's group. Ferry, apparently a nickname he got from spending time with a Sudanese soldier called Feriq, was a man of many talents. He possibly became chief of intelligence after Otti's death but no one knew for sure. Everyone was aware of Kony's affection for Ferry, who was abducted as a child and raised in Kony's home, once serving as his bodyguard. "Kony's blue-eyed boy," people referred to him. And when he decided to beat up all his bodyguards, the boss called on his protégé, who duly obliged.

All bodyguards were ordered to disarm and take off their shirts and shoes, then told to spread-eagle on their stomachs. George lay on the ground waiting with bated breath for Kony to specify the number of strokes they were about to receive. "One hundred," came his order, making George shudder. He closed his eyes, cursing the IOs under his breath and waiting for the blows. "*Gor gi idye ngee gi ki idud gi keken* (beat them on their backs and buttocks only)," Kony ordered, "*pe igo wigi* (don't beat their heads)." "No one is to make a sound," he said. "You will be killed if you do. It means that you are weak and I can't have weak people in my movement." "*Gamente na kara pwodi petek* (my government is not yet strong)," Kony kept yelling as he stood watching his bodyguards take the whipping in silence.

After the beating ended and the bodyguards stood up and slowly put on their clothes, Kony ordered his wives to come out of their huts. Out came a dozen trembling women, who were also ordered to take off their shirts and shoes. Kony ordered the women to be hit fifty times and if they cried, they were to be shot by one of Otika's men who stood over them with his rifle loaded. The women also kept silent but at least two had tears streaming down their faces as the blows rained on their backs and buttocks.

Seemingly appeased, Kony, who also witnessed the beating of his wives, called for a meeting. In his usual Sunday preaching style, he told the bodyguards and his wives that the beating should serve as a lesson to all those who might be thinking of committing adultery. "The women should not be deceived," he said. He then made it a crime for the bodyguards to talk to his wives one on one. The women were to use *ting-ting* or young boys as messengers and the bodyguards were not to shake hands with the wives or unnecessarily touch them. The women were forbidden from ever walking alone. "Even if you need to go into the bush to relieve yourselves, do not go alone," he ordered.

The bodyguards were to sleep in the open, not even under trees or bushes. "You are only allowed to use tarps and polythene bags to protect yourselves from the rain," he ordered. Kony then said the lesson was over but that the bodyguards were not to be given their guns back for twenty-four hours. "A wise decision," thought George, "as many were too angry and could retaliate, particularly against some of the IOs who enjoyed handing out the beating."

In the end, the bodyguards did not receive their guns for four days. The guns were locked in a small hut that served as an armory, guarded by men from Central

Brigade. More people from Central deployed as guards during the four days. Dog's Knee returned briefly but only as a simple guard. Otika had become too powerful during the whole thing and Dog's Knee could not compete with him any longer. During the four days, Kony called Otika to his hut often. George was certain Otika was telling more lies, defaming others so that he could strengthen his own position.

George hoped Otika would not see him as a threat; that surely he knew he had nothing to fear from George. But he decided he could not worry too much. "Such is life in the LRA," he thought. "One day everything is fine and you help the boss go to bed while the next you are beaten like a dog in front of him as he watches." He only felt sad that the joy of Independence Day, much needed after Otti's death, was short-lived. It also saddened him to realize how his hopes had been dashed in the last few months. It was almost the end of 2007, six months since his entry into the LRA. He had arrived hoping to become an important person in the rebel group. All he wanted now was to be insignificant enough that a young, uneducated, poor Acholi such as Otika would ignore him and let him live.

CHAPTER 8

WAR IS COMING

Tension reigned in the camps following Otti's death, which the killings of Aciro and Oloya only made worse. People were scared. Many worried they could still be accused of collaborating with Otti. Previous conversations about Otti and his people were often revisited and comments made casually in the past were reconsidered. The fighters sought to prove their loyalty to Kony by questioning others' affiliation to Otti. George kept quiet and tried to avoid any conversation. He was new, therefore there was little history to dissect.

The rumor that the newly arrived were involved in plans to unseat Kony did not die down but increased throughout October and well into November. George knew people suspected him of many things. It was said he was a spy for the Ugandan government, a former Ugandan soldier and even a religious fanatic who wanted to kill Kony because he was jealous of his divine abilities. It was mostly low-ranking fighters who threw around such accusations, when annoyed or when pretending to tease him. Senior commanders, to George's relief, did not pay attention; they were busy expressing their deep commitment to Kony and ensuring they were still in his good graces.

* * *

One senior officer to come to prominence at this time was Caesar Achellam, whose real name was Sicario Achellam. Achellam was well known in northern Uganda and in the early days of the LRA had briefly been in charge of the entire organization. Achellam enjoyed considerable respect in the LRA not least because of his responsibility for external relations in the mid-to-late 1990s. He communicated daily with the Sudanese Armed Forces (SAF), or the Arabs as everyone called them. One of the SAF commanders could not pronounce Sicario and called him Caesar instead. It stuck, and even Kony called him Caesar although it sounded more like Tcheegia.

Achellam was smart. He spoke Arabic and English and got on well with the Arabs. When Livingstone Okello, a senior commander, complained to Kony that Achellam lived a nice life with the help of the Arabs, Kony replaced him with Okello, but after a few months the supply trucks from the SAF were not running on schedule and relations with the Arabs deteriorated. "You don't know how to negotiate," Kony told Okello, and reinstated Achellam. He was given a large house in Juba, courtesy of the intelligence wing of the SAF, which he shared with Margaret, a young woman Achellam had abducted in Uganda and called a wife.

Margaret and Achellam stayed in Juba until at least 2001, a year before the Sudanese regime allowed the Ugandan army to enter southern Sudan and attack LRA bases there. Achellam and his family moved together with Kony to new bases in the Imatong Mountains of Central Equatoria, where the Ugandan army could not reach them easily. Achellam had to get used to the rough life, something he never really loved, according to Margaret who escaped in 2004 with two children born in the bush.

In the summer of 2004 Otti accused Achellam of having received money from the Arabs. Otti did not like Achellam, as was well known in the camps, where it was clear that Otti resented Achellam's influence on Kony, enabled by his personal connections in the SAF. Kony, who often said to his commanders that he did not like the Arabs, knew that he needed the supplies and support of the SAF, allowing Achellam to continue to be part of the decision-making process. As the relationship with the Sudanese deteriorated in early 2005, Achellam's influence waned, allowing Otti to convince Kony to agree to peace talks.

By 2005, as Kony decided on the future of the group, Achellam insisted that the LRA should try to continue the relationship with the SAF. This meant finding a way to their closest bases, a difficult trek via hostile South Sudanese territory to South Darfur. Otti wanted to pursue peace talks instead but the failure of the Sam Kolo attempt and talk of the International Criminal Court warrants for LRA commanders led to the compromise of moving to Congo. The move to Garamba was completed to ensure that Sudanese armed bases in Darfur could be reached by walking along the Central African Republic–Sudan border, north of Garamba, while also keeping open the option of peace talks.

Otti succeeded in convincing Kony to seriously pursue peace talks as the only way out of the bush. Kony agreed but he also continued to try and reestablish a connection with the SAF. At the end of 2006 he sent Odhiambo to Central African Republic and eventually Darfur to make contact with SAF officers. Odhiambo failed to find a way though and returned to Garamba at the start of 2007. He reported that the territory in Central African Republic leading to Darfur was hostile. Otti, who wanted to ensure that the peace talks would not be spoiled by revelations that the LRA continued to be affiliated with the SAF, used the failed mission to continue to press Kony to accept a peace deal.

In June 2007, as Achellam lobbied Kony for a second attempt to reach SAF bases in Darfur, Otti accused Achellam of continuous involvement with the Sudanese for personal gain, something Kony did not tolerate. Aware of the animosity between his two top commanders but unwilling to further consolidate Otti's power, Kony demoted Achellam but did not execute him as Otti's accusations of duplicity warranted. Achellam was confined to house arrest and interrogated by Kony, a favor not afforded to Otti later.

Though Kony often said that winning by talking was as significant as winning by fighting, he pursued all options available to him even when committing to signing the peace deal. At the end of 2006 he sent Odhiambo to Darfur, and Bok Abudema, further south in Garamba, to make contact with another Ugandan rebel group, the Allied Democratic Forces, in early 2007. Both missions failed but by the summer of 2007 Kony must have concluded that the peace talks had little hope of success. No one but Kony knows whether his change of mind was due to the information or belief he had about Otti's dealings or was simply due to his mistrust of the peace process. Kony did not trust anybody, let alone Ugandan officials involved in the peace talks, whom he considered "Musev-

eni's henchmen."Otti's demise in October 2007 also meant Achellam's exoneration. Kony pardoned Achellam but did not reinstall him as a top commander, certainly not awarding him Otti's position, for which he was a legitimate contender given his experience and seniority. Otti's position was assigned instead to Odhiambo, a younger but fiercer fighter than the diplomatic Achellam. Odhiambo was known in the LRA for his unquestionable loyalty to Kony, and carried out a veritable witch-hunt long after Otti and his people were executed. It was his chance to eliminate those he did not like or who threatened his position. Achellam read the situation well and kept quiet.

Odhiambo's resolve to root out internal enemies coupled with the persistent rumor that the newly arrived elements were involved in Otti's dealings caused fear among many but particularly those who had joined the LRA since the peace talks started. By the beginning of November 2007, a few weeks after Otti was killed, two commanders, Lieutenant Colonel Sunday Otto and Captain Richard Odong-Kau escaped for a second time and returned to Uganda. Otto and Odong-Kau were two exceptional cases in the LRA; they were the only fighters to have escaped from the LRA and later rejoined voluntarily only to escape a second time.

Otto and Odong-Kau were the first to confirm at the end of November 2007 that Otti was executed on Kony's orders. Various people involved in the peace talks had tried to reach Otti on his satellite phone but to no avail. Kony told the LRA delegation that Otti was sick but many started to suspect things were wrong when he failed to show up at meetings in Rikwangba or answer phone calls throughout October and November. Opiyo

Makasi, who left the LRA on 1 October, rightly guessed that Otti was in trouble and he told Ugandan security services that Otti had been arrested and most likely killed.

When Otto and Odong-Kau escaped from Garamba in the first week of November 2007, Kony, anticipating that they would divulge news of Otti's death, called Norbert Mao, a popular Acholi politician and then Gulu District Chairman, telling him that Otto and Odong-Kau together with Otti worked for the enemies of the LRA. Kony said that Otto was a mole for the Ugandan government and that Otti remained under house arrest.

At the end of November, Otto and Odong-Kau were flown to Uganda, having surrendered to the Congolese army and been handed over by them to MONUC. In interviews with the Ugandan press, they told the story of Otti's death, which Kony continued to deny until the end of January 2008. In a talk with Riek Machar, the meditator of the peace talks, Kony finally said that Otti was dead and that the LRA negotiation team was going to change. A new team leader, David Matsanga, replaced Martin Ojul, while other delegates were also replaced.

* * *

News of Otto's and Odong-Kau's escape brought some relief for George, who thought that it was now obvious that if indeed the most recent arrivals had collaborated with Otti, it would have been the two who just left, not him. By the end of November he was also told of the upcoming changes in the LRA peace team, indicating, at least superficially, that Kony remained interested in the peace talks.

All these events made George somewhat happier. He had come out of the Otti saga alive and maybe there still was a chance for the peace talks.

In the last two months of 2007 many changes occurred as a major reorganization of all LRA structures took place. The troops were divided into four new groups, called brigades, of about 150 combatants each, in addition to Central Brigade, Kony's personal security detail, which remained at full strength with about 250 men. Some commanders who were previously under Otti at Control Alter, one of the two towers of LRA leadership, were brought into High Command, Kony's inner circle. After Otti's elimination, the old model of command became obsolete as Control Alter ceased to exist. Kony formally amassed all leadership roles under his command, as had been the case for most of LRA's existence.

The leadership of the four brigades was assigned to relatively young commanders, most of whom were former personal bodyguards to Kony. The trend of putting young commanders in charge of large units was also continued with Central Brigade, which was taken from Colonel Lamola and passed to a younger man, Major Binansio Okumu "Binany." Another former Kony personal bodyguard, Binany was considered loyal to the boss and was rewarded with one of the top posts in the LRA. The positions of chief security officer and head of HPU were retained by Lieutenant Colonel Otto Agweng while Captain Otika and Captain Justine remained respectively chief bodyguard and personal secretary to Kony.

The young commanders displayed their loyalty during the Otti affair and they were repaid by Kony, who consolidated their positions in the LRA while cementing his role as supreme leader.

Of the senior commanders in the LRA, Odhiambo and Bok Abudema emerged strongest out of this episode. Odhiambo led the whole operation for Kony while Abudema was in charge of the execution squad and became Odhiambo's deputy. Other senior commanders were shunned, particularly those who showed sympathy or pleaded with Kony for Otti's life. Nixman Opuk, the oldest commander in the LRA, and two other commanders, Ochan Bunia and Dominic Ongwen, both former Otti protégés, kept their ranks but had no assigned offices or official tasks.

Crucially, orders emanated from Kony's High Command and went straight to the brigade commanders with little or no input from other officers. Agweng, Justine and Otika became more influential than senior commanders such as Bunia and Ongwen. George felt even more threatened by Justine. He could easily have senior commanders arrested or killed, let alone a fighter without rank, such as George. But the turn of events also meant that Justine felt secure in his role and George had little chance of ever challenging his position. George was smart enough to understand Justine's strength and made every effort to stay away. It was best to keep a low profile, he wisely concluded.

* * *

By the end of December 2007, Kony once again sent Odhiambo on a mission to Darfur with instructions on where to go and who to look for, information that Achellam helped gather by communicating with his old Sudanese Armed Forces contacts via satellite phone. A large group of about 100 people accompanied Odhiambo. Their orders were to make contact with the SAF and carry out reconnaissance in Central African Republic for potential bases in case Kony needed to leave Garamba. Despite continuing to publicly state that he was committed to the peace talks, Kony was also making contingency plans in the event that the talks failed. It was becoming increasingly obvious to many, however, that the peace talks had little chance of success and that Kony was preparing for future war.

* * *

During early 2008 George was deployed in Kony's personal unit. He learned to move as fast as the leader, walking all day. Kony traveled almost daily to other camps, talking to his officers and communicating on his satellite phone via his signaler with Odhiambo, who was somewhere in Central African Republic or maybe even Sudan – no one knew for sure. George witnessed Kony and Achellam talking on the phone to people he thought were part of the Sudanese army or government. He thought they were probably trying to ensure that Sudanese Armed Forces officers met with Odhiambo.

At the end of January 2008 Kony received a call from Odhiambo in Central African Republic. He had been unable to go to Darfur and asked for permission to return to Garamba. Visibly annoyed, Kony agreed but ordered Odhiambo to bring back abductees. "We need to build up our force," he added. He then ordered for a standby of 100 fighters to attack SPLA garrisons so that they could get more guns as well as abductees from South Sudan's Western Equatoria state.

George was surprised that Kony gave orders for mass abductions while still engaged in the peace talks. He was certain that these violent acts were sure ways of spoiling the talks. George was aware that fighters from other units had carried out attacks in the last year and a half of the peace talks. These attacks, he had thought, had been unavoidable: for example, coming across armed hunters, needing medicine for injuries or intimidating the local population when Kony felt exposed.

There had also been some attacks against the SPLA but that was understandable since, as Kony said, the SPLA, or the Dinkas as they were referred to in the LRA, "were sworn enemies." Yet George had never heard Kony being so explicit about attacks in South Sudan as he was in January of 2008. He thought that maybe Kony was ordering an escalation of attacks and abductions as a negotiation maneuver to get what he wanted from the peace talks, which had stalled since Otti's death.

By the first week of April 2008, the one-year anniversary of George's stay in the LRA, the standbys returned to Garamba. Those coming back from Western Equatoria arrived at the end of February, bringing along over fifty young South Sudanese, and ammunition and guns looted from the SPLA. Kony ordered that women of marriage age be distributed among commanders, taking two himself. The young South Sudanese men, all from the Zande ethnic group, were distributed among all units. They were to work in the gardens and also to be trained in basic military drills, including using guns and learning about discipline. George's unit received two sixteen-year-old boys from Source Yubu in Western Equatoria.

Odhiambo and his troops arrived on 3 April 2008. They had abducted over 100 people from Central African Republic, also from the Zande tribes which lived near the South Sudanese border. Kony congratulated Odhiambo and ordered most of the women to be given to commanders as wives while the men were to tend to the gardens and be trained in military matters. George's unit was given two men and two young boys of about twelve or thirteen. George learned that they were all from the town of Obo and thereabouts, near the South Sudanese and Congolese borders.

Faustin, one of the abducted men, spoke some English and he told George about what had happened. On the night of 5 March, Faustin said, there was a wake in a neighborhood of Obo. Faustin and other mourners stayed up late, eating and drinking as tradition required. At three in the morning they were surrounded by Odhiambo's men, who grabbed and tied them up while others looted houses nearby. In the morning the fighters and the abductees loaded with looted food and goods set off in the direction of Congo. They stopped six miles later to meet

Odhiambo, who waited by the river Mbomou, the border between Central African Republic and Congo, inside a forest the locals called the Forest of Darkness.

Faustin saw in the LRA camp other people who had also been abducted from nearby villages in the previous days. They spent three weeks waiting inside the Forest of Darkness while groups of fighters were sent on raiding missions to other villages. At the end of March they left for Garamba. It took them a week to reach the base. During the day they walked in a straight line, tied with ropes at the waist and carrying heavy loads. At night all the abductees were put together in one place and covered with a large tarpaulin secured in place with big rocks on its ends, making it hard to breathe inside. "We almost suffocated," he said.

Immediately after Odhiambo's return, on 4 April, Kony called a large meeting at his new base, called Swahili. He praised his commanders for all the good work they had done in bringing new people and making the LRA stronger. He said that the spirits told him that the LRA was strong and that no one should be afraid. "The year 2008 will be a good one for everyone," he said. "Victory is not far." Kony said that the peace talks had been a ruse by President Museveni to have Kony killed but that he had failed. He then paused and said in a somber tone, "*Lweny tye ka bino* (war is coming)."

There was panic among some of the people present and even some audible sobbing. Kony had not clarified when the war was coming, giving the impression that it was going to happen soon. Commanders gave orders for their units to regroup and for everyone to return to their respective camps. George followed Kony to his compound as Swahili emptied. Camp guards were doubled and security was put on high alert. George was certain that Ugandan soldiers were about to come through the bush at any minute. But nothing happened for days.

* * *

Ten days later Kony ordered Odhiambo to create a new base outside of Garamba. On 14 April 2008 Odhiambo, his deputy Abudema, and 80 armed men left Gangboo and walked about fifty kilometers west of the park towards the Congolese village of Bitima, where they settled. The camp was called Nigeria, a term that holies would later use to refer also to Odhiambo's group. The term Nigeria came from LRA's use of certain names, particularly countries and African leaders, as secret codes for radio communications. Mandela, for instance, referred to a key that corresponded to a particular coded system designed by commanders and distributed in advance to signalers, people in charge of radio and satellite phone communications. Otti had designed the Nigeria key, which Odhiambo must have chosen, perhaps ironically.

Kony's decision to relocate Odhiambo's base outside of Garamba was in part a strategic move. Kony could threaten attacks against Congolese civilians who lived in the vicinity of Bitima if his conditions were not met. But most importantly, Kony was convinced that the peace talks were not going to work, in which case he did not want all the groups based in one place, a potential trap. Being close to Congolese villages also meant food for the LRA, which until then had been supplied by international non-governmental organizations as part of the peace talks. If the peace talks were to end, the food supply would end too.

But the move near Bitima was also carried out with the aim of conducting reconnaissance further west and north in Congo. The ability to identify their surroundings was considered of primary importance for the fighters. One of the most striking things about the way LRA groups operated was the near-obsession with understanding the territory they used – a survival tactic. By the beginning of April 2008, as the LRA started to prepare for an eventual conflict, knowledge of territories as far away as a few hundred kilometers around Garamba had been acquired. In his attempt to reach Darfur, Odhiambo covered almost 250 miles north of Garamba. He returned with maps he had drawn of areas in Central African Republic where the LRA would eventually settle. Another LRA reconnaissance mission was carried out to the south of Garamba in February 2008, about 180 miles away from LRA bases. The holies were identifying escape routes and potential settlements, which would come in handy in the future.

* * *

It had been a year since George had joined, a time during which he changed significantly. He grew thin and spoke little. He could not remember the last time he laughed, but he was not sad. He thought he had finally become a fighter, a real rebel of the Lord's Army, one of Kony's own men. Long gone were the days when he was sent on guarding duty without a gun. He did little gardening these days but he was still part of the teams taking the Zande abductees to the gardens and sat in the *shamba*, making sure no one escaped.

He spent time with the training teams that taught the recent abductees how to behave like real soldiers, understand roll calls, military parades and officer ranks. They were not given guns yet but the abducted men were about to become *kuruts*. Just like George they would be trained how to fight but only given machetes and knives until they could earn the trust of the holies. It was only for the commanders and Kony to decide when the abductees would fight. It was unknown if the foreign *kuruts* could ever become real holies, like the Acholi fighters. It was rare for non-Acholis to be granted officer rank; even some of the South Sudanese Acholi who had been in the LRA for over a decade were still privates.

George knew that there was no way out of the LRA for him now and tried hard to learn everything he could about survival in the bush and rebel tactics. He understood that his life depended on it. Since he never showed any desire to become Kony's secretary, Justine ignored him and after a while everybody else stopped picking on him. It did not stop George from getting in trouble.

In the second week of May 2008 he wanted to go to Rikwangba to meet with the LRA negotiation team, hoping to get news of his uncle and the rest of the family back home. Kony was supposed to sign a final peace accord but he said he would not go to the ceremony, sending Achellam in his stead. George asked Major Okidi, the security commander of a group of holies to deploy to Rikwangba, if he could join them. Okidi said he needed to check with Achellam, his immediate supervisor. Okidi told George not to do anything without the group commander's express permission. But George decided to talk to Justine and see whether he would ask Kony to allow George to leave. Justine did and Kony agreed.

But when George joined the group leaving for Rikwangba, he found Okidi fuming. "This is not how it works here," he yelled at George. "There is a military order you cannot ignore," he said, and ordered George to be beaten upon arrival in Rikwangba. As a commander he had the right to kill George if he so wished, something that George had learned all too well in the bush. Throughout the past year, George had witnessed many people in the LRA, including experienced fighters, being beaten savagely on commanders' orders for the smallest of offenses. He understood he had no choice but to lie down and receive the caning without complaining, which he did as soon as they arrived in Rikwangba.

Even as late as May 2008, those outside the LRA, including the peace team members, were still unsure about Otti's fate or the reason for his death. Kony, who according to the Ugandan press told Riek Machar about Otti's death in January 2008, did not make any public pronouncements while forbidding LRA fighters to talk about Otti at all. George knew that he could not say anything to anyone about Otti or he would risk being executed. Okidi, annoyed at him for breaking his order, decided to send Omony, his coy leader, and Rie Rie as chaperones to ensure George did not spill the beans to the elders who knew George.

George was almost tearful from the pain of the beating the previous day, and having the two men staring at him as he asked after his uncle and family. He learned that everyone was doing well but all the elders were concerned at Kony's failure to show up to the peace signing. George did not say much but bid farewell, thinking it was probably the last time everyone would meet in peace. He was convinced the talks were finished.

* * *

The men in George's unit agreed that the peace talks were dead despite the attempts of the LRA negotiation team in Juba to extend the time period for the Big Teacher to sign the final peace agreement. Commanders listened to the radio, where threats of attacks from Ugandan officials were common. Kony often commented about the war drawing nearer and how the spirits instructed him to strengthen the LRA. Kony would then spend hours talking about preparedness for the incoming war. He said that standbys always needed to be organized to respond to attackers or be sent to fetch food and arms from the enemies.

One day in early June 2008, Kony said the war with the Dinkas had resumed. "The SPLA openly provoked us," Kony said. No one knew what Kony meant but there was talk of SPLA soldiers destroying LRA huts in Rikwangba.

Having been initially designated as an assembly place for LRA fighters, Rikwangba was located in the middle of a forested area, which had been cleared and a few rickety structures hurriedly put together. These were the huts where the delegations met and discussed the peace talks provisions.

A company of SPLA soldiers was stationed at the nearby site of Nabanga, also used a meeting place for LRA commanders and delegates. The SPLA was responsible for guarding the landing strip for helicopters bringing people from Juba. Rumors circulated in the camps that the Nabanga-based SPLA had destroyed the huts in Rikwangba and left messages written in Arabic stating that the holies were cowards and that Kony was a fake general who had never commanded the takeover of a single village. The same soldiers also destroyed a water pump that the holies used and stole food that the LRA had stored in Rikwangba. George did not know whether any of the stories about the SPLA were true but everyone else spoke about the grave offense the southern Sudanese soldiers had committed, leaving the Big Teacher with no choice but to retaliate.

In early June 2008, a large standby of eighty fighters under Otto Agweng deployed to attack Nabanga. At least one of George's coymates, Rie Rie, the same holy sent to guard him when meeting the elders in Rikwangba, joined the standby on Agweng's orders. Kony ordered that a B-10 pipe be used against the SPLA. Though erroneously referred to as a B-10, the weapon was in fact an

SPG9 recoilless gun produced in Sudan, also known as "the Soba," and was one of the biggest guns available to the holies. Weighing about 110 pounds and mounted on tripods, the Sobas, at least a dozen, had been given to the LRA by the Sudanese Armed Forces in the late 1990s. Kony wanted the standby to fire the 73 mm Soba first so that he could hear the attack. He also wanted to inflict as much damage on the SPLA as possible.

The element of surprise was crucial, with the attack planned for early morning on 5 June 2008 as the soldiers woke up. The idea was to shoot the Soba to create panic among the SPLA troops so that a sweeping force could then kill any remaining soldiers and loot the camp. Before their departure, the appropriate rituals to ensure the success of the mission were carried out. A controller, a type of priest of the Holy Spirit, usually a young fighter, anointed the fighters with "camouflage," the hallowed mixture that shielded the holies from the bullets of their enemies. It was made with shea-nut oil, water and ashes that had been blessed by the Holy Spirit. The controller smeared the concoction on the fighters' chests, near their hearts and their foreheads so that bullets would not touch them or would turn to water if they did. The standby left on 3 June 2008, swearing to defeat the Dinkas.

As Rie Rie told George later, Agweng decided to scout Nabanga on 4 June, a day after they moved close to the target and set up camp nearby. Agweng planned the attack for daybreak the next day. Indeed the attack started on 5 June with the shooting of the Soba, which Agweng oversaw. The rest of the holies moved on Nabanga from the south, west and east, pushing the soldiers and their families towards the north. Many were caught unawares and shot on the spot. Rie Rie told his coy mates that he counted forty-seven SPLA soldiers killed even though it was later reported on the radio that only fourteen were killed and a dozen injured. The holies looted everything they could take with them, including guns, bullets, boots, uniforms and three suitcases full of Sudanese pound notes. Agweng gave the money to Kony when the standby returned to Garamba.

George was annoyed when he saw Agweng's group return from Nabanga. Rie Rie brandished a shiny new AK he claimed to have taken from the dead body of an SPLA commander. Kony congratulated Agweng and his troops on a job well done and promoted some holies to junior officer ranks. George wished he had been part of the standby and yet he was still unsure he could survive in a real battle. He could easily suffer the fate of four holies from the standby who were killed in Nabanga, their bodies abandoned on the battlefield. As was the rule, no one spoke about the dead. It was as if they had never existed.

George would soon enough have his chance to partake in many sorties to loot food from the surrounding Congolese villages. One of his first missions had been to attack Kapili, a small village of fifty or sixty homes surrounded by banana and cassava plantations, in May 2008. The eighteen holies entered the village late one afternoon, shooting in the air to scare the inhabitants. Everyone ran away, allowing

George and his friends to loot as much food as they could carry back to camp. They spent the night in Kapili eating roasted chickens and *kwon gwana* they made from cassava flour. The next day they carried all they could to Swahili, where they shared it with HPU members.

Many such attacks on Congolese villages to obtain food and abductees were carried out throughout the months of June, July and August in 2008. Orders from Kony not to kill or gravely harm Congolese civilians still stood, so the holies restricted their gun use. George and eleven holies from HPU went to shoot antelopes near a small river in June 2008, a day's walk south of Swahili, when they came across hunters who, instead of running away as they usually did, stood their ground and opened fire. Taking cover quickly, the twelve returned fire with their semi-automatics, making the hunters flee. It turned out they had just killed a young elephant and were about to skin it when the holies appeared. They happily took the meat to camp and had a feast that night.

But the as the dry season came to an end Kony became angrier when talking to his commanders. He said that the Ugandan and Congolese armies had made a deal to attack the LRA because the peace talks were over. Kony blamed Museveni and the ICC for making him unable to sign the peace agreements. "I am not a fool," Kony often said, "to sign the peace agreement and have the ICC hang me like they did to Saddam in Iraq."

Kony said that the Congolese people should know better than to allow their army and the Ugandan army to attack the holies. "We need to teach the Congolese people a lesson," Kony repeated. As a result, attacks against Congolese civilians intensified in the second half of 2008. Prizes such as pistols, radios or food items were awarded to those who abducted the most people, or looted the most food. The bravest were also promoted, on orders that came directly from Kony. It was a time that George remembered as "fully experiencing military life."

Later that year George was to encounter for the first time what the LRA was best known for, attacking and killing unarmed civilians, not the romanticized version of guerrilla freedom fighting Kony spoke about. In the first week of September 2008 Kony was particularly angry at reports that the Congo army and MONUC were making plans to attack the LRA from the west while the Ugandan army would attack from the east. "I always knew that MONUC wanted to kill us," he said, "but they failed in the past and they will fail now."

In a public address to all senior officers present on 7 September 2008, Kony said that the Ugandan government did not want real peace but wanted to destroy the LRA militarily. The Congolese people are now allowing MONUC and the armies of Congo and Uganda to attack the LRA. "All orders not to harm Congolese civilians are rescinded," Kony said. The holies were now free to loot food and abduct as they wished. "Kill those you don't need," Kony said, "and abduct many children so that the Congolese would think twice before allowing their army to kill their own children."

Plans were drawn for simultaneous attacks against a dozen Congolese villages near LRA bases in Garamba. Odhiambo, who had become familiar with the territory near his Nigeria base, coordinated the attacks, which were carried out by over 250 fighters split into small standbys of ten to twelve combatants each. Over 150 abducted people from CAR, South Sudan and Congo also went to carry back all the loot. Attacks in Congo were planned for the week of 11–18 September 2008, while two other standbys were deployed to South Sudan to attack SPLA soldiers and civilians at the same time. George stayed in Kony's compound and listened carefully as standby commanders returned and presented their mission reports to Kony, who congratulated them as they recounted in detail the damage inflicted.

Most of the villages to the west of Swahili were targeted and gradually emptied of civilians, who escaped to Ezo, Tambura, Nzara and Yambio in South Sudan. LRA commanders reported killing hundreds of people in the Congolese villages of Duru, Kiliwa, Nandoro and Mambili. Other commanders attacked the villages of Kpaikpa and Nambia, which lay to the north of the LRA camps on the way to South Sudan. More than 200 children were abducted and brought back to Garamba, where they joined the other abductees from South Sudan, Congo and Central African Republic. The standbys from South Sudan returned during the third week of September bringing back many children taken from their homes. George was certain that there were now as many, if not more, recent abductees in the LRA as there were real holies. The camps certainly seemed to swell to almost double their original size.

Attacks against civilians in Congo and parts of South Sudan continued throughout the months of October and November 2008. Even though Kony continued to talk about a possible return to the negotiating table if the ICC indictments were withdrawn – a nearly impossible legal procedure, George would later learn – George was certain there was now no turning back from the path of war. A Ugandan army attack, possibly with the help of many other armies, appeared inevitable. The only question was why it was taking them this long.

On the afternoon of 14 November 2008, George stood guard in Kony's compound when one of Kony's satellite phones rang. Kony's chief signaler, the Technician, answered the phone in Luo and then quickly in English. The Technician then whispered to Justine that Museveni was on the line and he demanded to talk to Kony. Justine hurried to Kony's tent and relayed the news. Kony approached the Technician and signaled that he was not going to take the phone. He then turned around and started running.

Kony took off rapidly, giving his surprised escorts little time to follow. The escort leader started yelling and hitting the bodyguards to catch up with the boss. Minutes later they caught up with Kony, who continued running inside the forest. Together they made their way to Anyica. George knew from conversations he overheard between Kony and commanders that the LRA leader feared he would be killed by a missile guided by satellite phone. "That is how they killed Savimbi in Angola," Kony had often said.

Later that evening Kony gathered some of the commanders who traveled with him and said that the war was now inevitable and that Museveni was trying to find ways to kill him. "We are strong," he said, "and we can defeat any enemy who attacks us." George sat listening to the Big Teacher give his usual speech and wondered if the spirits had gotten it wrong. Kony first warned people about the upcoming war eight months ago, but here they were, still waiting for the war to come. It was not until a month later that the war finally arrived.

CHAPTER 9

KICKING THE HORNETS' NEST

The fourteenth of December 2008 started like most days had those last few months in Garamba. At dawn, many left to tend to the gardens. They were to spend the morning tending to cassava, sesame, peanuts, beans and tomatoes. Women and young girls set about cleaning their compounds, washing clothes in the streams and preparing food. The remaining holies gathered in the center of the camp, where after completing a roll call, instructions for the day were passed out. Day guards replaced the night guards while senior commanders relayed the daily instructions to their units. "Remain vigilant and maintain discipline." Some returned to their rest areas while others went to the *shambas*, the small low huts adjacent to the vegetable gardens.

In Swahili, George had a quick breakfast of tea and cold fried cowpeas before deploying to guard the abductees assigned to his coy to tend the vegetable gardens. Most of the food from the gardens belonged to Kony but the body-guards were allowed a little of it too. On previous days George had been in Kony's escort but that day he was told to guard the abductees. He was bored and wished he could be with the Big Teacher, as there were always interesting things happening in his company. Kony was in Swahili, but was about to leave for yet another outing judging from the mobilization of his bodyguards who waited outside his tent.

George left for the gardens as the sun started to feel warm, around 8 am. He sat on an anthill from where he could survey the abductees working on a cassava patch. Two hours later he chatted with Disco, a young Congolese boy of thirteen. Disco was smart and had learned Luo quickly. George would later learn that his real name meant "thank God" in French. But no one in the LRA could really pronounce it, which is why it had been altered to Disco. George asked Disco to bring him water but before the boy returned, George heard a strange noise in the distance that quickly grew louder. Something large and ominous was coming towards him.

Another guard yelled, "gunships," and ran towards a small forested area. The abductees also ran but George did not know what to do and stood in place. Disco ran to him, grabbed his hand and pulled him in the direction of the forest. Only then did George scramble, cursing himself for having frozen in place for so long. Disco had already disappeared inside the forest. George tried to join him but he could not get there in time and heard loud explosions close behind. Bombs.

He remembered the stories of past gunship attacks. Omony boasted how good he was at hiding from the searching eyes of the pilots who dropped bombs from low flying choppers. He often recounted using banana leaves to cover himself, shedding any white or brightly colored clothes. "You should always remember to keep your hands by your sides when hiding under a tree," Omony would say, "even your finger nails can reflect light when turned against the sun. You become an easy target." With Omony's lessons in mind, George jumped into a narrow ditch where a trembling boy also hid.

George saw people from the camp running towards him as the bombs exploded behind them making a wall of fire that appeared momentarily to swallow them. Smoke and dust made people cough and become disoriented. Some tried to jump in the same ditch George shared with the boy but he motioned them to keep moving towards the forest. "No room here," he yelled. Sitting inside the ditch with his head low he saw a young woman making for the forest clutching a yellow plastic jerrycan. She could not make up her mind which direction to follow but ran and stopped while clutching the jerrycan. "Drop it," George yelled but she did not move. He jumped out and ran to her. He snatched the jerrycan, threw it away, and pushed her into the ditch.

George had never witnessed anything like it. The exploding bombs turned the trees into a thousand pieces of flying shrapnel that made a horrible piercing noise. He feared death was imminent but tried to forget about it by counting the helicopters swirling around the camp. He thought there were seven of them dropping bombs everywhere in and around Swahili. It continued for about an hour, maybe two. Then the helicopters disappeared. George and his companions climbed out and ran towards the forest where they found the majority of Swahili's population. George was elated. He had somehow survived.

Kony was there, surrounded by his bodyguards who had mounted bayonets on their guns. He seemed calm and wore a slight smile. George joined the bodyguards and was assigned to a security fence around Kony's position. Throughout that afternoon, the noise of bombs was heard from the direction of the other camps. George was certain that all other bases had emptied once people became aware of the attack on Swahili and hid in the bush. Some from Gangboo, Anyica and Angula had already made it to Kony's group. It turned out that people in the other camps had seen the helicopters moving towards Swahili that morning. Two commanders alerted Kony of the incoming assault, which gave him time to run into the forest moments before the choppers circled his home.

Kony gave orders to provisionally camp where they stood while sending scouts to check on all other bases. Groups of *kuruts* and fighters were told to follow the scouts into the camps, particularly Swahili, where there was ample food stored in Kony's personal granaries, and bring back what could be carried. A party of eighty moved rapidly towards Swahili. George went as an escort but was expected to carry as much food and other goods as he could. It was no time to complain. George was amazed at the sheer destruction in Swahili. Most of the huts and tents were burned and large blackened holes formed on the ground where the bombs had dropped. Some granaries were destroyed but a few remained. Some dug out the stored food as others went to the gardens to uproot cassava and anything else they could salvage before the helicopters returned.

George and two others went on a mission to find missing people. He assumed many were killed by the bombs but was surprised to find no bodies. He could not understand how that intense a bombing had failed to kill. There were a few injured but nothing serious, mostly grazes caused by the flying splinters. George came across a group of three women, who were in shock. They were disoriented and thought George was a Ugandan soldier. "Don't kill us," they yelled. He helped them to the rest of the group, which was under strict orders to move fast, fearing an imminent arrival of infantry troops.

Back at the provisional camp George noticed that more people from the other bases had arrived and that Kony and a few of his bodyguards had moved to a nearby location. George knew that Kony always avoided staying with a large group, preferring instead to move with few people. George went with his group leader to meet him and deliver the mission report. George joined Kony's escort while his group leader reported what was salvaged, giving Kony some of his clothes rescued from Swahili.

In the morning, after the helicopters had made another round of bombing the empty camp, more people returned to Swahili to save what they could. George stayed with Kony, who called a meeting of commanders. The majority of the people from all camps had already arrived in the new base, although Odhiambo and Abudema were absent. Kony started the meeting with the usual routine of praying to the spirits and thanking them for saving everyone from the relentless bombing of the Ugandan aircraft.

"They cannot defeat us," Kony proclaimed, "because the Holy Spirit protects us, the spirit makes the bombs useless." He then reminded people of his warnings in the past that the war was coming. "Here is the real thing," he said, "and I knew about it long ago. But you did not listen. You became idle and not vigilant. Let this be a lesson to you to always take what I say seriously."

He then changed his tone, from almost humorous to outright menacing. He said the Congolese would have to pay dearly for being complicit in inflicting suffering on the LRA. "We are being uprooted from our home even though we did not start the violence, we only responded to protect ourselves," he said. "But the Congolese allowed the Ugandans and the UN to attack us. Now they will pay for what they allowed to happen."

Kony ordered that high frequency radios and satellite phones be used sparingly, because he suspected that the enemy was monitoring the communications. He said everyone would be moving as a large unit towards Bitima to join Odhiambo at camp Nigeria. They traveled to the northwest, moving carefully to avoid ambushes while listening to the helicopters dropping bombs. On the way to Bitima, Dominic Ongwen and his people joined the group. Ongwen had just returned from a sortie in South

Sudan where he had abducted people and looted large quantities of food.

Kony ordered the assembling of three small groups of about forty men, to rebury most of the military hardware rescued from Swahili and to collect intelligence on incoming infantry troops in Garamba. He also ordered that three large standbys of about 150 people each attack the Congolese towns of Faradje, Nagero and Kiliwa. Kony's revenge was to be delivered in a most brutal fashion.

* * *

The 14 December 2008 attack codenamed Operation Lightning Thunder (OLT) was months in the making. It became clear by April 2008 that Kony did not intend to sign the peace agreements, particularly since the issue of the International Criminal Court indictments was not, and could not be, resolved to his satisfaction. Ugandan officials, including President Museveni, openly threatened to attack LRA bases in Garamba after Kony's refusal to sign in March and April of 2008. But many of those involved in the talks understood that hope for a peace agreement had died with Vincent Otti. At least two top US officials discussed with their Ugandan counterparts the possibility of an aerial attack on LRA bases as early as December 2007, just a few weeks after Otti's demise.

When OLT commenced on 14 December it was hampered by many problems. The original plan was to unleash "a world of hurt from the sky," in the words of an American military officer who helped with the planning of the operation. The lightning was supposed to come from three MIG fighter jets that were to zero in on LRA camps, initially in Swahili where Kony was supposed to be that day according to intelligence, most likely gained with US help. Ugandan ground troops that were already camped in Congolese territory would then sweep through Garamba while SPLA and Congolese soldiers would ensure that fighters did not slip into South Sudan or further into Congo.

Accounts differ as to why that plan changed. The official Ugandan line was that the MIGs stationed in the Congolese town of Kisangani, about 160 miles from western Garamba, could not take off because of bad weather. An unofficial account from the Ugandan army posited that Congolese President Kabila refused permission for Ugandan fighter jets to operate in Congolese airspace, feeling perhaps that this was a step too far for an army that had been accused of stirring up conflict in the Congo in the past.

A third, and not unlikely scenario involved the foreign crew of helicopters contracted by the US government refusing to carry out their mission unless their pay was increased significantly. Whatever the real reason, it was decided that gunship helicopters, instead of the MIGs, would attack LRA bases, followed by ground forces. It meant that the ground troops that were supposed to have been delivered by the same helicopters had to wait until after the helicopters had delivered their payloads to be airlifted to Garamba.

Former LRA combatants, particularly those based in Swahili, indicate that between 9 and 10 am on 14 December loud helicopter noises emanated from the south. Kony, who was in camp that morning, left not long before the choppers flew over Swahili. He was alerted by commanders in other camps of the incoming aerial assault, most likely by a high frequency radio or satellite phone. LRA combatants, who were based at the time in camp Nigeria, located between Kisangani and camp Swahili, saw the helicopters directed towards Kony's location. Odhiambo's signalers in Nigeria would have radioed Kony's unit ten minutes or more before the helicopters reached Swahili.

In Uganda later that month, rumors abounded that Kony was informed about the impending attack. A common theory held that Riek Machar, the South Sudanese chief mediator of the Juba talks, leaked the plan to Kony. Other names were also mentioned, some being prominent members of the Ugandan army. There were rumors about a top Acholi officer in the Ugandan army or an Acholi director of a prominent non-governmental organization having tipped off Kony. But there was probably little truth in such conspiracy theories. Anyone in Uganda at the time who paid any attention was aware of the impending assault. A diplomat said, "We all knew the attack was about to happen from the newspapers writing constantly about it; it was not hard for Kony to find out."

Kony was indeed aware of the attack although he did not know the exact date and place. In the true tradition of "predicting the future" he often told his fighters that war was imminent without being specific. He initially made such predictions in vague terms at the end of 2007, soon after executing Otti. It was about the same time that President Museveni publicly claimed that if Kony refused to sign the peace agreements, he would choose "Plan B," the military option.

Throughout 2008, Kony's warnings of war had become so common that people in the LRA camps were surprised by the

December attack. "We dug our gardens during the day and did not think of fighting," one said. The majority of Swahili's population was out in their gardens when the helicopters appeared. It probably saved their lives. But even the children and women who were in Swahili when the helicopters arrived vacated the camp, alerted by the loud noise of the choppers before the bombing began in earnest.

Changing the plans to using helicopters for bombing as opposed to delivering ground troops, which was the initial intent, meant that the element of surprise delivered by the jets was lost. The slow, noisy helicopters gave Kony ample time to escape. The use of the helicopters also allowed many women and children to escape certain death. Infantry troops, who in the initial plan would have moved on to the camps immediately after the MIGs, only made it to the ground on 16 December, two days later than planned, when most of the LRA members were out of the camps but still in or near western Garamba Park.

There was no such thing as a coordinated offensive between the Ugandan, Congolese and South Sudanese armies. Many LRA groups filtered out of the Garamba camps unopposed and unchallenged by Congolese soldiers who could not deploy due to lack of transport. There were no SPLA soldiers helping either. The SPLA army high command was not even aware that OLT had occurred. A United Nations worker happened to be at the SPLA headquarters in Juba early on 14 December 2008 and recalled how the South Sudanese officers reacted in disbelief to media reports of the assault, an operation described as a regional effort between the three armies. "No one told us," an annoyed SPLA general shouted.

As the news of the poorly executed attack filtered out of Congo, Ugandan army officials tried desperately to present the operation as a success despite having little to show for the expensive campaign, some of which was planned and paid for with the help of the US government. A photo of the Ugandan commander of the Special Forces, the son of President Museveni, with his unit, posing with a wig, a guitar and jerrycans allegedly belonging to Kony, was published in the Ugandan papers, prompting ridicule. But people who knew the LRA's modus operandi and potential for violence were in despair. A humanitarian worker observed, "They just kicked the hornets' nest and set them loose."

* * *

In Congo the standbys deployed quickly to exact revenge for OLT and to show the world that the LRA was not finished, as some Ugandan officials boasted on the radio. Two groups led by Opiyo Sam and Charles Arop made their way to Faradje, over 100 miles southeast of Swahili. Kony's group, which included George, made the short journey of twenty miles to the north, near the South Sudanese border in the vicinity of Rikwangba, where food, supplied by international organizations during the Juba talks, was buried. What was supplied as a deterrent to LRA attacks on Congolese villages became fuel for fighters targeting civilians.

After a few days' walk south of Rikwangba, the group turned to the southeast following the road to the Congolese town of Duru. Kony wanted to connect with

Odhiambo who had a base north of Duru, near Bitima. Having received news of the arrival of Ugandan infantry, Kony ordered his fighters not to engage the soldiers but to move away and avoid confrontation, a well-known LRA tactic. "Save your bullets," Kony said, "use machetes, knives and *lut* (sticks) instead." Avoiding the Ugandan soldiers meant that the holies were always on the move, with little rest.

As Kony's bodyguard, George rarely stopped marching. Even when the large group rested for the night, Kony and his bodyguards continued to walk. In what became common practice, Kony left behind two scouts to direct others who followed, while he and his bodyguards moved to a different location, known only to the two scouts. Often, Kony moved many times, leaving behind a few pairs of fighters. Thus even the majority of his personal security detail did not know where he finally rested for the night. When ordered to deploy in the main escort unit, George often followed Kony's tracks to find along the way fighters who directed him to yet more guards, who eventually would take him to Kony's final location. It was exhausting.

As Christmas approached the entire group moving with Kony made their way towards Duru, a town that LRA fighters had targeted twice in the past. George knew a standby had attacked the town in September, when they looted and abducted many. Odhiambo was angry that some in Duru had helped people who had escaped from his camp. His men had killed a large number in retaliation.

On the way there George was part of the advance unit, a group of thirty that moved ahead of the main group, in charge of spotting ambushes and carrying out reconnaissance, usually by capturing and interrogating locals.

Kony's rhetoric of revenge and the annoyance of having left their base, coupled with tiredness and hunger, made the holies hostile towards Congolese civilians. While many local inhabitants had already left for South Sudan following the Ugandan bombardment of the LRA camps, some still remained, tending to their gardens. Members of the advance unit killed at least twelve farmers they came across. They did not use bullets but thick branches and machetes.

George worried he would have to participate in the killings or risk the wrath of his comrades. But he could not bring himself to do it. He wanted to use his AK but was under orders to save the bullets. He kept moving with his unit, hoping to delay as much as possible what he knew could not be postponed for ever. He had no problem using his gun to shoot others but using a machete or knife or, worse, a piece of wood to kill was something he could not do. He had seen others wield machetes and sticks, killing people by blows to the body and head and thought he would never be able to do it. It seemed so brutal and barbaric.

Approaching Duru, orders were passed to stop while two small teams were sent into town. To George's surprise Kony gave orders to limit the killing of people but to focus instead on abductions. Kony asked for a young girl to be found for him personally. The spirit had said he was to marry a sixteen-year-old from Duru. George, who was placed in one of the teams, was relieved to hear the orders not to kill. He thought that maybe Kony did not want too many deaths so as to avoid attention from the Ugandan and Congolese soldiers. Kony also seemed impatient to leave for Bitima to meet Odhiambo and Abudema. There were rumors they had already left for Central African Republic.

The standbys targeted three small settlements north of Duru where they abducted many young men and women, including a sixteen-year-old girl, whom Kony later took as a wife. The entire group then walked towards Bitima, spending the week leading to Christmas 2008 searching for Odhiambo and Abudema. By 25 December 2008, George's group was in Gangura in South Sudan, having attacked on the way the Congolese villages of Bitima, Nabiapai and a small town the holies referred to as Chakula, Swahili for food, but which was in fact Sakure in South Sudan.

Kony decided to set up camp near the South Sudanese border on 25 December and named it *Karama*, the Luo word for Christmas. He dispatched Dominic Ongwen to Nabiapai and Bitima to get food. More abductees were taken from the villages and brought to the main camp where Kony and the rest waited. Ongwen brought back chickens, goats, peanuts and maize, which was then cooked and distributed among the fighters. Everyone, including George, was happy to finally take a break and celebrate Christmas with some of the food the Congolese civilians had cooked for their own Christmas dinner.

* * *

While the majority of the LRA quickly regrouped and left Garamba intent on escaping the Ugandan soldiers, those unfortunate enough to have been disoriented and lost or left behind, were picked off at will by the infantry troops. President Museveni told Ugandan journalists in February 2009 that forty rebels were killed and 280 abductees were rescued. The arbitrary classification the Ugandan army used in labeling those killed as rebels and those captured as "rescued abductees" notwithstanding, it is unclear how many people killed by the soldiers were unarmed women and children. Testimonies from people captured and later brought to Uganda point to at least a dozen such cases.

Jacqueline, a Ugandan woman who spent over a decade in the LRA, was left behind with two other women and two young boys who had been abducted in South Sudan. They roamed the bush for a week after 14 December before Ugandan soldiers appeared. Jacqueline was the only person rescued while the two other women and the two boys were shot dead by the soldiers. All four had injuries, particularly the young boys who were in really bad shape, so the soldiers killed them, rather than having to carry them to their base.

Jacqueline said later that the Ugandan soldiers asked the two women in Luo where they came from and if they were hurt. The women replied they were Ugandans and that they were hurt. The soldiers shot them in the head at point blank and left the bodies in the bush. They told Jacqueline they did not want to carry the injured people and that she should be quiet or she would be shot too. She had hurt her knee walking in the bush but told the soldiers she was fine. She returned home to northern Uganda and recounted the story with reluctance and open fear; she could not understand why she was still alive and was certain the soldiers would come for her.

LRA combatants who were hiding in the bush and witnessed the killings by the Ugandan troops reacted in different ways. Most decided to run and try to meet with other groups. James lay hidden in a tree deep inside Garamba when he saw two members of his unit who fell behind due to exhaustion shot dead by pursuing Ugandan soldiers even as they put down their arms attempting to surrender. Convinced that the soldiers shot many surrendering LRA combatants to take their guns and sell them to Congolese civilians, James decided he would never surrender but die fighting. He later said: I saw firsthand what General Kony had been warning us all about. That Museveni's soldiers would kill us, and that we should never surrender. At that moment I felt sad for my companions who lay dead at the foot of the tree where I was hiding but I was also sad for my brother Moses who surrendered in 2005 when we were still in Uganda. I was sure that Moses was dead, probably my parents too; poisoned by the government, just as Ladit Kony had said.

James came down from the tree the night after and buried his two friends. He walked for two weeks, moving mostly at night until he found an LRA group going to South Sudan and eventually to CAR. In December 2010 he ran out of bullets and fell into an ambush manned by Ugandan soldiers in northeastern Congo.

He was captured alive and taken to Nzara in South Sudan where he was debriefed by military intelligence officers of the Ugandan army. He boarded a Ugandan army helicopter to Arua in northern Uganda, where he was put on a small bus and reached Gulu in February 2011. There he was reunited with his brother Moses and his mother, his father having died from liver disease.

While people like James found that the events of mid-December 2008 confirmed the deceitfulness of the Ugandan army they had long heard about in the LRA, others used the Ugandan army attacks as opportunities to escape, despite the high risk of being shot by the soldiers who due to operating in a foreign land and pressure from Kampala to produce results were nervous and trigger-happy. Peter, who had been in the LRA since 1997 and had risen to the rank of lieutenant as part of the intelligence unit in Kony's group, decided to surrender.

On 16 December, Kony sent Otika, Peter and a few other fighters, to gather intelligence on the state of Swahili, which Kony expected to have been overrun by Ugandan troops. The soldiers had yet to arrive but Peter escaped from the group and waited until 17 December when the first infantry troops arrived. He surrendered to the first group he encountered. He was questioned at length and taken to Dungu, and later to Kampala where he was debriefed for a week. He was then immediately sent back to the LRA front where he fought with the Ugandan army for five months. Peter later said that he had heard of many cases of LRA fighters being killed while trying to surrender. "Sometimes their LRA friends shoot them, other times Ugandan soldiers shoot them. It is a war and very hard to know what happens for certain." By the end of December

2008, the Ugandan army offensive slowed down as the majority of LRA members moved out of Garamba or hid in remote corners while the weak and injured were captured or killed by the soldiers. Far from being a success, as officials in Kampala claimed, the offensive had put in motion a series of events that would soon cause the death of many civilians, the exact scenario that many analysts and non-governmental organization representatives familiar with LRA tactics had warned about before OLT commenced.

* * *

Kony seemed concerned with the fate of Odhiambo and his troops, who appeared to have left for CAR. He sent messengers to find Odhiambo and have him return to Bitima. After celebrating Christmas in Karama, Kony moved the group back south, near Bitima, an area that was completely abandoned. Gardens were full of cassava and vegetables and life became easier as the holies could finally rest and eat again. But scouts who were sent daily on reconnaissance missions reported numerous tracks of soldiers. The Ugandan gunships that had attacked Garamba were still present; they heard them and saw them flying low. Kony ordered another move, this time south to Duru, Kpaika and Ngilima. He also sent more runners to find Odhiambo and direct him to Kony's new location.

One day in early January 2009, George, Okeny and Kokil went on a reconnaissance mission near Ngilima. Their orders were to be on the lookout for soldiers as Kony rested near Kpaika waiting for Odhiambo. The three made their way slowly towards Ngilima when they came across a building they thought was a school. Kony himself told the three to search the building as he was informed it was used by the Ugandan army. The three reached the building early in the morning, walking slowly and being careful not to step on the dirt path to avoid leaving footprints. When they reached the building, they split and circled it from a distance so that they could check from all directions. George moved slowly to the left and heard Kokil to his right signaling him to stop. Kokil pointed to the front of the school where it was written "L.E. Lilika" and what they thought was a word for school in French. Like many of the surrounding areas, Lilika was empty of people, who had clearly left in a hurry, afraid of the LRA.

Kokil then pointed to footmarks on the ground. He was certain they were made by Ugandan soldiers. "I recognize their boots from when I was in Sudan. The soldiers came after us all the time then," he said. Kokil said that these footprints were made two hours before. The soldiers had passed the night in the school. After further inspection the three concluded that the soldiers had pitched camp in the school for about two weeks. They saw that the trail went towards Ngilima, where the soldiers seemed to have gone.

They moved in and around the school, counted the positions where people had slept and calculated that this was a large squad comprising about 400 men. The three then checked the huts nearby, looking for food and other goods. They found chickens, goats, rice and peanuts, which they carried back to camp. Despite having been on a reconnaissance mission, George and his friends knew well that any opportunity to get food and other goods should not be missed because, as the saying in the LRA went, "a gun should make your stomach full and you rich."

On the way to camp, they walked slowly, loaded with food and excited to tell their commanders about their discovery. Suddenly a loud noise pierced the air and Okeny dropped to the ground holding his arm and screaming in pain. As other shots rang out George and Kokil threw away all the food and fell to the ground, pointing their guns to where the shots came from, returning fire. Congolese civilians were shooting at them. George knew about them, the self-defense groups, similar to the Arrow Boys in Uganda who defended their villages from LRA attacks. The holies called them "diehards" and were under orders to shoot them on sight.

But just like the Ugandan Arrow Boys, the Congolese diehards were poorly armed, mostly with guns that were only good for hunting small animals. They were also not trained in military matters and tended to run away when the real guns started firing. Sure enough, they had shot Okeny with a homemade shotgun and when Kokil and George returned fire with their AKs, the diehards ran away. George and Kokil carried Okeny back to camp. Kokil was angry as he had to leave some of the food behind in order to help carry Okeny. "Curse these savages," he yelled.

Back at camp, Okeny was taken to the sick bay located next to the main group, not far from Kony's position.

George and Kokil were dispatched to Kony's tent, a green army one that had been rescued from the rubble in Swahili camp. Kony listened to their report and congratulated them. "You behaved like real soldiers," he said. Then, turning to George, he said, "I did not expect you to survive by your gun but you have learned to be an excellent guerrilla." George was flattered, but dismayed when he realized Kony was not going to promote him.

* * *

During their travels between the South Sudanese border and the Congolese towns of Duru, Dungu and Bitima in early 2009, the holies were constantly harassed by Ugandan gunships which always appeared right after a small white spy plane. George, like everybody else, was aware of the harbinger of death. It usually took twenty minutes for the gunships to show after the white plane made its appearance. Like clockwork.

The all too familiar noise of the helicopters that made George's stomach turn would then be heard on the horizon, sparking panic and frantic activity among the people on the ground. Everyone threw away their yellow jerrycans, white clothes and every other colorful item they carried. Those who could run fast tried to find cover under trees before the helicopters spewed fire and death from their mounted machine guns, usually after dropping many small bombs. The dead were usually women, children and the recent abductees, who were too slow to shed their loads and run.

The attacks were almost daily on given weeks, then absent for days and even entire weeks, which was strangely unbearable. Waiting for the helicopters to appear was tantamount to torture. George almost wished they would come, shoot and go away so that the group could get on with the rest of the day. But waiting for the helicopters to appear was hard to take.

Everyone was uneasy, nervously expecting the white plane or the gunships to appear in the sky and pound them to oblivion. George prayed to be finished quickly if he were to be killed by the gunships, hopefully by a bullet to the head. He had seen many people burned to death by the flaming bombs or cut to pieces by the flying shrapnel. He did not want to suffer the same fate.

One day in February, after a helicopter attack, George did the usual sweeping routine, alongside three others. The four helped everyone get back on their feet to resume marching and ensured that no one tried to escape. As George approached an open area the helicopter attacked, and he saw a baby crawling over what seemed like a log. He recognized baby Joy as his friend Sergeant Padibe's daughter. George had often played with Joy when the group stopped for the day. Getting closer, he realized the black log was Joy's mother Angela's burned body. She had tried to run holding to her daughter but was embroiled in flames and threw Joy on the ground to save her from the fire.

Joy survived with serious burns. Kony ordered that she be raised by a young Congolese woman from Kpaika, who was also to become Padibe's new wife. George often thought about Joy, who was later captured by Ugandan soldiers together with her Congolese stepmother. Having been born in the bush, Joy knew little else but the bush. If she was still alive, she was now probably Congolese, not Ugandan like her biological mother and father. George hoped that Joy was loved and not treated like an orphan.

George could not stop thinking about Angela's death, wondering about her painful end. He had nightmares, dreaming about her final moments of agony and woke up covered in sweat, terrified that he was burning also. He wanted to talk to Padibe about Angela and Joy but Padibe refused to talk about anything at all. He had stopped talking altogether.

Kony seemed impervious to all the death and destruction around him. He was always the first to run when the helicopters appeared. Only his personal bodyguards saw him when the groups were on the move; he usually walked faster than the rest and separated from the main group. His presence was only felt when someone from his unit escaped. He then emerged in front of the main group, yelling orders and berating people who walked slowly. But he was also nice, uttering words of encouragement and patting people on the back, smiling as if nothing had happened. It was almost as if he enjoyed the war.

While the main group was moving back and forth between Duru and the South Sudanese border, one day in early March 2009, a young Congolese girl who did chores in Kony's compound escaped. Kony sent a large standby to look for her while forbidding everyone else to move that day. He ordered the standby to look for the girl in Duru and return in the evening to report to him. "Kill anyone you find who cannot serve my government," he ordered.

George and eighty others moved towards Duru looking for people to capture and interrogate. They captured three people and after questioning them they learned that a girl who escaped from an LRA group had just left for Duru. They killed all three Congolese and moved to Duru where they came across more villagers in the outskirts. After more questioning it transpired that the girl came to Duru but left for South Sudan. Annoyed, the commander ordered that all those captured in Duru – twelve people – be killed.

Men from George's unit bayoneted eight people to death. It was the first time George had killed without firing his gun. He affixed his bayonet, a long rusted knife he used to cut cassava and yams, to the top of his gun and rammed it into an old man's chest. He closed his eyes and repeatedly stabbed the man until he stopped moving. He looked at the face of the old man, who seemed peaceful, and a feeling of guilt overcame him. "His spirit will haunt me forever," he thought. "What have I done?" But as he stared at the old man, George felt a sharp pain at the back of his head and realized one of his coy mates had slapped him on the neck. "Move," he yelled, urging George towards the remaining few homes in Duru's outskirts.

That night George thought about the man he killed, even imagining he looked a bit like his father. He prayed all night, hoping he would eventually sleep and forget about the man's eyes, which seemed to stare at George every time he tried to close his eyes. "It is not my fault," he repeated to himself. "I am just a soldier, only obeying orders. Soldiers obey orders; commanders are responsible for giving the orders."

Soon he stopped thinking about the old man and his reservations about killing faded away. In two short months George killed several people, usually by hitting them on the back of the head or by piercing them with his large knife. He also learned how to tie people up well. He was particularly good at the *kandoya* method, tying the arms together behind just below the elbows. *Kandoya* was introduced in Uganda by Museveni's NRA rebels, so Kony joked about it being the only good knowledge the President had ever imparted.

George did not know why he was no longer squeamish about killing. He thought that he had no choice; he would either kill or be killed. "The people I killed would kill me given the chance," he thought. He also thought that he was now a real LRA and that was what the holies did. He followed orders and killed when his superiors told him to. It was what everyone else did and he could not be different. As the Big Teacher often said, "A soldier has to kill. There is a special place in heaven for soldiers because God understands that soldiers are different from civilians and God judges soldiers differently from civilians."

CHAPTER 10

A REAL REBEL

One day in March 2009 on the way to Bitima, George and three other men trailed Kony's group guarding against soldiers. George carried Kony's tent and mattress and his own personal belongings. His load was so heavy he openly cursed Omony for ordering him to stay behind and keep guard while burdened by Kony's stuff. He did not dare throw away the boss's things. Holies were executed for far less. As rearguards, George and his three comrades were supposed to walk about a mile behind Kony's unit, as the entire group moved slowly through a forest, away from main roads.

In the afternoon, the group stopped by a small stream, where Kony met with another commander. The four guards moved to a cassava garden at the back of Kony's provisional camp. George was exhausted and was happy to finally sit down and take off his gumboots to tend to his sore legs.

Minutes later he saw six Ugandan soldiers at the entrance of the garden, only 200 yards away. He almost jumped to his feet in fear but calmly tried to become one with the ground and motioned to his colleagues. One of them panicked and ran away, alerting the soldiers, who started shooting. The rules dictated that the blocking force was not to engage but only shoot a few rounds to alert Kony and delay the soldiers, who usually took cover and hesitated in their pursuit. It gave Kony ample time to disappear.

George and the remaining two fled from the soldiers, who continued shooting. He ran inside the forest alongside Okello, who had been shot in his right thigh. They continued to run without stopping. They heard the noises of bullets intensify and realized it was Kony's unit returning fire. The soldiers had come too close to the Big Man so the bodyguards held back the soldiers, allowing Kony to run away with one or two guards in tow.

Later George learned that Agweng had ordered most of the fighters in the external security wing to set an ambush outside of the cassava garden and wait for the soldiers to come running, thinking that all the rebels had fled. George was told that the soldiers fell into the trap and fifty-seven were killed and eighty-two guns were captured. His coy mates would later tease George about how he missed the glorious battle of Bitima of March 2009.

The two ran further into the woods, only stopping when the shots became distant noises. Okello walked with difficulty, clutching his blood-soaked thigh. After a while he could no longer walk. He cried in pain, saying he was bleeding to death. George cut a large tree branch that Okello used as a walking cane. George said he knew the location of a sick bay where Okello could get help. "Don't worry," he said, "I will take you there."

George remembered the position of an LRA base near Bitima, by a small stream, where a sick bay had been established two months before. When Kony's group walked back and forth between Bitima and the South Sudanese border following the raid on Garamba, the group was attacked by Ugandan gunships. Binany, who was in charge of security for Kony's families, was injured trying to usher Kony's wives and children to safety. During the chaos, one of the wives* escaped with her two-year-old daughter, who had been fathered by Kony.

The former Aboke girl was known to the holies as *Mego* Aboke (Mama Aboke) but her real name was Catherine. The camp established near the place of attack and her disappearance became known to the holies as "Mego Aboke." George remembered going in late January 2009 with Kony to visit the injured Binany, who had set up the sick bay not far from where the attack took place. George was certain that Binany was still based in Mego Aboke and decided to take Okello there. He figured it was about a day and a half's walk even with a limping Okello.

Okello agreed to George's plan. They walked slowly and quietly towards a small river. They worried the

---

* She was the last remaining of thirty young girls abducted from Aboke secondary school in Apac on 9 November 1996. The Italian nuns, who ran the school, managed to negotiate the release of 109 girls the day after they were taken from their dormitories, but the commander in charge of the operation refused to release them all. The nuns and the parents of the abducted girls advocated about the plight of their children, meeting Pope John Paul II and other prominent world figures, bringing the world's attention to the LRA and Kony for the first time since the start of the rebellion.

soldiers were searching for them but George knew they could not hide and wait. Okello risked bleeding to death. Upon reaching the river, George told Okello to crawl under a shrub and wait while he went searching for food. They had dropped all their food when running from the soldiers and were now hungry.

George knew the area well, having passed through it often in the last months on the way to the South Sudanese border alongside Kony. He remembered a small hamlet not far from where he hid Okello so he went to find food there. He had walked for three miles when he came across small huts surrounded by vegetable gardens including a large cassava field. He could hear people talking only a hundred yards away from the cassava garden so he crept slowly and quietly uprooted as much cassava he could.

He ran back with the cassava to where Okello hid and found him unconscious. Thinking that Okello had died, fear gripped him. George grabbed him by his shoulders and shook him. "Please Okello don't die, don't leave me alone," he yelled. "Wake up, I have cassava for you." Okello opened his eyes and said, "I am here my friend, just as you left me." Relieved and embarrassed by his desperate plea, George began dinner preparations. They had walked nonstop from noon until 6 pm when George uprooted the cassava. It was now getting dark and George knew they could no longer carry on. They had to wait until the morning to resume their journey to the sick bay.

George took out a plastic torch he carried in his pocket and searched for small pieces of dry wood to prepare the fire. He put together a few twigs, covered them with dry leaves and placed slightly larger pieces of wood on top of the heap. He lit a small piece of paper with matches he always carried on him, making sure that the small leaves and twigs were lit. He then fanned the fire quickly with a small, flat, aluminum plate to make sure there was enough oxygen to keep it going, slowly adding pieces of wood to the glowing embers at the bottom.

When the fire was ready, George warmed some water in a small pot that Okello had tied to a small bag he had managed to keep, and washed Okello's wound, bandaging it with a piece of cloth. Okello seemed better, saying he was hungry. George smiled and said the cassava would give them back their strength. He had placed the roots near the fire to roast as he dressed Okello's wound. The cassava was soon done, and they both ate it with a bit of salt. Like matches and torches, soap and salt were absolute necessities for all holies.

After they finished eating, George prepared a sleeping place for them, but before going to sleep they chatted about the day's events. They marveled at how they were still alive and how God must have truly been on their side. George asked Okello if he was feeling well. Okello said he was feeling fine but that he worried about being separated from the group. "Congo," he said, "is a foreign land to us and it is not good to be away from our people." George said not to worry because he knew Mego Aboke was near. Okello said he was happy to hear it and prayed that they would get to the sick bay as soon as possible.

Okello then started to talk about his life, as people usually did around the fire in LRA camps. He started his speech by lamenting the fact that he had no family of his own and that the LRA government was now his family, and Kony his father.

My father died when I was born, or that is what my mother told me. I had an older brother named Paul who people said was crazy. Paul was not crazy, I knew him well. He had a sickness that made it difficult for him to understand others, but he was nice and always helped me and my mother. We lived in Minakulu, by the big road that links Gulu with Kampala."

The holies came to our village in 2003 when I was thirteen. It was early in the morning but it was still dark. Kidega was the commander, I know him well now. They kicked our door and grabbed us while we slept. One of the *youngus* (child soldiers) held a razor blade to my neck and told me to go out. Someone grabbed mother and Paul, who was sixteen, but tall and strong. Paul refused to be dragged but ran towards mother who was being whipped by Kidega because she was too confused to sit on the floor like he asked.

Kidega's guard yelled at Paul to drop on the floor but Paul did not understand. He tried to help our mother but Kidega's guard shot him in the stomach. They beat him up in front of us and let him bleed to death. We saw him die slowly, his blood just poured until he dried out, like a sheep being prepared for cooking. Kidega said mother was stupid for not controlling Paul, who now was dead because of her. "You are a bad woman," he said, and slit her throat.

Okello continued, his voice quivering when mentioning his mother:

I was scared. When I saw Paul and my mother dead on the ground covered in blood, I could not move my hands or feet. It was like an evil spirit pinned me down. I was sure I was going to die and I wanted to. Kidega pointed his knife at my head and said, "You are now with the LRA; forget your family." The others pulled me up as I could not stand up and tied me with other children from Minakulu, also taken that night. We walked for hours until we reached the bush.

But these people here teach you to be strong. You have no choice but to obey and be strong or die weak. The day after I was taken as we walked towards Kitgum, one kid called Olweny, whom I knew very well because we played nine-stones together, tried to escape but they caught him and brought him back to where we stopped. Kidega then ordered all abducted children from Minakulu, thirteen of us, to pick up sticks and beat Olweny to death.

We were all in a circle around Olweny, who was really scared. He was little, maybe eleven years old. He asked us not to kill him and started crying. Kidega made fun of him because Olweny pissed his pants. Kidega said, "If you don't kill him, we will kill you." I picked my stick and hit him in the face, then everyone else hit him many times until he stopped moving and his brain came out of his head. I felt bad but I knew I had become a man then, a soldier.

Kidega told us to throw Olweny's body in the bush, warning us that anyone who tried to escape would suffer the same fate. "You are now real soldiers of the Lord," Kidega said, "and you belong to Joseph Kony, our father." This is how I ended up here. This is now my family because God wanted me to be Kony's child, and you are my brother.

George listened quietly. He wanted to tell Okello his story of joining the rebels but he was certain Okello knew. George felt that his story could not compare to what Okello and other holies had gone through so he kept quiet. In his first few months in Garamba George had listened to many such stories around the fire but this time with Okello was different. He spoke directly to George, telling him things that one only discussed with a close friend or a brother. George was grateful that after so many months in the LRA, he felt trusted. He was particularly happy at the mention of the word *omera* (my brother)."I am tired," said Okello, which George took as the sign that their conversation was over. He packed the remaining cassava and helped his friend lie down. He then walked around slowly to make sure there was nothing suspicious and went to rest on his sleeping mat. Okello spent most of the night groaning in pain, only sleeping late at night.

* * *

Early in the morning they walked towards Mego Aboke. Five hours later, around 10 am, George thought the area looked familiar and that the sick bay was not far. He helped Okello hide and continued to walk slowly alongside a small river. His walk had soon turned to a slow crawl as he listened intently for any noises. In the last two years in Garamba he had learned to talk and listen like a real fighter. Most of the holies spoke softly and in short sentences, always aware that an enemy could be near.

George waited for a while by a small anthill when he heard a voice coming from the direction of the sick bay. George was now certain this was the place where Binany was based but wanted to make sure the Ugandan soldiers had not overrun it. He realized that the words he heard were in Luo, spoken by holies. Waiting a little longer he was then able to distinguish a few different voices, recognizing the voice of Ladere talking to one of his escorts. George knew them both and was happy to have finally found the base.

He slowly stepped outside of his hiding place, walking carefully towards the group, knowing that any abrupt movement could make the nervous camp guards shoot him before realizing he was not a foe. He was seen by one of the guards who yelled at him to stop and asked him to reveal his identity. "*Group pa Kony*, I am from Kony's group," George answered. He walked towards them slowly, keeping his AK on his shoulder pointing down to the ground. Ten holies surrounded him and asked him many questions. Knowing that the interrogation was obligatory George answered every question carefully. "How did you separate from Kony? In which position were you shot? How long ago was it? Is there anyone else with you?"

The guards escorted him to Binany's tent. Binany interrogated George for over twenty minutes. George told him everything and said that Okello needed help. Binany then ordered an escort to go with George to find Okello. Binany asked Okello the same questions. George knew that Binany wanted to make sure their stories matched and was relieved to hear Okello repeat the exact same story. He could get in trouble if Binany thought he was lying or hiding something. There was little trust among the rebels.

Okello was treated with traditional medicine and some pills the fighters had looted from a clinic nearby. George stayed with a small group of Binany's bodyguards, who praised him for his bravery in escaping the soldiers and carrying a wounded comrade. They told George this was what it meant to be a real soldier.

George felt proud, especially because he still had many bullets left. He had one magazine in his AK and three extra magazines in his pouch. "Weaker people would have thrown the heavy magazines away before running from the soldiers," he thought. He asked a boy to get his hair dreadlocked *rasta* style, the signature style of the real holies. As he sat on a small bench feeling his hair being pulled into small bundles, he felt good. "I need to get hold of myself," he thought. "I am becoming really good at pursuing these guerrilla tactics."

George stayed for three days in Binany's base before Binany ordered him to join another group which roamed nearby, that of Opiyo Sam. George bid adieu to Okello, who said he was forever grateful to George for saving his life. George shook hands with all of the fighters in the sick bay and smiled when they patted him in the back. "I hope to see you again soon friends," he said.

* * *

On 15 March 2009, the Ugandan army officially ended Operation Lightning Thunder, handing over to the Congolese army. Unofficially, 2,000 Ugandan soldiers stayed in Congo to continue the hunt. As some Ugandan troops left Congo, the death toll perpetrated by the LRA against Congolese civilians started to emerge. The numbers have never been certain since investigations were hard to carry out in remote villages, but by the end of February 2009 the LRA had killed more than 1,000 people, mostly in Congo but also in South Sudan.

Over 300 people were killed in Doruma while they celebrated Christmas. Kony's group killed at least another fifty people between Bitima and Duru. Standbys attacking Faradje on 25 December 2008 killed 150 people, abducted 160, mostly children, and destroyed close to 1,000 homes. Another LRA group moved to Nagero, where the Garamba Park rangers were based. The LRA attacked on 2 January 2009, killing ten people, including four rangers. The fighters destroyed the building that housed the main offices, setting fire to two planes and looting guns, ammunition and uniforms.

Wildlife rangers in Garamba National Park, July 2015.

Another LRA group left Garamba on 16 December 2008 and set off due west for Banda in Bas Uele. After walking for nearly three months, attacking villages on their way, the eighty fighters reached Banda on 15 March 2009, just as the Ugandan army officially left Congo. The population of Banda, including workers from international NGOs and the national army, did not expect the LRA to attack so far west into DRC and were caught unawares. The LRA killed more than thirty people in and around Banda and abducted fifty-eight, including two Belgian women working for a medical organization on polio eradication programs. The aid workers were kept overnight before being released unharmed on the morning of the 16th.

By March 2009, LRA groups were scattered throughout northeastern Congo, with Kony's groups in Bitima and Sakure in Congo's Haut Uélé, Ongwen alongside river Duru following it into South Sudan near Yambio, Arop and Opiyo Sam to the southeast of Garamba, and Achellam Smart to northern Bas Uélé on the border with CAR. Thus, in the aftermath of OLT, the attack intended to destroy the LRA, Kony had under his control a network of groups extending over a radius of about 600 miles, inside Congolese and South Sudanese territory.

* * *

George joined a group of eighty led by Opiyo Sam and was immediately placed under Sam's personal escort of thirteen other men. They walked towards Naibapai near Bitima where they were to meet Kony. During the trip George became friends with Ochan, who said that they had attacked Faradje where they had killed many and looted lots. Ochan said that they walked back from Faradje with 200 abductees and met Kony in Bitima at the end of January. Kony was happy to see them and praised them for their bravery.

While resting with Kony's group near Bitima, Ochan said that an intelligence officer reported to Kony in February that Ongwen was collaborating with Kwoyelo and talking to Museveni. Kony ordered Sam to find and bring Ongwen to him. Ochan heard from other commanders on the way to South Sudan that Kwoyelo had deserted to the Ugandan army, further proof that he was indeed a traitor. By the end of February 2009, Sam's group caught up with

Ongwen near Maridi, South Sudan. Ongwen agreed to go with Sam to see Kony, which seemed like sheer madness to George. Kony had killed people for far less; talking to the enemy was considered high treason.

Ochan thought plans had been made to execute Ongwen, as Kony had also not forgotten Ongwen was the only commander who asked for Otti to be spared, but in the end Kony decided not to kill him. The holies thought that one of Kony's wives, also Ongwen's sister, was the real reason Kony always spared Ongwen, even when he got drunk or disobeyed the Big Teacher. The Big Teacher loved Ongwen's sister very much.

One time in Garamba Ongwen has been so intoxicated that he had drunk the water used for washing hands. He did it right at Kony's table and the Big Teacher was so mad, he almost had him shot. "How can this drunkard lead troops in battle?," he yelled. But his wife pleaded for her brother's life and Kony spared Ongwen.

When Sam brought him to Kony from South Sudan, Ongwen's escort was replaced; some of his bodyguards were transferred to Sam's group, being swapped with Sam's old bodyguards. Kony ensured that commanders did not spend a lot of time with the same escort to avoid bonding and shifting of loyalties. After the regrouping, Kony told Ongwen and other commanders that everyone was about to go to Central African Republic, Ochan reported to George. Sam and his fighters were ordered to find all others left in Garamba and return north to meet Kony. They were to walk to CAR.

When George joined Sam's fighters, they were on the way back from their mission in Garamba, having failed to find any other groups. Sam told his men to hurry since Kony wanted to make his way to CAR by the beginning of April and he had asked that Sam join him on the way there. Kony sent a message to Odhiambo and Abudema, who were already near the CAR border, to return to Congo and allow Kony to go first. Sam's group was now close behind Kony, who, as George knew well, moved relentlessly.

George braced himself for a long and tiring journey trying to catch up with the boss. He hoped that they would reach Kony soon so that George could finally return to his old unit. But trying to find Kony was always a difficult task. "No wonder the Ugandan army could not get close to him, the way he tore through the jungle," George thought. When the group failed to find Kony in Bitima and made their way northwest towards CAR, George lost hope that Kony could be found in Congo at all.

Sam walked even faster than Kony, but there was no sign of the Big Teacher. Each day began at 4 am when the group started to walk at a brisk pace with no stopping until 2 pm. The short stop was necessary to drink water, have a handful of food – mostly peanuts or other dry food items that did not need cooking – and at 2.30 pm the march resumed. Walking continued until about 6 or 6.30 pm, when they tried to find a stream or river bank to spend the night. Everyone was then busy cooking, bathing and taking care of their sore bodies.

Aching and blistered feet were washed carefully and when possible rubbed with shea-nut oil, animal fat or cooking oil. By 8 pm everyone ate assembled around fires made in small pits in the ground. By 9 pm everyone was asleep except for the night guards, who were replaced every four hours throughout the night. Most nights George would fall asleep listening to the faint noise of a small radio Sam listened to, usually the BBC World Service. George felt his eyes get heavy just as the melody announcing the news played. It made him think of home, when Quinto listened to the news as George read – a distant memory.

Two weeks after he joined Sam's group George was exhausted. He grew thin and felt unceasing pain in his ankles, knees and feet. There was little food, usually peanuts and boiled maize he kept in his bag and of which he ate only a handful a day. Sam did not want to stop and loot food from villages, fearing that he would miss meeting Kony. Hunger became acute and everyone foraged in the forest while walking, eating all the wild fruit and berries they could find. Often the group stopped for the night and people found they had nothing to eat so they searched for roots and leaves while the more optimistic tried to catch fish with torn mosquito nets or long sticks they used as spears. George went to bed so hungry he could not sleep even though he was exhausted from all the walking.

They were chased by soldiers who could not keep up with the group's pace. George was used to the sound of bullets flying past, making an unmistakable hissing sound as he ran. He did not think about dying, something that had preoccupied him almost constantly in the early weeks following the Garamba attack. Now he worried only about finding water and food and being able to walk. But once in a while he thought about the soldiers catching him. They would surely kill him. They had no reason not to, he was convinced.

* * *

One morning in late March 2009 George was deployed as a blocking guard with Ochan and another holy George did not know well. Unlike rearguards who walked behind the main group to sweep those who lagged behind, blocking guards stayed put behind the main group, deploying for days at a time. The blocking guards delayed or stopped soldiers, giving the main group enough time to escape. They were instructed to ambush and briefly engage soldiers, then scatter in a different direction from where the main group was in order to confuse and divert the soldiers' attention.

The first day in the new assignment was quiet, which George enjoyed. The night was also quiet as the frogs were silent, which made sleeping much easier. George was happy to cook as Ochan kept guard. George proceeded to roast some wild roots he found, and some cassava Ochan gave him. George then joined Ochan in the guard position while they slowly chewed the food George had cooked. The other man they jokingly called *Ladit* took a nap.

George and Ochan had to position themselves in such a way that they could see what was coming but not be seen. Usually it meant high ground, an anthill or a small tree with a clear line of vision of at least 200 yards. Noon came and passed and all was quiet. George and Ochan sat close, talking in a low, almost inaudible, voice. Ochan joked about

Ladit, who talked in his sleep as George kicked him gently to make him stop. Ladit would fall quiet for a while but would then resume snoring, causing the two to giggle quietly.

At around 4 pm George heard the sound of broken twigs in the forest. "What was that?" George whispered. "Monkeys jumping in the trees," said Ochan. "I don't think so," said George, slowly putting on his backpack, motioning to Ladit, who was now awake and chewing boiled peanuts, to move. Ochan and Ladit understood that people were coming towards them and prepared to shoot. Seconds later they heard the sound of footsteps approaching. They lifted their guns and crouched behind the trees.

They saw a group of soldiers walking in combat formation. Their uniforms were green with the Ugandan flag on their arm. The three waited until the soldiers came to an open spot before opening fire. Some of the soldiers fell, others ran back and a few took up defensive positions. The three ran in three different directions from where Sam's group had gone, to throw the soldiers off the group's trail. After running separately for an hour, the three met again at a prearranged location where they made camp for the night.

That evening they chatted happily about their successful ambush and how well they executed their orders, just like real soldiers. They discussed their long and hazardous journey back to the main group. Sam had provided them with directions for the next RV (rendezvous) point. The three agreed they had to be careful as the soldiers would be looking for them. "The strange nature of the bush life," George thought. "One day you are the hunter and the next you are the prey."

They woke up early and started their journey to the RV, which was at least a full day's walk. They were hoping to reach Sam's group by the end of the day or they risked being on their own for a long time. No holy wanted to be alone in the bush. They knew that Sam was not going to wait but would continue the journey to the CAR border to join Kony. Throughout the day, the three walked carefully.

When they reached open spots, free of trees and shrubs, one crawled while the other two waited until they received the all-clear signal, usually a whistle or a quick wave. In the afternoon, when the sun burned brightest, they stopped for a quick bite and water. They spoke briefly about their good luck and not coming across any soldiers. "Pray the Lord it will be like this till nightfall," Ladit said.

They resumed walking and reached a little creek at the foot of a small hill. They entered from the south, a nice forested area that continued to the north where they were headed, but the creek itself was completely bare. It was perfect for an ambush, an open area with a high vantage point. Ochan went first, crawling to the top of the hill where he could get a good view of the forest on the northern side. George and Ladit waited until Ochan whistled and slowly walked in the open towards the trees. Ochan was walking down on the other side of the hill when shots were fired. George realized they had fallen into the same type of ambush they had carried out the day before.

Unlike the holies, who fired a few rounds and ran away, the soldiers did not stop shooting. George knew he had to get away. He dropped to the ground and yelled to Ladit to do the same but it was too late. Ladit was shot in the face and chest and fell in front of George, his body shaking for a few seconds before becoming still. "Ladit is gone," George thought, and briefly regretted never learning his real name.

George had no time to think as the bullets rained around him. He shot at the soldiers hiding behind the trees and when Ochan did the same from the top of the hill, George ran. He stopped and shot at the soldiers from the edge of the forest hoping to force them to take cover and give Ochan a chance to escape. George saw three soldiers running toward him. They ran and took turns shooting at him, not letting him return fire. He shot a few more rounds and ran into the forest, scared that the soldiers would injure or capture him when he ran out of bullets. He was sure that Ochan had run away too and hoped to meet him as they had agreed in the place they had lunch earlier in the day.

George ran for at least an hour before the sound of bullets died down. He was still alive, though he did not know how. He thanked God for having saved him once again and made his way to where he thought he could meet Ochan. He found "Position Lunch" and waited for his friend to appear. He realized it was almost his second anniversary in the LRA and thought of when he had first joined the rebels. "I must have looked terrified," he smiled. "So much for being a secretary, a man of letters," he thought. "I am now a real rebel, fighting fierce battles with the army." He was elated.

PART TWO

WAITING FOR THE WHISTLE

CHAPTER 11

THE BLESSED LAND
OF PEACE AND REST:
PART TWO

When the prayers to celebrate their arrival in Central African Republic concluded, Kony asked everyone to walk away from the river without looking back. It signified the entry into a new country, a new future, leaving behind all the suffering that the old country and the past had produced. He then divided the troops in three. One group was to return to Congo to gather the remaining holies and bring them to CAR. A second group led by Otto Agweng was to travel to Darfur in Sudan to locate the barracks of the Sudanese Armed Forces. The third group, a standby, was to leave for the villages north of Obo and bring back food. The standby left that night and returned two days later with plenty of food, including peanuts, maize, cassava, rice and meat. Everyone was finally able to rest and eat.

Kony ordered the remaining people to continue moving. They no longer walked in the same manner as in Congo but took more breaks. The main group stopped for longer periods of time as small units deployed to survey the new land. On the second day of the walk, northeast of Obo, they came across a trail littered with cow dung. Kony dispatched people to meet the cow herders nearby. George could hear the cows mooing, less than two miles away. One of the commanders who had been in CAR with Odhiambo said that these were Muslim cattle herders called Mbororo. The Mbororo moved with their families and many cows, maybe as many as 1,500–2,000. "They are like the Karamojong in Uganda. But no one is to harm them," Kony said, ordering them to ask nicely for cows.

The standby, including George and led by Lukwang, moved quickly on the trail of the Mbororo. Approaching the herds of cattle, they saw men dressed in black who ran away when they saw them. The holies followed them, trying to signal that they meant no harm. The men in black eventually stopped and greeted them reluctantly in Arabic. As Kony had ordered, an Arabic speaker told the Mbororo that they came in peace and wanted to talk. He said that the LRA was on its way to a distant place and needed assistance. "What assistance do you need?," one of the Mbororo asked. "We need food, cows," the reply came. "We don't have the authority to do that," the man said. "We need to wait for the *sultan*."

While waiting for the sultan, as the Mbororo called the boss, a woman appeared with a mat made of dry grass and invited them to sit. "Please visitors sit," she said in Arabic. "No thank you," Lukwang said. "We are simple soldiers and not allowed to sit idly." She said that she was the wife of the sultan and tradition demanded that she

A young Mbororo man and woman in Mboki, CAR, March 2010.

welcomed them. "Our *sultan* does not permit us to sit,"
George said in Luo, making the others laugh. "No," said
Lukwang.

She smiled and walked away emerging later with two
large bowls of milk. LRA rules dictated that no food given
by outsiders be consumed for fear of poison but the men
were hungry. It also seemed that the Mbororo became
tense when they had refused to sit down, so declining
the offer of milk might be regarded as a sign of hostility.
After quick deliberations in Luo, the standby members
accepted the milk, which they drank in big gulps.

An old man eventually came to meet them. He wore
grey pants tucked in his boots, a white shirt and a black
vest. He introduced himself as the sultan and invited
them to sit and talk. The Arabic speaker replied they
had to stand up and discuss business. "What is your
business, how can I assist you?" asked the sultan. "We
want cows, our people are hungry and we need to travel
far," replied Lukwang, who spoke broken Arabic. "But
we have no money and need you to be kind and donate
us the cows." "How many cows do you need?" the sultan
asked. "Thirty," said Lukwang, after some talk in Luo
among the Arabic speakers who struggled to remember
the correct term. "Thirty is too many," the sultan said,
"I give you fifteen and we remain peaceful." "We need
thirty," the holy replied, this time raising his voice. "We
have many people to feed. You want us to fight among
ourselves because there is not enough food?" They eventually agreed to take twenty-one.

The sultan ordered his men to bring twenty-one cows, which they did quickly, as if they knew already which cows were to be sacrificed to the LRA. The standby commander asked the Mbororo to help slaughter the cows, also done rapidly. These men knew what they were doing. They slaughtered and skinned the cows in about an hour. After the Mbororo left, the standby commander ordered small teams of four to cut each cow and distribute the meat to all members of the standby. When the happy men returned to camp with the meat Kony smiled and said that God was on their side.

In the first few days in the new country, gorging on cow's meat and feeling his legs heal, George thought about his new home. He was happy there. The country was beautiful and rich in the things that the holies appreciated, like wild fruit and roots. There were many wild yams, the rivers had abundant fish and baboons and chimpanzees provided good meat. And as a particular treat, the area also had many honey trees. Kony had been kind enough not to forbid eating honey, which some took as a challenge to eat as much as possible. George was quick to join them.

The groups continued to move without pitching camp permanently. They walked between the northwest and southeast of Obo, often crossing the busy route that connected Obo in CAR with Tambura in South Sudan. It was unclear to George why the Big Teacher kept walking after he had promised that they would live in CAR as they did in Garamba, in permanent camps. But Kony insisted that CAR civilians should not know where the LRA camped, thus the constant moving. "We should be invisible," he said.

Kony also ordered standbys to loot food in South Sudan and Congo but not in CAR. "We need to show the people of Central Africa that they have nothing to fear from us," Kony said. Soon after the cows' meat was finished a large group was organized to bring food from South Sudan. George was part of the group that numbered 200 people and was led by Otim Ferry. George was happy to have the opportunity to find food.

* * *

Sitting outside his house in Mboki, CAR, one day in March 2010, Ardo Chevu agreed to talk about the Mbororo, "my people," as he called them, and the LRA. He wore a long white djellabah that ended at his toes and a yellowish turban that wrapped around his forehead and neck. He held a long walking cane in his right hand even when he sat down. He was thin and tall with faded green eyes. Chevu was the chief of the Mbororo based in Mboki, a position he said he had accepted reluctantly. "Because my people move around a lot, we don't stay in one place for long." But he had already settled in Mboki with a large number of other Mbororo families.

Times have changed for the Mbororo. Many move with cows and only stay in the forest but some decided to stay here in Mboki. We used to stay away from the south of CAR because the tsetse fly killed our cows. There is medicine now for sleeping sickness and people are forced to move further south every year because there is little water in the north. Mboki used to have thousands of refugees from South Sudan and Darfur but with peace in Sudan, they went back and we bought their houses. We now live peacefully with the Zande. We marry them and have children with them. Our men marry Zande women, it must be said.

My people are suffering. We are cattle people; we walk with our cows. It is what our forefathers did and it is what our children and grandchildren will do. But everyone attacks us. We are peaceful people but we are always threatened. In Sudan the Janjaweed take our cows and milk. In South Sudan, the SPLA attack us, they say we are President Bashir's people. In Congo, soldiers harass us constantly.

We had a lot to cope with in the past but now we are facing a big threat, the LRA or the tongo-tongo as they are known here. These people are wild; they steal our cows, take our children and kill entire families. Maybe fifty Mbororo were killed by the tongo-tongo last month alone. No one finds out about it because whole families are killed and left in the bush. They are nomads, they are coming from different countries, no one knows about them. We only find out when other Mbororo find the bodies in the bush. The tongo-tongo come, they ask for cows and when our people refuse, the tongo-tongo kill them and take the cows anyway. Who is to stop them?

They also take our children. They abduct the kids to use them as hostages so that they get more cows or force the fathers to spy for the tongo-tongo or to buy things for them in the market. I know of at least fourteen Mbororo who are now with the tongo-tongo, taken from their families by force. Three young girls and one woman with two children were abducted recently. My own *son was taken by the tongo-tongo in Bambouti in South Sudan and was forced to stay with them for a whole year. They used him as a guide and as an interpreter. He escaped and came here two months ago, but he was not well mentally. I sent him to Sudan to get treatment and told him to stay. I don't want him back here.*

We don't want to have anything to do with the tongo-tongo but they use our cattle paths to move in the bush. People here accuse us of helping the tongo-tongo. One day in Zemio the police took a Mbororo man and put him in prison, accusing him of being a spy for the tongo-tongo. The next day 100 people from the town stormed the police station where he was held and killed him. They beat him to death with no proof at all that he was a spy for the tongo-tongo. The gendarmes put him in prison for no reason at all and did not protect him.

* * *

In early June 2009, George left the temporary camp in CAR with Ferry's standby and headed northeast, with Tambura in South Sudan as their destination. The first day they moved in true LRA fashion, starting early in the morning and walking until nighttime with only a short stop for lunch. They chose a secondary road that ran parallel to the main road linking Obo and South Sudan, a shortcut in the forest that traders and cow herders used. It headed towards Tambura, at times cutting across the main road. The holies heard the sound of motorcycles on the road but were under orders not to attack inside CAR.

On the first day the group did not come across any human settlements. At night everyone was excited, talking around the fire about their escape from Congo and their new life in CAR. The next morning they left early, hoping to finally find food. Five miles later they found a trail they thought looked familiar. It was made by Ugandan soldiers with the unmistakable army boot tracks visible on the ground. The soldiers had walked in their usual four-line formation, coming from South Sudan, going towards Obo. The tracks were one day old.

Ferry decided to send two messengers to alert Kony. The rest were to proceed with their mission as people were hungry and food was badly needed in Kony's camp. At noon scouts sent to explore the area reported fresh tracks nearby. George and ten others went to investigate. They followed the footmarks leading to a small river where they found the remains of an antelope. Local hunters were somewhere close, probably cooking the meat. A plan was made to surround the hunters' camp and capture them.

Six holies crossed the river twice so that they could approach the hunters from behind while George and the remaining four rushed in front of the hunters, allowing them little time to escape. Four men were in the process of smoking the antelope they had skinned. They must have been at hunting camp for about a week. They had a lot of smoked meat, and sizable quantities of cassava flour and peanuts they must have brought from their village.

The standby commander conducted the interrogation. The hunters were Zande from South Sudan who spoke Arabic and came from a small village five miles east. They said there were no military or security forces in their village and explained the position of other villages in the area. After the commander acquired all the necessary information, he made a sign to the rest of the men, who bayoneted the hunters. There was no debate as to what to do with them. Once they revealed they were from South Sudan, their fate was sealed. The Dinkas, as they called all inhabitants of South Sudan, were sworn enemies of the LRA and were to be killed. It did not matter if they were Zande or any other ethnic group, all non-Arab Sudanese were "high-profile enemies," as Kony referred to them.

Ferry was later told of what happened, including the information received from the hunters. He decided to attack the hunters' village early in the morning. The orders, given that night, included looting everything possible, abducting people that could be useful, such as young men and women, and killing the rest. That night around the fire everyone was happy, eating the meat of the hunters and discussing the forthcoming attack. Many said they were excited to see some action again. "Everyone has been writing us off," one said. "We will show them we are not finished." Since they entered CAR, Kony told them that people on the radio were saying the LRA was finished and that he was dead. "Museveni can only kill me with words," he joked.

At 4 am, as the standby prepared for the day's attack, the two runners sent to alert Kony returned with an urgent message from the General. The standby was to return immediately to Kony's camp. There was to be no attack. People were annoyed. They were so close to the food they badly needed but instead of eating they would now have to walk. Again. Hungry. The thought of more marching and no food made everyone angry. But they knew better than dispute orders and the group was quickly on the move.

The pace doubled as Kony only gave them a day to return even though it took them two days to walk from Kony's camp to the South Sudanese village. The heat combined with the fast pace made George breathe heavily. His feet were bruised and his thighs were irritated, making every step he took painful. Not stopping for lunch, they walked late into the evening. At 9 pm Ferry ordered everyone to sleep. There was little to eat, a few handfuls of wild berries picked hastily while walking. It was all George had had all day.

At midnight they resumed marching. Most of the walking was usually done during the day, but in emergency cases, and particularly when the path was well known, groups also walked during the night. Ferry, like Opiyo Sam in Congo, was keen to obey Kony's orders and wanted to meet the boss on the deadline he was given. No commander wished to make Kony unhappy. Ferry kept pushing everyone to walk faster. The women and children in the group were crying out in pain, but there was to be no stopping.

Around 9.30 am the standby finally reached the old camp, but Kony was not there. Two scouts said the General ordered that they follow his trail without stopping until they reached him in his new position. Everyone was

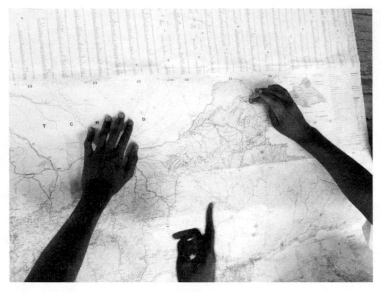

Young children who had recently escaped from an LRA group where they spent more than six months show the long distances they walked, about 400 miles away from their home. Obo, CAR, June 2015.

exhausted and had already collapsed on the ground. "My God," cried Ferry, "when shall we rest today?"

Having spent a lot of time as Kony's bodyguard, George knew that the boss was able to walk for the entire day. He had witnessed Kony go all day without stopping to rest, drink or eat. This journey would take a long time. He was not sure his legs could take it but he saw the women and children getting up and starting to walk slowly, initially limping then building up speed, and felt ashamed. He continued to walk without complaining, staying in the middle of the group. He did not want to be in front and ordered to cut a path in the bush or at the back and be whipped by the rearguards, a bunch of cruel bastards.

They walked all day, following Kony's trail until they found his group at dusk. Ferry went to report to Kony as George and the rest of the group dropped to the ground exhausted. George looked around and was reminded of a scene from a movie, a story of slaves who had to walk for days to the ocean where a boat waited to take them away. "We are like those slaves," he thought. He never dared utter those words aloud but at that moment in time, when his spirits were lowest, George wished he had never set foot in the LRA. He wished he had been born somewhere far away where people did not know Kony or his so-called holies.

* * *

As Kony and his group moved across CAR, the LRA Congo groups instigated a campaign of violence reminiscent of the killings of December 2008 and January 2009. By June 2009, over 15,000 Congolese refugees crossed into South Sudan and CAR, seeking refuge from LRA violence. An area west of Garamba, between Niangara, Ngilima and Bangadi, was baptized by the local community and NGO workers "the triangle of death."

One night in early June 2009, François Mbolingiye, a father of six living with his family in Nakwa, near Bangadi, was having dinner outside his home when he noticed twelve armed men surrounding his family. The men, in dirty military uniforms, wore their hair "rasta" style and reeked. After taking out all the food in the house, they ordered François and his family inside his hut, locked the door and set it ablaze. François could see the men outside who sat and ate the food François' wife had prepared while he and his family choked from all the smoke and burned alive.

François forced the door open and ran outside, trying to pull his two-year-old son and the rest of his family out with him, but the men shot at him. He ran into the bush, wanting to call for help. He was shot in the shoulder as he ran but managed to get deeper into the forest before collapsing. He was found unconscious in the morning by two men from Nakwa and taken to a clinic in Bangadi and eventually to Dungu, where an international aid organization ran the town's hospital. He found out in Dungu hospital that his entire family had succumbed to the fire.

It seemed that the Congo attacks, particularly in the triangle of death, were carried out to divert attention from Kony and the majority of the LRA moving to CAR. But the Ugandan army was aware of Kony's intentions as various fighters who defected had spoken of Kony's attempt to enter CAR since the end of 2006. The army had made contingency plans and was prepared to act quickly once it became known that Kony had left Congo for CAR.

Despite Kony's orders to maintain secrecy and not to mistreat the civilian population, news filtered out at the end of May 2009 about an LRA attack on a small hamlet north of Obo called Kourukou I. Village chief Ellie Leande explained how a large group of people, including women and children, which he referred to as tongo-tongo, a term for the LRA that came from the Luo word tong, meaning "to chop," attacked Kourouko I, killing ten people with machete blows to the back of the head and stealing all the food they could carry. Apparently the commander of the standby could not prevent his troops killing people as they looted Kourokou I, let alone force them to ask for food nicely, as Kony had ordered.

The preparedness of the Ugandan army coupled with news of LRA attacks in Obo's vicinity brought about a swift movement of Ugandan soldiers into CAR territory. Kampala had taken care of the diplomatic side, having already reached an agreement with CAR authorities to grant entry to Ugandan soldiers in Mbomou prefecture in the southeast of the country. Located over 600 miles from the capital Bangui, Obo was indeed, as a French diplomat put it, "a forgotten and forgone territory" to the President of CAR, François Bozizé, who worried more about his own regime propped up by France and guarded by Chadian soldiers than a handful of rebels in a remote corner of the country.

The lack of any institutional capacity and security forces in the area was beneficial to Kony. His belief that he would be left alone in CAR benefited the Ugandan army, giving it an element of surprise that it historically lacked in its dealings with the LRA. Ugandan troops moved quickly into a makeshift base in Obo and attacked LRA groups. The rapid response on the part of the Ugandans, who had already established a forward operating base in Nzara, in the nearby Western Equatoria state of South Sudan, caught the LRA commanders unawares, a rarity in the entire history of the long conflict.

* * *

George opened his eyes with difficulty and saw a coy mate standing above him. "Wake up Yankee," he said. "Time to move." George got to his feet, unaware of where he was. It was still dark but he slowly started to recognize the forest and soon realized he had slept since the afternoon of the previous day when he had returned with Ferry's group. His body felt better and he could walk normally. "Thank God," he thought. "I am still able to walk." He walked to Kony's unit where he saw the Big Man address senior commanders.

"So far we have refrained from attacking inside this country, because there was no proof the Central Africans were part of the anti LRA alliance. But it is clear now that they opened their borders to the Ugandan army. These actions destroyed the relationship that the LRA government wanted to develop with Central Africa," Kony said, using the term "Central Africa" to refer to CAR, as did all holies. "It makes no sense to search for food and recruits outside of Central Africa when the people of Central Africa are now fair game," a commander argued. "We are within our rights to invade this country," Kony said, and all the commanders agreed. "Let us now plan the invasion of Central Africa," Kony ordered.

A standby was to attack Obo, the largest inhabited center nearby. Ferry and Lieutenant Okello Palotaka were in charge. At 10 am on 18 June 2009, the standby comprising eighty people including women and children set off for Obo. George was chosen to participate in the attack. The group walked towards the southwest guided by three scouts, who had been on reconnaissance missions near Obo before. The group crossed a few small streams and broke through a large forested area. The scouts urged people on, insisting they would reach Obo soon.

Everyone was hungry and weak. There was nothing to eat but berries and other wild fruit, and roots picked while walking. As the day came to an end, the group prepared to find a place to spend the night. They walked over dry plains until late at night, when they came across a small pond at the bottom of a large field where they stopped for the night.

George felt exhausted. He went to the pond to drink some water and wash up before going to sleep. An impossibly bright moon enabled him to discern his reflection in the water. He thought he saw the face of his grandfather, the famed Abonga he had seen in family pictures, staring at him from the water. "My God, I look like an old man," he worried. He wished he could talk to his mother and explain how tired he was and receive a few words of encouragement as when he was a small child back in Uganda. George knew what his mother would say: "Put on Christ's heart and carry on." But George would reply that even Christ's cross seemed not that heavy to carry compared to the pain George experienced. "No one to help me," George would say if he could, "like Simon who gave Jesus a hand. There is no one here for me."

The night hours brought little relief. His feet were swollen and throbbed with pain. Staying still made the pain worse. He rubbed his legs but the pain seemed to move throughout his body. "As if my blood is sickly," he thought. He wondered what his mother would say to encourage him but could not come up with anything. He chided himself for being childish.

He did not know how long he slept but it felt like minutes. "How could it be four in the morning already?" After more hours of walking without seeing anyone or any villages, people became annoyed. "These scouts don't know where we are going," someone said. The guides said they were close and that there was no time for arguments. Palotaka had to bark orders at the starving men to keep quiet and not to beat the scouts. Around 5 pm they came across an abandoned homestead. People cheered up and picked up the pace, but Ferry ordered a military formation, which meant an advance and rearguards, while the rest walked in single file with the women and children in the middle. They were to walk carefully, guns at the ready in case the soldiers appeared. Everyone wanted to be at the front of the group, to be the first to get their hands on food. Hunger seemed to have made everyone mad, "like a pack of wild dogs," George thought. He squeezed to the front of the line, ready to walk into the village and eat the first edible thing he saw. But he saw Ferry's bodyguards positioned at the head of the group handing out serious beatings to those pushing to get in front. The punches and canings had the intended effect. Everyone stopped and waited for orders.

Palotaka organized the formation with four men ahead as the advance party and two as rearguards with the rest in the middle. George was annoyed he was only in the middle of the group but carried on in silence. The path became wider, with evident signs of human activity. There were small gardens of vegetables and soon the group heard voices in the distance. With every step towards the village George felt his stomach hurt more and realized he salivated upon hearing the voices. "My God," he thought, "what is this hunger doing to me?"

Two people caught just outside of the village said that it was called Ligoua and Obo was only six miles away. The Ugandan army had arrived and set up base in Obo a few weeks before. Ferry quickly drew on a piece of paper where the Ugandan army camp was located based on the description of the captured man and woman. He asked about the location of all households in this village and the number and whereabouts of all inhabitants. The two said that all the civilians were at home at that hour. Ferry gave orders on how to raid the village. He did not specifically order the killing of anyone, including the two who had just been arrested, so people focused on finding food.

Ferry wanted to secure the village before eating since the group was going to spend the night there. George and a Congolese *kurut* wielding a large butcher's knife guarded a path on the eastern side of the village. George kept an eye on the path and slowly moved to a cassava garden where he uprooted a couple of stems and tried to eat the cassava raw. The *kurut* did the same. George entered a house and continued to eat. Peanuts, half-cooked rice, sugar cane, *kwon gwana* and vegetables still cooking in a pot. He felt an urge to keep moving, to keep looking for food, to eat everything.

* * *

Al Hadji Fofana said his father was from Senegal but came to CAR twenty-five years before and married a Zande woman. His dad continued to go to Senegal and bring back fabrics and other goods he sold in Mboki's central market but Al Hadji and his mother stayed in Mboki. Like many of his friends whose fathers were originally from Chad, Sudan and Mali, Al Hadji felt comfortable living in Mboki, a little town in the southeast inhabited by a mix of ethnicities. But life became hard when the tongo-tongo attacked the town on 24 July 2009.

That morning Al Hadji left his home early and walked into the bush, close to river Mbomou. He joined two friends, Congolese refugees who had taught him how to make small tents out of bamboo and palm tree leaves they sold to people in the market to use as roofs for their stalls. Manda and Japonais were from Digba in nearby Bas Uélé in Congo. Al Hadji knew that both boys had left with their families because of attacks from a group of rebels called tongo-tongo. He had heard that the rebels were violent and that they had now come to CAR, but only east of Mboki, to Obo and near the South Sudanese border. He never thought he would meet them.

The three youngsters were surrounded by a group of armed men who were emaciated and smelled bad. Their hair was dreaded and covered in dirt. They wore ripped shirts and had plastic bags over their feet stuffed into gumboots. One said in Arabic they were Ugandan soldiers. Then he continued in a language Al Hadji did not understand but someone emerged from the back of the group and spoke in Pazande, one of the local languages. The Pazande speaker said he was from Ezo in South Sudan and wanted information on Mboki. The armed man said through the translator that they should not be afraid and that he only wanted to buy food from the market.

Manda and Japonais did not say a word and seemed frightened. They kept their hands on top of their heads while sitting but Al Hadji stood up. When the armed man learned they were Congolese, he directed his questions solely to Al Hadji. The commander asked him about the number of soldiers and police in Mboki, their bases and the number of Ugandan troops. Al Hadji said there were no Ugandans, only five Central African soldiers. It was clear these men were not part of the Ugandan army, which the commander of the group acknowledged. "We are from the Lord's Resistance Army," he said, "but do not fear us, all we want is food."

The LRA men engaged in conversation, which, with the help of the Sudanese translator, Al Hadji understood as a debate on whether to attack the town that morning or later at night. Some of the fighters said that they should not attack Mboki in the middle of the day. It was too dangerous. They said they had little ammo for their guns and could be killed if soldiers appeared. They said that they should attack the small villages outside of Mboki, to get cassava and vegetables from the gardens. Then the commander ordered everyone to walk into the forest. After an hour, they reached river Mbomou, where Al Hadji saw over 100 people. There were many armed men, as well as women and children. They were all skinny and covered in mud.

Al Hadji noticed others from Mboki who had also been abducted that morning. Two women who had been caught fishing by the river and two other men. A six-year-old, probably a daughter of one of the women, was also among the abductees. He noticed some people who must have been abducted in Congo earlier. They were unarmed and were in really bad shape, emaciated and covered in bruises. The people taken that morning were made to sit on the ground while two young boys with machetes stood guard.

An LRA man holding a large gun asked one of the girls next to Al Hadji in Arabic if she was married. She said no and the man asked her to follow him into the bush. Al Hadji told her not to go and she did not move. Annoyed, the fighter grabbed Al Hadji and pulled him towards a small anthill where another fighter sat, surrounded by others. It seemed that he was the commander of the entire group.

The armed men surrounding the boss told Al Hadji to sit down but he refused. He was certain they were going to kill him, so "why make it easier?" he thought. He felt the blows at the back of his head and face but stood tall. The fighter who brought him to the commander pointed his bayonet in Al Hadji's face and prepared to plunge it in his right eye. The commander stopped him and called for the man from Ezo to translate.

"Sit down and don't be afraid," the commander said. Al Hadji agreed while wiping blood from his split lips. "All I want is to talk," said the commander, "and there is no need to be a fool because these fellows here will kill you." He then asked the same questions the junior commander had asked in the morning; about Mboki's defenses and the goods in the central market. He asked whether there was any sugar and tea in the market because he wanted to buy some. "Also soap and maize, I need those things badly."

Al Hadji said there was all that and much more. "What about the army, where are they based?" "Three miles from the market," Al Hadji answered. "Can you take me there?" "If you promise not to kill us," Al Hadji said. "Yes, but if there are more soldiers that you did not tell us about and we fall into an ambush, I will personally kill you," said the commander.

The armed men proceeded to tie everyone caught that morning. They tied four together; Al Hadji first followed by Manda and Japonais and last the young woman. They were bound by their waists, walking in single file. The remaining three people were also tied together, sparing the six-year-old, who followed behind. All eight walked in the middle of a large cluster of fighters, women and children. A young Congolese boy of nine held a huge knife and pulled the rope that tied Al Hadji and the others.

The group set off for Mboki, about six miles away. When approaching the town, the loud noise of cows the Mbororo herded into a large pen scared the fighters. "Just the cows mooing," Al Hadji said contemptuously. Before reaching Mboki, the fighters dispersed and entered from three different directions. They caught the Mbororo and stole their watches and clothes, also bringing some of them along. After entering the town, the commander asked Manda if there was a quick route to the base of the army. Manda said he did not know because he was not from Mboki. Al Hadji said there was one but that the soldiers would shoot them with machine guns if they went to the base. "I will kill you if we are attacked on the way to the market," the commander threatened again, and ordered them to continue.

Entering the main road that led to the central market, the fighters at the front of the line told people in Arabic and English that they were Ugandan soldiers coming from Obo. It

momentarily stopped the flight of the townspeople but as other
fighters filtered in from many directions and people saw the
tied men and women, they resumed running. The commander
ordered all abductees to sit down by the side of the road while
the fighters descended on the market. The merchants did not
put up resistance, telling the LRA fighters in Arabic to take
what they wanted and not harm anyone. Al Hadji witnessed
in silence what he thought was the biggest act of destruction
and looting he had ever seen. "Those people were possessed,"
he later said, "like they had never seen food before."

The tongo-tongo took sugar, maize, soap, oil, boots, matches,
batteries and everything else they could find and loaded the
abductees with all the loot. But a nervous fighter shot in the
air to scare people, and violently shoved a young boy against
a wall. A large gash on the side of his head spewed blood.
Suddenly people appeared with bows and arrows and attacked
the tongo-tongo. Annoyed, one of the LRA men shot the young
boy whose face was covered in blood and could not get out of
the way quickly enough. He died on the spot, prompting a loud
shriek from his father, a Chadian merchant. It turned into a
rallying cry as the Chadian traders who until then had allowed
the tongo-tongo to take their goods, grabbed machetes, spears
and knives and turned on the looters. The LRA men and women
took cover inside some of the abandoned shops along the main
road. Convinced that the commander was not going to spare
them, Al Hadji turned to Japonais and told him they should try
to escape. "Help me untie this rope," he said.

Japonais said he was too afraid they would be shot and kept
his head down. Undeterred, Al Hadji dropped the heavy load

and managed to loosen the rope from his waist. He started to run away from the market, towards the town's Catholic Church. When Japonais saw the rope was loose in front of him he untied himself and ran behind Al Hadji. Some tongo-tongo saw them and fired many rounds, striking Manda who was still tied up by the side of the road. He died soon after.

Three men gave chase to Al Hadji and Japonais, shooting at them from about fifty yards. Al Hadji heard the bullets whizzing past him and heard screaming. He saw Japonais writhing on the ground, blood spurting from a large wound in his back. The tongo-tongo continued to pursue Al Hadji, who was certain they would kill him. He saw an abandoned bike and climbed on it quickly, managing to get away. He was not sure if they were saving their bullets or their guns jammed because they did not shoot him. But he had no doubt that God had saved his life by placing that bicycle in his escape path. He was grateful to make it out alive and went immediately to the army station to alert the soldiers.

At the market, Chadian merchants and Mbororo armed with bows and arrows forced the LRA to leave. Two tongo-tongo men were stabbed and died on the spot. A woman from the LRA group was hit by a poisoned Mbororo arrow, which caused her death on the outskirts of Mboki as she tried to return to the bush. At least nine other tongo-tongo were injured and taken back to the bush by their friends. Many Chadians, Mbororo and Zande men armed with machetes and bows followed them deep inside the bush where they found three more bodies, bringing the total number of LRA deaths to six.

Four people were killed by the LRA – Manda and Japonais, the eleven-year-old Chadian boy and a young Sudanese trader.

Despite being based only a short distance away it was more than an hour after the LRA returned to the forest that soldiers from the local barracks turned up at the market. In a grainy photograph from that day, the soldiers pose triumphantly over the emaciated bodies of the three slain LRA members.

Nine months after the attack, Gregoire Dedieu Dagaya sat next to Al Hadji, and recounted in detail the events of that day. Dagaya was the leader of the auto-defense group of Mboki. A former soldier in the Chadian army, in 2002 he had settled in Mboki, where he taught philosophy at the lycee, the town's high school. "We, the auto-defense, followed the tongo-tongo deep into the bush. We had no guns, no AKs like them, just bows and arrows, knives and the anger that boiled our blood. We would have followed them all the way to Congo if we could but we have families to take care of. We needed to come back to look after our children. The Central African army and the Ugandan army refused to do a thing. But that is fine. We showed the tongo-tongo they cannot screw with us."

CHAPTER 12

THE DEVIL'S CHILDREN

The group spent the night in Ligoua eating, gathering food, preparing the loot to be brought to camp and eating some more. George found a ten-liter jerrycan of cooking oil, some shea-nut oil, matches, salt, soap and a couple of torches and small batteries. He loaded it all inside a big backpack where he had also stashed peanuts, maize, rice and *kwon gwana*. It was his private stock that would ensure his survival for at least a few extra weeks.

Continuing to eat, George witnessed the devastation they had brought upon Ligoua. The houses were gutted and chicken feathers and goatskins still dripping with blood dotted the ground. The holies continued to roam around the village, packing food and other goods to bring back to camp. The unfortunate few from Ligoua who has been unable to escape were forced to shell peanuts and peas and pound rice in wooden mortars.

Late at night someone found a radio and tuned to a channel with American music. People started to dance to the beat of disco music, making fun of each other's moves. But then Ferry found a Ugandan channel and to everyone's delight Ugandan music burst out of the small speakers making everyone jump to their feet and dance. The eating and music made George feel like he was at home celebrating a birthday or a wedding.

Before long, the day broke and the group prepared to return to the bush. Everyone was burdened with heavy bags and jerrycans filled with peanuts, rice, peas and cooking oil. The loads were tremendously heavy, some over eighty pounds, loaded on backs, shoulders, heads and arms. The abductees from Ligoua suffered the most. They were laden with even heavier luggage and whipped with sticks to force them to move.

Upon entering the bush the group stopped as the commanders assembled for a brief meeting. Some wanted to go back to the main camp and bring food to the people there who were starving. Others said they wanted to continue to Obo, as was the standby's initial order. Since Obo was only a few miles away, they had to hide the food in the bush and proceed to their destination. Ferry agreed and the group made for Obo. But on the way they caught civilians who said there were 5,000 Ugandan soldiers in Obo. Considering there were only eighty people in the standby, not all of them fighters, Ferry ordered a return to where they hid the food from Ligoua.

Ferry worried there was not enough food and goods to bring to Kony and ordered another standby to loot more food from Ligoua. He wanted to bring back enough food to keep the boss happy, expecting Kony to be annoyed at the failure to attack Obo. The group went back to Ligoua and returned to the bush at 3 pm with yet more food.

George was amazed that Ligoua was still empty and fully expected the Ugandan troops to appear. People who had escaped the night before would have made it to Obo already, alerting the Ugandans. And yet no one appeared, even though it was late in the day.

Palotaka told the abductees from Ligoua to put the food down and pay attention. He spoke in Luo, which the Congolese recruit translated. Palotaka said that they were free to go back home but that they should not live in Ligoua but move to Obo and stay there. "Ligoua is our village now," he said, "we will be coming often to get food here." He continued, "We are the Lord's Resistance Army and we don't kill people for no reason. All we want is food so don't be scared of us but don't disturb us either, because we will retaliate." After he finished talking, the dozen people were set free after their terrifying twenty hours. They ran away without looking back.

Early the following morning, they started their return trip to Kony's camp. Everyone, including small children, carried heavy loads, which slowed the pace of the walk and made people cry in pain. George fantasized about dumping everything on the ground but feared the bodyguards' lashes. He also thought of all the times in the past he had been hungry and knew that what he was carrying could help fend off that hunger a little longer. It could keep him alive a while longer, giving him hope for the future.

The all too familiar foot pain returned. People around him took off their gumboots and put on plastic slippers to relieve the pain while continuing to walk slowly. He wanted to do the same but was afraid he would not be able to lift his load back on to his shoulders. He kept walking, trying not to think of the pain. He thought of the butterflies. There were so many beautiful butterflies in CAR; he had never seen so many stunning insects before.

The group stopped late at night to eat and sleep, leaving again early in the morning. George was selected to be part of the advance party, a task he hated. The heat made it hard to breathe, let alone cut through the bush with a blunt machete. He was exhausted and thought he was like a wounded lion desperately trying to escape a trap. He kept falling down. Ferry's bodyguards who walked behind and supervised the line yelled at him. He was desperate to reach a stream or river so that he could finally take a break and wash off the sweat that covered his head and body. He whispered "Thank you Jesus" when at 5 pm two messengers appeared. They were sent by Kony to escort the standby to the General's new camp.

George could not believe his ears when he heard the messengers say Kony's camp was four miles away. He did not think he could walk even a few extra steps. He had a strong urge to sneak into the bush and hide. To his further dismay, the messengers said they had strict orders from the General not to let the standby rest but to walk without stopping until they arrived at the new camp. People there needed the food badly.

George thought he would prefer to kill himself than resume cutting through the forest. He readied his gun and thought about emptying the magazine in his head. When

Palotaka called the advance party, George stayed back waiting for the threats to commence and preparing to do something crazy. Maybe he could shoot Palotaka and then himself, or just refuse to get up. But the two messengers joined the advance party and no one noticed George's absence. He slowly followed the crowd of people, quietly thanking God for having come to his rescue again.

When the group finally reached Kony's camp George was shocked at the condition of the people, who seemed on the verge of death. Two small children and three abductees from Congo had already died from hunger. He saw everyone staring with big sunken eyes as he and others from the standby unloaded the loot from Ligoua. He worried that they would pounce on the group, raiding the food just as the group had done in Ligoua. Everyone received some food, which they devoured in silence.

That night people gathered around the fires eating large quantities and sharing painful stories. Those who were left in the camp spoke about their hunger while George and his standby friends described the long march to and from Ligoua. People were happy to still be alive and lamented that the next morning the painful walk would resume. They did not know where they were going. There were rumors that the Ugandan soldiers were close, chasing the group as they had done in Congo. No one dared mention Kony's prophecy about CAR being the land of blessed peace. They were grateful to be alive.

In the morning the group followed Kony, walking towards the northwest. It became clear that the Ugandan soldiers were following the group when the small white spy plane that haunted the holies in Congo appeared in the CAR sky. George felt that familiar, yet briefly forgotten, feeling of nausea associated with seeing the white plane. But no gunships followed so Kony, concerned that the soldiers were behind, deployed a blocking unit. The blocking unit was given an anti-personnel mine and told to plant it in the middle of the group's trail and wait until the soldiers stepped on it before shooting. The blockers returned at the end of the day, reporting that no one had appeared.

Happy that they were not being followed, Kony ordered the group to pitch camp for the night. There was enough food to go around and people finally had a chance to rest. The food looted in Ligoua was running out already so Kony called a meeting of senior commanders to make plans for securing more food. "It is as if nothing has changed," George thought. It was only a few weeks since the Ugandan soldiers entered CAR but as far as the holies were concerned, things were the same. They escaped the army and killed civilians to take their food so that they could survive another day. It was the way of the LRA.

* * *

Jean-Pierre Mbolikinton lived in Ligoua, CAR, for almost all of his forty-five years. During his lifetime in the small village located almost exactly the same distance, just over twelve miles, from the South Sudanese border, the Congolese border and Obo, Jean-Pierre interacted with many armed men: SPLA from South Sudan, Congolese rebels and CAR soldiers, but the LRA, the feared tongo-tongo, were completely different. They were wild, with wide eyes and shriveled faces, intent on killing and eating, "like hyenas," he later described.

It was about 6 in the evening when Jean-Pierre and his neighbor Paul sat outside their homes, talking about the harvest and the hot weather. Their families were still in the gardens, tending to the cassava and maize. Soon, the conversation turned to the noises they had heard from the direction of the Congolese border and the arrival of the Ugandan soldiers who had taken over the airstrip in Obo. The soldiers were there for the rebels.

"The rebels who attacked Obo in 2008," explained Jean-Pierre, "the tongo-tongo, or the devil's children," as some people called them. The tongo-tongo seemed like possessed human beings, people from Obo said, they killed humans the same way one would kill an animal. Two weeks earlier hunters had seen tracks of a large group of people walking from Congo to CAR. Everyone in Ligoua was afraid it was the tongo-tongo. "Protect us from this evil," the pastor said at Sunday's mass.

As the two men sat on their small tripod chairs, Jean-Pierre noticed four armed men running towards them. He did not move but Paul jolted. There were shots, one hitting Jean-Pierre's chest and his left underarm. He heard Paul yelling loudly as he fell on the ground clutching his neck. The armed men – they were just boys really – surrounded them. One hit Paul on the head with a hammer until he stopped moving, his head becoming a bloody mess of brains, bones and red dirt.

Jean-Pierre fell on his knees and began to pray, only then noticing the blood pouring from the left side of his chest and arm. A large group of armed men, women and children descended on the village. Jean-Pierre was terrified as he witnessed the wild people storm the houses, eating while chasing the villagers. A child of about ten entered Paul's house and came out with a large bag of peanuts. He sat next to Paul's dead body shelling and eating peanuts and staring at Jean-Pierre in silence. "The devil's children," thought Paul as the child looked at him unflinching.

Jean-Pierre ripped his shirt and tied a small tourniquet around his arm, holding the rest of the ripped shirt tight against his wound. He started to walk slowly on the main path that led towards Obo. He was sure he would be stopped by one of the people, who reminded him of locusts attacking a maize garden. But no one paid any attention.

Jean-Pierre noticed people running toward the bush. He recognized other inhabitants of Ligoua escaping the wild crowd. He joined them, eventually finding his children and wife. Paul's first-born inquired about his father but Jean-Pierre could not bring himself to tell him what had happened. "I don't know," he said. "Maybe he has gone to Obo already."

Jean-Pierre and his family left for Obo early in the morning. He met a Ugandan army officer who took him to the army's field hospital. While he was being stitched up, the officer asked him about the attack. Jean-Pierre explained with the help of an interpreter. The officer listened carefully and said he was ashamed to say that these people were indeed from his country, the feared LRA. Jean-Pierre asked, "What are they doing here, killing us in our own country?" The officer smiled and shrugged. "Don't worry," he said, "we are closing in on them and will soon capture them like grasshoppers in a bottle." "I hope you do it soon," Jean-Pierre said. "I want to go home."

Jean-Pierre did not go back to Ligoua, which was attacked seven times by LRA groups between the end of June and August 2009. More attacks followed until March of 2010, by which time Ligoua was entirely deserted, becoming indeed the village of the LRA. All 500 inhabitants relocated to Obo, living predominantly in a camp for displaced people dependent on international organizations to provide food, water and other goods.

* * *

It was almost the end of July 2009 and Kony's group continued to move in and around Obo, attacking small villages for food and abductees who could carry the loot, while trying to avoid the Ugandan soldiers. Kony decided to move north of Obo and eventually to Darfur. It all depended on what Otto Agweng accomplished during his trip to Darfur. His return, expected at the end of July 2009, was eagerly anticipated. If all went to plan, the Congo groups would make it to CAR at the same time as Agweng returned and then everyone would leave for Darfur.

Kony said that no one would harass them in Darfur. The Arabs would not permit the Ugandans or anyone else to enter their country, unlike the cowardly Congolese and Central Africans. Darfur was definitely the promised land of peace and rest. The only question was whether Agweng had persuaded the Arabs to grant permission for an LRA base inside their country. Kony asked everyone to pray for a favorable outcome to Agweng's mission.

But days passed and Kony grew impatient and angry. Reports of Ugandan soldiers engaging LRA groups increased. Some holies were killed or captured and many escaped. Kony blamed the hunger for making people weak. "We need food," he said, "for people to eat but also to prepare for our long journey to Darfur." He ordered a standby to bring food from South Sudan. He said that despite the treachery of the Central Africans allowing the Ugandans into their country, the LRA should continue to be patient and focus on attacking the sworn enemies that were the Dinkas.

Colonel Leonard "Lubwa" Bwone, a senior officer who had been in the LRA since the early days, headed the standby. A former accountant, Bwone was one of the few relatively well-educated officers remaining and his loyalty to Kony was never questioned. Bwone was rumored to be a rich man as he had been in charge of LRA finances for a long time. But people joked that his money could not buy him monkey droppings in the bush.

About 200 men, women and children were selected for Bwone's group. George was part of the standby, which made him happy. He had already finished all the food taken in Ligoua, even his own private stock, and looked forward to getting more. Previous scout missions had discovered a new path northwest of Obo which sloped eastward into South Sudan. It was probably a path made by hunters or villagers and was usually frequented by the Mbororo.

George was excited about the new adventure even though some of his friends warned him to be careful in South Sudan. "The Dinkas are wild and all have guns in their homes. They will kill you if you are not careful," they told George. "Water is also hard to find," they said. George had heard stories of holies dying of thirst in the heat of some parts of South Sudan. Some spots were barren with scattered trees, which made the work of the Ugandan gunships easier. They bombed and killed holies at will. Numerous lives were lost there, which made many in the LRA feel hostile towards the South Sudanese.

After a few long days of marching, the standby stopped in a forest while still inside CAR. All bags and other heavy materials that could slow down the group were hidden in the bush to be picked up on the way back. Very early the morning after, the main group set off for the border, following an advance team of twelve deployed to extract intelligence from the locals. George was in the advance party and soon after they left their night position they saw two civilians on bicycles riding towards the South Sudanese border.

George and his companions tried not to scare the riders and greeted them in Arabic. "We are members of the Ugandan army," they said as they walked slowly towards the two men, who hesitated briefly. It gave the holies enough time to get close and direct their guns at them. George was the first to reach for his pistol, a Sig Sauer Kony had once given him as a present, and aimed it at the riders. The men were interrogated for over half an hour. They said they were from a nearby Sudanese village called Zangambaro where there were only four policemen, who were usually drunk by noon. Zangambaro was only two miles away.

Bwone told the standby to prepare to attack Zangambaro. It was 3 pm, too early to attack as they needed to wait until dark. They waited inside a small forest, cleaning their guns, while a small reconnaissance team deployed to check the surrounding territory. The team returned at 4 pm and reported having seen tracks of Ugandan soldiers leading to a village to the east they understood was called Namutina. The trail was made by maybe 100 soldiers. Bwone said everyone should be careful and prepared to encounter soldiers in Zangambaro.

Bwone then passed on the orders of the day. If they came across soldiers or security forces in the village center they were to battle fiercely until they chased them away. "We are not going away empty-handed," Bwone emphasized. He said that any civilians who were of a good size to serve the LRA movement were to be abducted while the rest were to be killed. By good size, he meant young men and women who could be used as fighters, porters, wives and servants.

At dusk the group walked towards Zangambaro. As they drew near the village center they heard a lot of noise, unusual in the bush. A small motorcycle, kids shouting and the unmistakable halting noises of wood chopping. Upon entering the village, they reorganized their line. Those wearing Ugandan army uniforms secured over the years moved in front so that the villagers would not run away. They needed abductees to prepare the food and carry the loot back to camp.

The group walked in a single file, women and children bringing up the rear. People ran when they saw the armed men but those ahead of the line took off their caps, waved them in the air, yelling in Arabic that no one should be afraid; they were just the Ugandan army troops coming from Namutina. Hearing these words, some stopped running and hesitantly walked back towards the group. But as they came closer and were able to see the women and children in the dim light they ran again. Two policemen at a small post near the village's clinic quickly realized what was happening and fired a few rounds but the return fire was overwhelming, forcing them to flee.

The brief firefight caused a massive flight and within minutes the village had emptied. Teams of fighters were positioned on Zangambaro's main entry points while the rest of the people started the much dreamed about looting of everything in sight. Orders from Bwone were clear; only take food and other useful items but not clothes as the Dinkas had powerful witches among them who could have poisoned the clothes. "Those who break the orders and take clothes will be harshly punished," Bwone said.

Someone yelled, "*kic*, honey." Everyone ran to where the cry came from, to discover that the market of Zangambaro was awash in honey that filled many plastic bottles and jerrycans. "Hallelujah!" they yelled, and rushed to grab it all. George snatched two five-liter jerrycans and threw away everything else he had in his backpack, hiding the honey at the bottom of the bag. "This honey will save my life," he thought, and quickly moved on to find more food. Peanuts, dry cassava and maize were always favorites. They made good dry rations that lasted a long time and filled the stomach.

There were no abductees to force to shell peanuts and peas or to carry the food back to the bush but eventually one man emerged, too drunk to fully understand the peril he was in. He approached the fighters, talking to them in Arabic, and offered to help them with reading the labels of the drugs stored in Zangambaro's clinic. He could read Arabic and English well and seemed to have a good understanding of the uses of pills and potions in the clinic. He then said he was not afraid of the LRA and that death did not scare him.

After most houses were looted, Bwone ordered the group to pitch camp for the night in Zangambaro. Night guards were deployed around the village while the main group split into smaller units scattered around Bwone and his escorts. George and his fellow bodyguards from Kony's protection unit were also placed right in the middle of the circle, next to Bwone. Captain Obwoya was their new leader as Omony had stayed behind with Kony. As custom demanded, Kony's people were considered part of the high command and always sat in the middle of the protective circle of fighters, next to the senior commanders.

While the young *kuruts* in his unit, recently taken in Congo and CAR, prepared the fire and started to cook food, Obwoya sent George and three others on a mission to find a radio for Kony. Obwoya was responsible for bringing enough food and other items to keep Kony happy. He knew that the boss appreciated a nice radio, particularly one that played cassettes or compact discs.

Kony enjoyed listening to the BBC and playing music for his wives and kids.

George was placed in charge of the group of four. He was eager to please Obwoya as well as the Big Teacher who might eventually find out which fighter secured him the best radio ever. After searching almost every house in the village, George found a large black stereo that had a radio and played both cassettes and discs. To his amazement, he also found a stack of tapes and discs, some of them with Ugandan music. In the same house, which must have been some sort of a shop, George discovered four large jerrycans filled with a locally made wine. He ordered the three others to bring the wine, while he held on to the stereo.

George gave Obwoya all that he found, which earned him a pat in the back as well as some wine. The four were then sent to rest with their unit, where the young *kuruts* were already spit-roasting chickens. As in Ligoua, everyone ate initially all the raw food they could, only cooking after the initial hunger pains had dwindled.

They spent the night inside the village. The only time the LRA ever held territory was in the immediate aftermath of looting a place. Unlike in Ligoua, orders were given to burn everything they could not carry, an expression of hatred towards the South Sudanese. All small huts with thatched roofs were set alight, including the small clinic inside which the drunken man burned alive. George could hear his screams as he sat nearby around his unit's small fire eating chicken.

Obwoya sent for George to join him for dinner. George was served more chicken and wine and Obwoya put on some nice Ugandan music. Obwoya lauded George once again, saying he was going to make the General happy. They ate, drank and danced late into the night as Zangambaro burned. No one was afraid that the Ugandan soldiers might attack. "They are scared of the dark," Obwoya had said earlier in the night when they discussed the presence of the army in Namutina. "During my fifteen years with this government," he said, "Ugandan soldiers never attacked us at night." "The deal is that they get the days and we the nights," he joked.

The morning found everyone busy packing the looted items to be carried to the main camp where Kony and the rest waited. George had been in the LRA long enough by now to understand the importance of putting together enough of a personal stock to last as long as possible. It meant the difference between life and death. He was also expected to bring back food for the rest of his unit waiting in the camp. Kony said one always had to think about the movement first and foremost, but George knew not to neglect his own needs, otherwise he could die of hunger, like many others he had personally witnessed in the past few months.

He packed two five-liters jerrycans of honey, ten pounds of dried, shelled peanuts, seven pounds of cassava flour, three pounds of sugar and some batteries, soap, salt, matches and torches into his backpack. It was heavy enough a load to be carried by two strong men. He had not forgotten the sweet taste of the wine he found the night before and managed to sneak five liters of it in his small pouch where he usually carried his gun's magazines or bombs. He filled his small aluminum water canteen with wine and took small sips occasionally. Returning to camp was going to be enjoyable.

* * *

Sister was angry. She looked in the distance, over the green savannah that stretched all the way to Congo and said, "These people come from there and kill everyone just to steal their food. Take the food, take everything, but why kill?" By the end of 2009, Sister, a Catholic nun of the Comboni order, had spent over a decade in South Sudan's Western Equatoria state. Based in Nzara, near the capital Yambio, she and four other nuns ran a small clinic, a school, a food distribution center, a shelter for Congolese refugees as well as overseeing a large garden of vegetables which supplemented the diet of the refugees, the nuns and their visitors.

"Here is some pizza," Sister said, quickly adding, "sorry if it is not something you might have eaten before. It is a version we make at home in Trieste." "Plus we don't have all the good ingredients here." She then continued to talk about LRA attacks, clearly something that pained her deeply. "This Kony guy needs to go, he is a very bad man," she said. "He has inflicted so much pain here. I know how the LRA works, I spent thirteen years in northern Uganda and I speak Luo. I know what he makes these kids do, he turns them into killers. He needs to go."

"Come talk to the Congolese refugees from Duru, Kpaika, Tomate and all other villages leading up here to South Sudan,"

she continued, now fairly agitated. And all the attacks here in Western Equatoria. Some of them attack from Congo all the way up to Yambio and some other groups attack from CAR in Source Yubu and Namutina. They have razed whole villages, burned them all. All the people have come to Yambio and here to Nzara, almost dying of hunger. Who will care for them?

We try as hard as we can but we are too few and we can't cope with all the numbers. We are afraid for our lives also. At night we only sleep because we know that Richard is out there with his friends patrolling. No SPLA soldiers turn up to help us. It is as if this is not their country. Even the Ugandan soldiers based here have been more helpful than the SPLA. Let me call Richard.

Richard, a twenty-four-year-old from Nzara, had just finished distributing food to 300 Congolese refugees living in a little house next to the nuns' residence. He was covered in flour, which he did his best to shake off his trousers. "The sacks get all ripped up on the truck from Kampala to Juba then here," he said. It takes over two weeks for the food paid for by the sisters to get here from Uganda. We also have many internally displaced people from all the counties next to us, Tambura, Namutina, Ezo, even nearby Yambio and Nzara. They are escaping the tongo-tongo and have nothing to eat. I don't know why the tongo-tongo are only targeting us, the Zande people.

We have no help from the SPLA. They turn up much later after the tongo-tongo leave the villages. They maybe are afraid of the rebels or maybe they just don't care. You see, the SPLA here is mostly made up of Dinka and Nuer while all Zande and Equatorians are deployed in Blue Nile and other states away from home. Our President, Salva Kiir, says it is done so that the army does not become tribalized. That might be a good idea but it is not working for us. People are dying but the SPLA refuse to deal with the tongo-tongo. There are 3,000 SPLA here in Western Equatoria alone, why can't they take out a few hundred rebels? They have nothing else to do. They just sit around and accuse us of killing each other. "You Zande," they say, "you cannot be trusted. You are killing each other and blaming it on Kony."

I and many people were fed up and took matters into our own hands. We call ourselves Arrow Boys because some of us are only armed with bows and arrows to fight the tongo-tongo. Some Zande brothers from Congo came to teach us about self-defense. Not many people know this but the Zande self-defense groups in Congo were initially formed to deal with SPLA attacks. When the SPLA was still a rebel force before the signing of the peace agreement with the North, SPLA soldiers used to go into Congo, like the tongo-tongo now, and steal food from our Zande brothers there. The self-defense groups protected their people from the SPLA in the past.

Now the self-defense groups in Congo are trying to fight the tongo-tongo but the Congolese army is giving their own people trouble. These Congolese soldiers are themselves former rebels and from different areas in Congo. They came to the Zande lands in the north of Congo and began to harass the civilians, starting with the self-defense groups. At least the SPLA here are mostly indifferent, but they are not killing and raping us like the Congolese soldiers do to our brothers and sisters there. These are hard times for the Zande everywhere.

We have had our trouble with the SPLA in the past but things are calmer now. In 2007, there were riots in town when a Dinka colonel killed an Equatorian soldier. People rose up and burned the barracks and lynched three Dinka soldiers. The Dinkas hate us; they accuse us of having been collaborators with Khartoum during the struggle. They say, "you Equatorians like Bashir so much and you fought against us so now fend for yourselves." They talk about the Equatoria Defense Forces that fought for President Bashir in the past but that does not mean that all Equatorians want to be ruled by Khartoum. We all want to be part of independent South Sudan. We don't like the Arabs.

And Kony, he is in President Bashir's pay. If Bashir loved us so much he would not send Kony to kill us. But the Congolese Zande brothers have taught us to fight. We know how to make guns that we use for hunting animals in the bush; we are now using them to kill the tongo-tongo. We are only making big hunting guns now, powerful enough to kill a lion, not just small animals. Our people are smart, they are making shotguns that can use Kalashnikov bullets which are cheap and easy to find.

There are 1,000 Arrow Boys throughout Western Equatoria. We do night patrols around our villages, keeping the tongo-tongo away. They don't attack villages when they see us around; they are afraid of us. We have killed and captured more tongo-tongo than the SPLA and the Ugandan army combined. The Arrow Boys mimic the tongo-tongo tactics, which is why we are good at this. We wait for them at river crossings where they pass or spend the night and then we shoot them like wild dogs.

During the day we also deal with security issues which the SPLA neglects. Drunkards, and other people, who disturb the peace. Our biggest problem is the Mbororo. These Arabs come from the north with their cows. They are all paid by Bashir. They

So-called Arrow Boys carrying locally manufactured guns on the road to Tamboura, South Sudan, June 2013.

give the tongo-tongo food and guns and they fight together, killing Zande. We don't like the Mbororo and we have told them many times not to destroy our lands with their cows but they do not listen. They even poison our streams to force the cows to move away. The Arrow Boys are now using their guns to keep these Arabs out.

But we need help, we need better guns and military training. The tongo-tongo are trained soldiers, they fight hard and they have big guns, Kalashnikovs and RPGs. The Arrow Boys have to shoot first and then run, because we don't have automatic guns. We have to reload and shoot but the tongo-tongo respond with their guns and can easily kill us.

Powerful people in the United Nations say they can't give us guns because they don't want to turn us into a militia that the Governor or local politicians can use for their own agendas. They say we will be like the rebels in Congo that started as self-defense groups and are now militias. We don't want that, we are farmers and hunters, we don't want to fight but the tongo-tongo have left us with no choice.

* * *

By 10 am when the sun began to burn, the whistle was blown, the signal for George's group to leave the village. Two hours after leaving Zangambaro, heading towards CAR, people at the back of the line heard the noise of the small white spy plane. Commanders barked out orders to hide. Most of the men ran away in the bush, trying not to stand next to the women, who were so loaded with stuff they could barely move. It was well known among the holies that women were usually the first to succumb to the gunships.

Some men took up defensive positions in an effort to try and shoot at the incoming aircraft while others did their best to hide. George broke some large leaves and put them over his body and loot. Bwone ordered that the group be split into four, and that everyone should scatter in different directions to confuse the pilots.

It took only a few minutes after the white plane passed before a large green helicopter appeared and started to drop bombs. Everyone panicked and ran like crazy. George followed his unit, trying not to drop any of the food he was carrying. It seemed that everyone else dropped their loads to run faster but George knew he could die of hunger without that food. He might as well die now of bombs than postpone his death by a few weeks.

He breathed heavily and the loud noise made his ears ring but he continued to walk as fast as he could. He stopped once in a while trying to hide behind bushes or low trees and took swigs from the wine-filled canteen. Soon he felt drunk. I might as well die happy, he thought, like the guy in Zangambaro who burned alive. "I hope he died happy in the end," George thought, suddenly feeling a slight sense of guilt. "I did not kill him," he told himself.

The gunship returned throughout the day, leaving for a while and returning to drop more bombs. Everyone kept running, returning to pick up the dropped food when possible and continuing to run when the gunship appeared. As night fell and the helicopter disappeared for good, the group was finally able to come together in a resting place near a small stream. Four Congolese women, part of Kony's unit, were missing. A search patrol went to look for them.

It was dangerous walking back to where the gunship first bombed the group. The search patrol risked coming across Ugandan soldiers. But as bodyguards to Kony and his family, the primary responsibility rested with Obwoya and the fighters he had designated to take care of the women. They now had to ensure the women were found dead or alive. Obwoya assigned George to the patrol, led by Second Lieutenant Abe. George was surprised to find he had already drunk more than half of his wine bottle, about three liters.

The group walked slowly for two miles until they reached an open place. Large burned areas were visible while lots of tracks on the ground led in different directions, the footmarks of the large group of people running away from the chopper. George headed down a small hill and saw what he had feared all along, the dead bodies of the women scattered on the ground.

There were only three bodies and George recognized all of them. Marie was one of Captain Justine's wives while Faida and Mbolikina were *ting-ting*, young servants to Kony and his wives. Their bodies had turned white as if they had been dipped in white paint. George felt frightened at the sight of the white corpses but he was terrified of Kony's reaction. He knew he could be punished for not protecting Kony's family members. It was after all George's only duty.

He whistled to the others. Abe said the women must have been burned by white phosphorus. "It burns everything," he said "but bodies turn white like ash from burned wood." He ordered the women's boots to be removed and the bodies to be hidden in the bush so that the enemy could not find them. "Part of our mission here is completed," Abe said, adding that the fourth woman was probably dead too but the search patrol had to return to camp.

They took the boots and threw the remains in the bush and collected all the food the women had dropped. George tried to wipe some of the blood smeared on the bag of food he was carrying but soon gave up, preferring instead to drink his wine as he walked back to camp. A cold rain started to fall on them, washing the blood off the bag he carried on his head. He was certain the blood washed over his hair, trickling down his face and neck, but he did not care. He just wanted to get to camp to eat and be warm. He felt nauseous and thought he should not have drunk all that wine.

At camp they handed over the gumboots to the operations commander, certain they would be returned to Kony and Justine. The rule was to never appropriate the property of others. They returned to their unit where their coy mates asked about what they found. George felt freezing and hungry and was in no mood to talk but he worried his coy mates would be annoyed and accuse him of keeping secrets. He sluggishly said that the women were killed in the airstrike and reached for the food his comrades had prepared.

His coy mates made fun of the dead women, saying that ladies do not know how to act militarily. "You can teach them all you want," someone said, "they would still end up dead the moment a gunship comes." Everyone kept vowing to never stay close to a woman during an air raid as women were known for freezing with fear and were unable to escape gunship attacks unharmed. George stayed silent. He wished he had more wine left so that he could get warm and chase from his head the images of the white corpses.

CHAPTER 13

DISCO

George knew it would be difficult to sleep despite his tiredness. He hoped the wet spot at the back of his head was due to the rain. It could also be the blood of one of the Congolese women who were blown to pieces earlier trying to escape the Ugandan helicopters. He did not want to check. He wanted to sleep.

Late that night he managed to drift off, covered in blankets under a tarpaulin that kept most of the rain out. He dreamt he was walking the streets of Gulu, alone in what seemed to be an abandoned town. He saw his father, or his image, staring at him from the old photograph his mother kept in a wooden frame next to her bed. In the dream his father asked him how he felt. "I am fine," George replied, and woke up. For a fleeting moment he did not know where he was. He yelled for his cousin thinking he was at home but he heard people talking and understood.

His group prepared for the day's march. He felt the familiar pain in his legs as he stretched his limbs and wished that he was home. "I am not fine, *baba* (father)," he whispered and slowly stood up. Once on his feet, he moved quickly as he was now accustomed to, tying the luggage he was to carry that day and loading it onto his back. He thought about the meaning of the dream but the group commander blew the whistle and people started walking. They were trying to reach Kony's camp before nightfall. They knew that people there were starving.

Four groups moved separately. George walked with Obwoya, the unit commander of Kony's personal body-guards. It was still dark when the group set out but soon the sky began to brighten. They walked into an open area covered by clouds of white fog, which they took as a blessing from God. The fog kept them hidden from the gunships' sights, at least for a while. Spirits rose as they crossed the South Sudanese border and entered CAR. There were dense forests now, which meant increased protection from air raids.

They expected to be attacked. Officers tried to ensure that no more women or children would be lost to the gunships. Obwoya ordered his fighters to look after Kony's families and not allow anyone to fall behind or escape. At around 11 am, the hated spy plane appeared. Soon after someone yelled from the back, "The big one is coming." It needed no explanation as everyone heard the loud and terrifying noise of the Ugandan helicopter. George ran to three women Obwoya had assigned him to protect and told them to move quickly behind him. He told them to be calm and follow his orders. As he reassured the women he heard, "There are two helicopters." "*Ring* (run)" George yelled, and sprinted forward.

Running for hours, all the bodyguards, women and children managed to survive. The forest made it easy to foil the helicopters. The pilots continued to drop bombs even when they were unable to see underneath them. George was happy the women under his protection had made it out alive, but found out to his dismay that they had dropped all the food they carried. He still had most of his load and was annoyed that he now had to share his food with them.

The gunships continued to follow them until around 5 pm but the bombs never got close enough to hurt anyone on the ground. Obwoya's unit reassembled and continued without stopping until they approached Kony's old position at dusk. All other groups arrived around the same time. As anticipated, Kony was not waiting for them where they had left him before the Zangambaro trip. He never stayed in a single camp for two consecutive nights.

Bwone ordered two scouts to be sent to Kony's old position, confident that the Boss had already relocated. Bwone hoped that Kony had left men behind to guide the group to his new location. The unit's Regimental Sergeant Major or RSM, the person responsible for assigning tasks, picked George as one of the two scouts. George felt exhausted and in pain after the long hike, during which he had not dropped any of the food he had carried all the way from South Sudan. He asked the RSM if he could send someone else instead, fully expecting to be whipped for asking. No holies disputed orders, but George was exhausted. He preferred a beating to more marching. To his surprise, the RSM agreed and sent Oninga instead. George was grateful to finally get a moment's rest.

Shots were heard at the back of the group. People started to run, trying to escape from the Ugandan soldiers who had caught up with the group's rearguards. Officers yelled orders to hold on to the loot. They would be embarrassed if they came all this way and lost the food just before meeting Kony. He could accuse them of being weak and doing nothing to rescue his people from hunger. He could even humiliate them by demoting them, taking their wives and servants or having them publicly caned.

After crossing a small river everyone regrouped and walked in single file. Commanders tripled the rearguards and ordered them to shoot on sight and keep the soldiers back. They also increased the pace and ordered beatings for those who dropped food. The high speed combined with the total darkness made people stumble and often fall to the ground with muted thuds. George could barely keep up. He heard some of the women next to him cry out and felt he was about to do the same. When the group was ten miles away from Kony's old position, Bwone ordered them to stop. The soldiers had given up the chase so the group rested for the night. Everyone fell to the ground and sat there, lacking the energy to bathe, eat or even chat.

George took off his gumboots and inspected his feet with a torch that made dim light. He could see that his feet were stained with blood. He could barely move his toes, which, like the rest of his body, throbbed unbearably. As he sat contemplating whether he would ever be able to walk again, a young recruit told George that the RSM had ordered him to deploy as a night guard on the western side of the encampment. George sat in silence and ignored the order. He did not care. "Let him kill me," he thought. "That way the pain will go away."

There was no cooking that night as people were exhausted and far from water, turning instead to dry rations from their personal stocks. Those who had lost their food during the air raids had to rely on the charity of others or spend the night hungry. Grudgingly, George gave a few handfuls of peanuts to the three women. He also gave some food to two friends from his coy under Sam. He knew that these men could one day save his life. A holy without friends was a dead holy.

When morning broke, he stood up feeling exhausted and seriously doubting the strength of his legs to carry him an extra yard. He thought about what to do, then crawled behind a large tree carrying a small bag. He took out some *moo ya*, the blessed shea-nut oil, from his bag and smeared it over the bruises and cuts on his legs and body. He ripped a spare shirt and used the pieces of cloth to wrap his feet and keep the *moo ya* on his bruises before putting on his boots.

He got up and joined the group just as the whistle was blown for the start of the march. Around midday, the group came across Kony's messengers, who said he was five miles away. Once again, exhausted and impatient for rest, George knew that if they were to meet Kony that day, they would have to start a fresh journey with no breaks. Of course it was easier for Kony, George thought, as he never carried a thing. Kony's aides even carried his guns. Kony only held on to a small Beretta pistol that people in the LRA called "Star," which he never used but only waved around at times. "To look like a military man," George thought.

One of the two scouts from the night before appeared, saying the Ugandan soldiers were on their heels. He had exchanged fire with them earlier in the day and Oninga had been killed. George was sad to hear of his friend's death, a frequent occurrence these days. "I live only by the grace of the Almighty," he thought. He said a prayer under his breath, thanking God for saving him again.

A drawing of LRA captives by a formerly abducted twelve-year-old child. Obo, CAR, March 2010.

As the group hurried to reach Kony the spy plane appeared. Knowing what came after it, commanders yelled for everyone to hide. Obwoya asked George to take charge of two young Congolese abductees and keep them safe. George knew one of them, the thirteen-year-old Disco. He did not know the other, called Marate. The appearance of the helicopter made everyone scatter. George grabbed the boys and hid in a ditch, waiting for the explosions to end.

* * *

Long after the aircraft disappeared, George, with Disco and Marate in tow, followed the footprints, trying to rejoin the group. They heard voices from the hillside they had just crossed and thought they belonged to their friends. George ordered the boys to hide and be ready to shoot. Only Marate had a gun; Disco was unarmed. Hiding behind shrubs, they realized the words spoken were in Kiswahili, the language of the Ugandan soldiers, who appeared from behind the hill. They were too close to run so George ordered Marate to shoot right after George opened fire.

He waited until he saw the soldiers clearly, about fifty yards away, and let loose with his AK. Marate followed suit and the three took off into the bush before the soldiers could retaliate.

George found a trail he thought was made by Kony's group and ordered the boys to follow it, turning to the southeast, across another river. They crossed the water with difficulty and continued to run until they heard a familiar whistle. George stopped and whistled back. He saw two boys emerge from the forest. Sammie and Dan, nine or ten years old, abducted in Congo a year before, long enough to have adapted to the LRA life. Sammie and Dan had no guns but, like Disco and Marate, they were trusted boys. George asked them about their group and they replied that they had been with Kony but separated during the gunship attack.

George continued to follow the trail, placing Marate at the back, walking in front himself while the three unarmed boys stayed in the middle. They heard footsteps so they hid. The plan was to shoot and run if they saw soldiers. But the person walking towards them was Diana, a young Central African girl, *ting-ting* to Kony. She too had been separated from the main group and was lost. George jumped in front of her, which made her flee. He ran after her, caught her and pinned her down, repeating that they were the same people. Shaking, she agreed to join the group and continue to search for Kony.

They walked all day, following the trail alongside the river. At nightfall they decided to enter the forest to spend the night. They had nothing to eat, which made sleeping hard. Marate and George took turns as guards. As they rested silently, they heard noises a few hundred yards behind them. There were people talking loudly and cutting firewood for the night. "Ugandan soldiers," George thought, "using their machetes. Holies never make such loud noises when they pitch camp for the night." He motioned to his companions to be quiet.

As darkness grew and forest sounds subsided, the soldiers' voices were clear enough for George to hear. He could even distinguish some of the Kiswahili words they used: beans, *posho*, battle, women. He whispered to the boys not to be afraid. "Ugandan soldiers don't walk at night in the bush," he said softly, urging them to sleep. He looked at the youngsters trying to fall asleep and felt a strange sense of calm. He knew they trusted him, which made him feel brave. "It is my duty, as the oldest, to protect them," George thought.

He decided it was not safe to follow the trail alongside the river, an open area. He was certain the soldiers would walk beside the river rather than cut through the dense bush. "At least we will get a break from the soldiers and gunships," he thought. Early in the morning, he instructed everyone to move silently to the east, away from the soldiers' camp. He did not have a compass but directed the group using the position of the sun.

They walked for five hours, cutting through the bush, until they came upon Kony's trail. It was clearly an LRA trail, judging from the grains of maize and small dots of cassava flour, the gumboot tracks offering further proof. George was happy his plan had worked. He knew they needed to walk fast to catch up. Soon they came across two men Kony had left behind to direct those who were lost, Sergeants Black Ninja and Okeny, who hid behind a tree and whistled when they saw the small group. George knew them. They were bodyguards to Kony and deployed together often. He was happy to see them.

They said Bwone had already made it back and met with the General but many people from his group were lost when the gunship attacked. They said Kony was not happy when he found out about the death of the Congolese women. He was even angrier at people showing up empty-handed as those remaining in the camp were famished. He was so annoyed that he ordered Bwone, who was exhausted, to return immediately and attack villages near Obo and bring food.

Around the fire that evening Okeny said Kony had told people to prepare to leave for Darfur. All the groups were to move northwest in CAR where they were to wait for Agweng to return from his scouting mission to Darfur and lead the way back there. Okeny and Black Ninja were under orders to spend the week in the area in case Agweng returned to Kony's initial position, not knowing the group had moved northwest. They were to join Kony a week later in the new position after spending five days waiting for Agweng.

George decided to wait with Black Ninja and Okeny. His decision was made easier when he saw that they had ten liters of honey, some peas and cassava flour that they had received from those who looted Zangambaro and returned to camp before the air raid. George had not eaten in two days and the thought of walking again made him feel sick. Instead, he rejoiced at the idea of spending time with his friends, washing in the river and eating fried peas and honey.

Since the group had now grown to eight, Black Ninja and Okeny decided to set up an ambush on the road linking Obo with Tambura, the South Sudanese border town. They needed food and the traders on the road most likely had plenty of it. The next day, all eight walked toward the main road. Diana and the three unarmed boys waited inside the bush in a small trench to keep out of harm's way. The four with weapons proceeded to set up an ambush. George stayed near the side of the road, close to a sharp curve so that he could easily see in both directions. The other three took positions to his left, ready to pounce at his signal.

Two hours passed but no one appeared – a bad sign. People must be aware of the LRA presence and had stopped using the road. George heard loud voices from the direction of Obo. They were too loud to be locals. As the people on the road approached the curve, he realized it was Kiswahili, a sure sign soldiers were coming. The four crept back into the bush, close enough to see the road, and waited.

The voices grew louder, as did the clanking sounds of jerrycans and aluminum utensils the soldiers carried on their packs. "Ugandan soldiers," George thought, "making so much noise you could hear them from miles away." He watched the long line of soldiers dressed in long-sleeved green shirts that had UPDF – Uganda People's Defense Force – emblazoned on the back, their caps pointed backwards like the American soldiers George had seen in movies. He smiled and looked at Black Ninja and Okeny when he heard a few of them speaking Luo. "Acholi, just like us," he thought, "maybe even former holies now chasing their old friends."

Around 120 men marched in a straight line carrying mortars, RPGs and other heavy guns clearly intended for use against the LRA. "All this only to come after us," George thought. "Their only aim is to kill me and my friends and there are probably hundreds more of them. Much better armed, fed and clothed than we are. All grown men, trained soldiers. Most of us are teenagers and children, like Marate and Disco."

The four decided it was not safe to stay there. George felt disheartened as the group of eight started the long walk toward the rendezvous point where Agweng was supposed to join them. It was near Parayard, the same place north of Obo where Kony first set up camp after entering CAR, at least five days' walk through the dense bush. George did not look forward to walking the long distance with little food, trying to avoid the gunships, the mortars and the bazookas he had just witnessed up close.

"Will this ever end?" he wondered as the group walked in silence. "Who knew for sure that Darfur would be the peaceful place Kony had promised? He said the same thing about Garamba Park and CAR. He said CAR would be the blessed land of peace, right at Parayard. Kony's prophecies were wrong. Now the army was here in full force to hunt them down. How long until the soldiers kill me or hunger defeats me?"

They walked for three days, marching cautiously during the day and resting at night. George organized the night guards, which usually meant Marate and Sammie on the opposite sides of the camp. Disco and Diana were in charge of making dinner, which was always the same; fried peas followed by a little honey. On the fourth day, the group approached Parayard, and since it was already 5 pm, they decided to rest for the night. They sat around the fire talking and hoping that they could soon meet Agweng and leave for Darfur. They hoped their suffering would end once they reached the bases of the Arabs. Black Ninja said he remembered when the holies first took him from his home in northern Uganda and brought him across the border to Sudan, where the Arabs gave them food and guns. "Praise the Lord it will be the same when we get to Darfur," he said.

* * *

In the morning the group prepared for the journey ahead, filling their jerrycans in the little stream. There was no water for the next few miles. CAR was a strange place when it came to water: some places were blessed with many rivers and others were completely dry. The lack of rain in the present rainy season did not help either. Everyone remembered well when they first moved into this area from Congo and could not find any water. George could not forget how close Disco had come to dying back then.

A few months earlier, when George was on duty guarding Kony as the group crossed into CAR, he asked Rambo, a fellow bodyguard, to monitor Disco while he walked close to the Big Teacher. Unlike Congo, which had an abundance of rivers and streams, that piece of land of CAR seemed devoid of water. George thought this was strange, as the land was covered in green, lush vegetation. Each and every one in the group was tired and extremely thirsty. Some fell to the ground clutching their throats, begging for a drop of water.

George drank slowly from the small canteen he kept around his neck, emptying it quickly. He hid his five-liter *jerekan* in his backpack. He was certain that if officers saw his large jerrycan they would take it. As the thirst grew unbearable, George would leave the main group and go into the bush during the day with the pretense of needing to relieve himself. There, away from everyone's desperate eyes, he would take small sips of water from the hidden jerrycan.

After one of his trips to the bush when the group stopped for the night, George came out to discover Disco collapsed on the ground. Rambo explained that he had tried in vain to keep Disco walking but that he seemed finished. Rambo then told George to get rid of him. "*Ka yweyo*, have him rest," Rambo said, using the ubiquitous euphemism for killing. George tried to talk to Disco but he would only point at his mouth.

George was surprised Disco's *jerekan* was empty. He knew Disco was used to walking with little water. When George asked others, they said Rambo drank all of Disco's water. George was annoyed but could not say a thing. He knew the rules, the lower the rank, the worse the chances of survival were. Disco was a mere abductee from Congo, a *kurut*, who could do nothing if someone stole his water or food. Rambo was within his rights to do whatever he wanted with Disco, including killing him as he had just asked George to do.

George was unsure how to proceed. Abductees who could not walk were killed without hesitation. George decided against it. He helped Disco walk into the dense bush. They came across other fighters sitting on the ground preparing their dinners and beds for the night. Someone asked, "Where are you taking that *punu*, that pig? Why don't you kill him there instead of wasting your time and draining your energy carrying him around?" "I want to take him further away so that we won't smell his rotten odor all night," George replied.

He carried Disco farther into the bush, dug out his water bottle from his bag and poured half a liter into Disco's container. Disco drank vigorously, finishing the half-liter in seconds. George let him rest for a while and told him to stand. "Please *lapwony*, teacher, more," Disco pleaded. George did not want to share more of his water. "I need to save it," he thought, "otherwise I will die of thirst tomorrow and no one is going to help me." But he was certain that by giving Disco so little he was only delaying his death, so he looked inside his bag and found a one-liter bottle of water he had also stockpiled. He gave Disco the bottle and saw him sweat heavily and breathe faster while he drank. "You saved my life, sir," said Disco. "I can now walk by myself."

People were surprised to see Disco alive. George said Disco survived by the grace of God. "I wanted to kill him," he said, "but he got up and started walking." Before they reached their coy's position, he warned Disco not to tell that he had given him water. Omony questioned them but their stories checked out so he believed them. He told Disco to stop being lazy and that there was no sick bay for him. Those who refused to walk were killed. "He who cannot survive the harsh conditions of the rebel life will die without help," said Omony. "If you allow the walking to defeat you, no one will help you," he told Disco, looking at George. George knew what Omony meant. He remembered eight *kuruts* and two holies who died of thirst and exhaustion during the trip to CAR. Their bodies littered the path the group had followed from Congo.

The next day the group came across some *It Lyec* "elephant ears," the climbing vines whose stems are full of water. One had only to cut both ends of the stem and cool water would flow. It was even better than river water, sweeter and smoother. Everyone scattered like bees, attacking all the vines they could find with their machetes and knives. George saw Disco cutting stem after stem, directing the water straight into his mouth. Laughing, Disco waved at George which George tried his best to ignore. The last thing he needed was for Omony or someone else to see and accuse him of fraternizing with the abductees. It was beneath real holies, George knew.

* * *

They took off in single file towards the rendezvous point with Agweng, George choosing to be the rearguard, walking about half a mile behind the group. Two hours into the day's walk, he realized he had fallen farther behind than he had intended and picked up his pace to catch up with the group. He came across Disco sitting on the ground, crying that he was in pain.

George stopped to inquire. Disco said he had been over-loaded with bags by Black Ninja and Okeny and he could not carry everything. He said his load was so heavy he could not breathe. He asked George to help tie the bags to his back so that it was easier to carry. George stopped to help, but the others continued to walk. After securing Disco's load the two hurried after the group but could not see anyone. George tried to follow their trail but after climbing a small hill, he was no longer able to discern which direction the group had taken. The six must have stopped walking in a single file and started to move sepa-rately, creating many trails in order to confuse the pursuing Ugandan soldiers. They had done a good job as their own rearguard could not figure out which way they had gone.

George climbed to the top of another hill and made the various LRA whistles he knew but there was no response. Black Ninja, Okeny and the rest had disappeared. George was angry. He did not want to be alone in the bush again. He blamed Disco for keeping him behind. He ignored Disco's pleas to forgive him and slapped him on the neck. Then he kicked him when he fell on the ground. "*Tima kica ladit* (Forgive me sir)" Disco pleaded, "I did not mean to get us lost."

George continued to punch and kick Disco but the pleas and tears made him stop. He sat down and tried to calm down. "I am not a bad commander," he thought, "like those who beat me when I was new. I can find the position; it is not very far from here, maybe a day's walk." Known as *dyang pyera aryo wiye acel*, meaning Twenty-One Cows, the exact location was near Parayard, the place where they once ate the twenty-one cows they took from the Mbororo cattle herders. That was where Black Ninja and Okeny were supposed to meet Agweng and move north to find Kony.

George thought he would be able to find Twenty-One Cows before the others left to meet Kony, but he knew that he had to hurry. Agweng would not wait. George told himself he was a seasoned fighter and could take care of things. He had the energy and mental strength to succeed. Without saying a word to Disco, he continued to walk in the direction of Twenty-One Cows. Disco followed, breathing deeply under the heavy load George had tied to his small frame.

CHAPTER 14

WHEN THE WALKING DEFEATS YOU

George had known Disco from when he "joined" the rebels. He was part of the unit that attacked Disco's village in Congo, not far north from the LRA bases in Garamba, in May 2008. It became clear at the time that the peace talks with the government were not going to succeed after Otti's execution in October 2007. George remembered how angry Kony became when scouts reported in early 2008 that the Congolese army was joining forces with United Nations peacekeepers and the Ugandan army to plan an attack on the LRA in Garamba. "The Congolese people will regret it," Kony yelled. He then ordered standbys to attack Congolese villages and bring back abductees, boys to be turned into fighters and girls into servants and eventually LRA commanders' wives. "*Citu omak dano*," Kony said, "go abduct people."

George was part of one such standby that attacked villages and brought back many children, including Disco. George did not remember whether he personally took Disco away from his family. It was dark when the unit attacked Disco's village. About twenty holies first

caught two men who were tending to their crops outside
the small village. The two were then forced to lead the
fighters inside the village.

The holies broke down the flimsy wooden doors and
shot in the air while grabbing people and bringing them
to an open area. They tied together those they caught,
about two dozen, including women and children. The
holies took as much food as possible and loaded it on the
heads of the abducted villagers, who were tied with rope
around their waists. The adults carried the food as far as
Garamba and were then released. Five children, including
Disco, were taken to the LRA bases inside the forest. They
were to become *kuruts.*

George knew that his name was not really Disco. It was
something in French that meant "Thank you God," as
Disco later explained, but some holy thought it sounded
like Disco and that became his name.

Like thousands of other abducted children and teenagers from Uganda, South Sudan, Congo and CAR, Disco
was just another *kurut,* a corruption of the English word
"recruit." Almost everyone in the LRA, with the exception of high commanders, had at some point been *kurut.*
The term referred mostly to boys who would be trained
to become real holies. They willingly participated in
missions to attack soldiers or loot food and bring back
more abductees. It was a model that Kony had perfected
to keep his movement alive for more than two decades.

George wondered how it was that the children, especially the non-Ugandans, continued to stay in the LRA even

when the groups operated near their homes. "Why," George asked himself, "did they stay?" Disco was in Kony's group for many months, often moving near his village before the group left for CAR. George understood that many Ugandan fighters did not attempt to desert because they were far from home. "But why did Disco continue to stay when the groups moved to CAR?" Disco was a Zande, the same tribe as the people in the area of CAR where Kony and his group had operated for the last few months. He spoke the local language, which was similar to his mother tongue, and could find his way home if he came across locals.

George figured that, like many others, Disco was too afraid or too weak to attempt to leave. Disco and George knew well that if they tried to escape and were caught they would suffer immensely and likely meet a painful death, usually blows to the head with heavy sticks or machetes. George had a good idea of what Disco might be thinking about if and when contemplating escape. It was probably the memory of one of his friends who was abducted at the same time as Disco.

George vaguely remembered the face of Disco's friend who was accused, probably falsely, of having tried to escape. Disco and the three other children abducted from the same village were told to surround the young boy, who had no idea what was coming. Another Zande speaker translated the order from one of Kony's top bodyguards. *Gor ineki onyo itoo*, "Beat him to death or you will die."

The four children tried to hold back their tears as they took turns hitting the young boy on his head and body.

He initially screamed in pain and yelled, apparently calling each of his friends by name, asking them to stop. But the terrified four, including a young girl, continued to strike as four fighters pressed their guns on the young ones' backs. The beating stopped when the boy fell silent, a crimson mass seeping out of his battered skull. The LRA commander said to the four through the translator, "this is what will happen to you if you try to escape."

George had become accustomed to this tactic. He understood it perfectly. Forcing the children to kill other abductees, or their friends and family members, made them never think of leaving. It made them feel scared and guilty. It changed them forever. Now they were killers, like most in the LRA. It was a thing they had in common, a bond of sorts that was reinforced by frequent beatings. "We have to beat the weakness out of you," officers were fond of saying. "If you survive you have the strength to be a real guerrilla, if not, then you can't be part of this movement." George was grateful he had not been forced to kill friends or family members in order to become one with the movement. But he had received beatings, and he had also killed.

George did not know if Disco had killed. Chances were he had. He knew that young *kuruts* were the first to be sent on looting missions. He had always thought that this was a way to test them, to ensure that they were good material. But an old commander once told him something George found curious. The commander had joined the LRA in his sixties, in the early days of the war. He even claimed to have known George's father, so naturally George tried to talk to him often.

During one such conversation the commander said that he was too old for the LRA and that the movement was perfect for young boys. "*Youngus* kill with ease," he said. "You only need to show them first how to do it, just like Odomi. He is one of our bravest fighters. I remember when he was first taken. He was very small, he could not even walk very far."

The LRA might have been a movement for the young, but George knew that *kuruts* like Disco, Sammie and Dan had the lowest chances of survival compared to almost everyone else. They were constantly picked on and harassed by other fighters. The *kuruts* assigned to various units were often given the most menial and onerous tasks. Disco was part of Kony's group, and had to do chores, work in the Big Man's compound and carry foodstuffs.

Because Disco was not an Acholi from northern Uganda, he would never be considered a real holy. Even non-Acholi abductees from Sudan who had spent over ten years in the LRA were still not fully trusted by the Ugandan fighters, who considered Acholiness, especially Ugandan Acholiness, as a key LRA ingredient. Non-Acholi were never promoted to senior ranks and were generally treated badly; they were required to learn Luo quickly and not utter a word to one another in their mother tongue. Disco, who had been in the LRA for more than a year by August 2009, spoke Luo relatively well.

* * *

As George and Disco walked towards Twenty-One Cows, George was annoyed at being lost again. He was also worried. He remembered that this area did not have much food and water. He knew that if he did not rejoin his group, the two would be in trouble. George also hated that he had to cut through the bush by himself. Disco was too young to help, so George used his machete to cut a small path in the forest. He made sure not to make much noise to avoid attracting the attention of any Ugandan soldiers who were probably not far away. Soon he became tired and told Disco to stop for a rest. Disco was relieved to have a chance to stop carrying the huge load on his shoulders. He sat down and said, "Thank you sir. I am sorry I got us lost but I am sure you will figure out how to get to Twenty-One Cows, I know you can do it." "Shut your mouth," said George, still annoyed, although flattered by Disco's praise. He was also amused that the thirteen-year-old was trying to encourage him.

George was grateful they still had food and told Disco to save his water. "Remember what happened last time we were here?" George asked. "I do, but thank God, Rambo is not around," Disco replied coyly. George, who hated Rambo as much as Disco did, could not help but smile. "Sorry sir," Disco said, "I know he is a real guerrilla from your tribe." "I don't care," said George, "and don't call me sir." "Should I call you Yankee, what, sir?" Disco asked.

George looked at him for a while and then in a high-pitched voice, clearly imitating Kony, said, "Call me *Lapwony Madit*, Big Teacher." Disco seemed stunned, for a second staring at George incredulously. No one was allowed to make fun of Kony, this was a serious offense. He started laughing. George laughed too, mostly at the way Disco giggled as he tried to but failed to untie his bags, constantly falling on his side. George helped unfasten his luggage and told him to prepare food. Disco had some cassava flour in the bags he was carrying which he mixed with water and made into a paste. George poured out a little honey, which they ate with the cassava paste. They drank a bit of water, all in complete silence.

The rainy season already seems over, George thought, and the green grass they would come to once leaving the forest was not even tall. There would be no cover from the soldiers. The water in the rivers was not enough to stop the soldiers from chasing them deep into the bush. He recited prayers hoping that God would spare their lives and keep the soldiers away as they sought to find their LRA brethren.

They continued to walk in the afternoon, George cutting a path in front, followed by Disco carrying a large load of items, most of which belonged to Black Ninja and Okeny. At nightfall, still in the forest, George found a place to rest for the night. He told Disco to find firewood so that they could warm some water to prepare the cassava. George made a hole in the ground where he started a fire with the wood that Disco brought. This way it was hard for anyone around to see the glare from the fire. It was a trick George had learned in his early LRA days.

George took a saucepan from Disco's bags, placed it on the fire and put a bit of *moo ya* in it. Disco looked in amazement as George mixed cassava flour with warm water, turning it into patties which he then fried in the *moo ya* with a bit of salt. Disco knew that it was not permitted to eat *moo ya*, the holy shea-nut oil that Kony said was to be used only for rituals and as a medicine. George too was aware that if other holies found out that he ate *moo ya* he would be in trouble and receive a beating. But he did not care. He worried that they would run out of food and water or be killed by the soldiers.

"We might as well enjoy ourselves before the Ugandan boys take us down," George said looking at Disco as he handed him a fried patty. Disco snatched it and bared his teeth. "Don't worry boss," he said smiling "I will shoot them first." "You don't have a gun," George said. "I will take their gun and shoot them and then I will shoot them with this," Disco said, pointing at his groin. They both laughed and proceeded to eat all six patties, dipping them in honey. They drank water and George said they should be careful and not drink it all. "We will be ok," said Disco, "I am sure we will be at Twenty-One Cows tomorrow. There is a small stream near that position." George said nothing, but hoped that Disco was right.

They started early in the morning. The sun was bright but cool. George felt hopeful the march would go well and that they would spend the night by the river near Twenty-One Cows. George knew that if it took them too long the group would leave. George and Disco had at most one more day to get there. They moved out of the forest, walking quickly through two large plains before entering into another forested area. They ran as fast as they could when in the open, Disco always lagging behind under the heavy weight. George told him to run, adding, "These fields are usually scoped by Ugandan snipers sitting on the hilltops. We are easy prey in the open."

George searched intently for a path made by the Mboro-ro's cows, which he remembered led to the camp where their friends would be waiting for Agweng. He estimated they would reach the position right after the sun burned brightest, just before dark. The two walked without resting to eat, hoping to reach their destination. But as darkness fell, they were still walking, unsure where they were. That evening they ate the last of the honey and the cassava paste. They were also running out of water. George had a small bottle in his bag but Disco had finished his.

He told Disco to look through the bags he carried. Disco did not want to, fearing Black Ninja and Okeny would beat him if they found out he went through their stuff. George said not to worry and that they needed to check if there was food and water inside. Disco agreed and opened all the bags. They checked every single one. There were clothes, military uniforms, small batteries, pots and pans, a Motorola two-way radio that did not work and a Nokia cellular phone without a Sim card. No food, no water. George was annoyed. "I have to be responsible for him too," he thought. "I need to get to Twenty-One Cows before they leave."

In the morning they started to walk when it was still dark. George felt really hungry. He knew Disco was not doing well. Around noon they stopped to eat wild berries. Disco looked terrible. He had no water left and asked George for some. George said he did not have any. They ate all the berries they could find and resumed walking. Disco walked slowly, and George told him to hurry up. "Throw all that stuff away," he told Disco. "They will kill me," Disco replied and carried on. George said, "Keep walking then, we should be near now."

By mid-afternoon when they walked out of the forest and into a large plain, George realized they had been going around in a circle. It was the same area they had walked through the day before. Disco muttered, "This looks familiar," but stopped when he saw George's angry face. George was irritated and about to yell at Disco when he heard two loud bangs and felt a sharp sting in his left arm.

"Run," George yelled, clutching his bleeding arm. He saw soldiers positioned at the top of the hill to his right. They fired more shots as George and Disco ran ahead trying to reach the forest in front of them. "*Oyot, oyot*," George yelled, "quickly, quickly." Disco kept falling under the heavy load. Two bullets hit the pots he was carrying on his back. They finally reached the forest and ran inside, unsure if the soldiers were following them. Disco could not throw away the load tied to his back so he was moving slowly, dangerously slowly. George helped him and they ran away together.

They finally stopped for the night. George tended to his wound, which he was happy to see was not very serious. Disco sat down on the ground without moving. George cut all the ropes that kept him pinned down. "Leave this shit here," he said angrily. "Don't carry this anymore. Forget Black Ninja, we are being killed." Disco nodded. He had no food or water so he just tried to sleep. George looked at him as he fell asleep. Disco seemed so small even for a thirteen-year-old, all skin and bones, with his clothes hanging off his tiny body even as he rested on the ground.

George took out the small bottle he had in his bag. There was a little bit of water left. He wanted to drink it but decided to save it. He knew it was now too late to go to Twenty-One Cows as the group would have already left to find Kony. George was no longer even sure how to get there.

He sat thinking and came up with a different plan. He thought he could go back to position *Tee*, (Bags), the place where people who attacked Zangambaro hid their luggage. It was right by a stream, and there was a forest nearby that had many wild yams and even trees with beehives and honey. "We ought to go there," George thought, "because the holies who escaped the air raids returning from Zangambaro will retrieve their luggage. There must be food and water in some of those bags." He thought they could make it there in two days, especially if Disco did not carry anything. "I will give him some water tomorrow and he will be fine," George decided.

In the morning, he told Disco the plan, after he gave him a drop of water. He had another drop for himself and the water was gone. Disco agreed, he even seemed happy. At least he did not have to carry the heavy bags.

They changed direction and walked toward the east. They moved through the forest, then alongside a large flat plain where they tried to lick the wet dirt as their thirst became unbearable. They kept walking since they had nothing to eat or drink.

Late in the afternoon George saw a "honey tree." He was ecstatic and asked Disco if he knew how to harvest it. George remembered the last time he tried to do it and preferred not to get stung again. "Sure," Disco affirmed. George took out a small pot from his bag and handed it to Disco together with his lighter. "Put the combs in the pot," said George, "so that we don't waste any." Disco took some dry grass and burned it in front of the hive. He then put his hand inside but got stung many times, and could not get out any combs. He fell to the ground in pain.

"You don't know," said George, annoyed that Disco had lied to him but also impressed with the boy's courage. He took the lighter and did the same thing. He was able to find and bring out combs, all the while getting stung. He put the combs in the pot and came down from the tree. He did not want to show Disco that he was in pain, but his hand was swollen and throbbing. "We should not eat these until we find some water," he said, as he tried to put the pot in his bag. "No, sir, please give me some," said Disco. "I am so hungry I cannot walk." "If we eat this and don't drink any water, we will die of thirst," said George. "Just a little bit," plead Disco.

Reluctantly, George agreed. Disco took the combs carefully and immediately put one in his mouth, only to spit it out quickly. "Not good," he yelled. George looked closely at the combs and realized they were full of bee larvae. He was irritated that his hand was still in pain and that the stuff was not even good honey. But he could not help smiling at Disco's facial expression. Disco thought the larvae tasted bad and still ate some because he was hungry. He swallowed a little bit and claimed that it was not bad, still a little sweet. Soon he asked for water. "We'll keep walking, there has to be a stream around here," said George.

That night they felt terrible. Disco constantly asked for water and George had blurred vision. They fell asleep clutching their throats and desperately licking their lips with dry tongues. George prayed for rain that night but none came. George woke up to an intense pain in his stomach and his head felt heavy. He kicked Disco awake. He got up but he could barely walk. "I am dying," he told George, his voice barely audible. "No, you are not," said George and took him by the hand.

They chewed on leaves and sucked on wet dirt, which helped a little. They ate wild berries and continued to walk. "We move slower than a snail," George thought. Disco fell to the ground twice. "A bit longer," George said. "We are close." Disco walked for a while longer but then collapsed and could not get up. George yelled at him and then kicked him. He even pleaded with him but Disco did not move. He kept his eyes closed and whispered that he needed to sleep. "No," yelled George, grabbing Disco by the shoulders as he lay on the ground. "It is not sleep."

"*Wot tye ka ngani.* (The walking is defeating you.)"

"Get up."

Disco did not move. He did not make a sound. George shook him by the shoulders, telling him to rise but eventually stopped and stared at him. Disco seemed small, even smaller than two days before. As George kept him in his arms he thought he held a baby. Disco felt light, as if empty inside. He scanned Disco's withered face and limp body for signs of life but nothing moved. "Maybe he is asleep," George thought, then saying in a whisper, "It is fine, *ywe* (you rest). I will go find water and food and come back." He got up and continued to walk without looking back.

George felt disoriented but was certain he was near position Bags. Two long hours later, he found it and went through the bags frantically. He found a large bottle of water and drank voraciously. He quickly turned back and walked to where he left Disco. As he walked and drank, his vision cleared. His head ceased buzzing, a sound that had driven him crazy in the last couple of days. He stopped walking and sat down to rest at the top of a small hill.

He felt hungry so he took out the pot with the honeycombs and looked around. The beauty of his surroundings amazed him. The sun was setting and everything was bathed in a lovely orange color. He stared into the distance and chewed on some larvae. "One day tourists could come here and enjoy this beautiful place," he thought.

CHAPTER 15

NO JOY IN THE WORLD

The Brigadier sat at the head of a large dining table set in the open next to Nzara's airstrip, a dusty track of red land surrounded by leafless trees. A small town in South Sudan's Western Equatoria state, Nzara had become home to 700 Ugandan soldiers who provided support to colleagues chasing LRA groups in CAR, Congo and South Sudan.

On the table, next to an enormous square map covered with red cloth, sat a pile of documents and a few small maps covered with annotations and other scribbles. Prominent on the table was a copy of Clausewitz's **On War,** *but the Brigadier read the* **Red Pepper,** *a Ugandan tabloid featuring photos of scantily dressed women. The back page carried the caption "Horny beach bums going crazy over Regina's round bottom," in a large font.*

He folded the paper and welcomed the visitors to the large dining table, shouting, "Bullet." A short man in military fatigues and red slippers emerged and stood to attention next to the Brigadier. "Water for our visitors," the Brigadier ordered and Bullet disappeared, quickly returning with a few bottles of Rwenzori. "From Uganda," said the Brigadier proudly. "We bring everything from Uganda, even the water. From our own Rwenzori mountains. This place has nothing."

The Brigadier was the Ugandan army commander in charge of the LRA offensive as well as the permanent commander of the fourth army division based in Gulu. Apart from being responsible for providing security to northern Uganda, the fourth division was also the main supplier of troops engaged in the LRA offensive outside of Uganda. An Acholi, the Brigadier was well known for his loyalty to President Museveni. It had earned him rapid promotion and leadership posts including the overall command of the anti-LRA offensive.

The Brigadier owned plenty of land in northern Uganda, including Gulu, where he also owned the biggest hotel in town, a popular hangout spot for foreign workers and state officials. There were various reports in the Ugandan press questioning the source of the Brigadier's wealth. A particularly damning article in the Daily Monitor of 23 July 2008 accused him of being involved in land grabbing in Acholiland when the local population was herded into the so-called protected camps to escape LRA attacks. The article claimed that the Brigadier used his position in the army to take the land of the people forced into the camps, rather than defending the camps, which became easy prey for the LRA. The Brigadier denied the accusations but never really explained how he acquired his riches.

The Brigadier was also known for being in charge of the group of soldiers that stormed Gulu prison in 2002 and executed Peter Oloya "Yumbe," a member of a political party which opposed the ruling party of President Museveni. Despite a public outcry over the execution of Yumbe, the Brigadier continued to increase his influence. People in Gulu spoke of Museveni's affinity to the Brigadier, due to his willingness to assist with the President's electoral campaign in Acholiland, a traditional opposition stronghold.

A report by the Ugandan Human Rights Commission implicated the Brigadier as the officer in charge of the squad that killed Yumbe. At a subsequent case brought in front of the Ugandan High Court in 2003, the presiding judge concluded that the killing of Yumbe was a blatant case of extrajudicial killing and that he was shot on the orders of the then lieutenant colonel, later promoted to brigadier.

"Kony is in CAR," the brigadier said. We are chasing him and his criminals wherever they go. We chased them in Congo and they moved into CAR. We are chasing them there too. There is no place to hide for these evildoers. We will catch them. But we need help, helicopters to go after them, as they move fast. We need funds for vehicles and fuel. We need airplanes to bring food and water from Uganda. Our partners, the Americans, have helped us but more is needed. But we will take care of Kony. These attacks in South Sudan and in CAR are the last kicks of a dying horse. Kony will be finished soon.

And with that the Brigadier said he was busy, bid the visitors goodbye and resumed perusing the Red Pepper.

* * *

George waited alone at position Bags. He made a small tent with leaves and branches inside the forest, a few hundred yards away from Bags. He worried the soldiers would find him so he spent most of the day in the forest. Early each morning he walked carefully to the luggage and rummaged for food. He was not concerned about water as the small stream near Bags was still alive, though it appeared to be drying out. "So much for the rainy season," he thought.

One day he found a notebook, a pen and a small radio set in one of the bags. He did not know the bag's owner but worried it could be a commander, or worse, Kony. George knew that he could get in trouble for taking things from the bags of the boss. He decided he did not care. At that moment he was not sure he would survive the day. He wrote a short message on a piece of paper he ripped from the notebook. "Yankee separated from the group, waiting nearby," was the message he scribbled quickly and put on top of one of the bags, under a rock to keep it in place. He then returned to his forest hideout and went to sleep.

Ten days passed but no one appeared. George became concerned that all the groups had already left for Darfur. "Maybe I am all alone now," he thought. He considered attempting to surrender to the Ugandan army or waiting to see if other groups, coming from Congo, would pass there on their way to Darfur. He could join them and put his life in the hands of the rebels once again. Surrender seemed risky. What if the soldiers recognized him from when he shot at them with Ochan or with Marate? What if they put him in prison for a long time? He was sure he preferred the bush to prison.

And what if the soldiers killed all the holies who tried to surrender? Some commanders said that the government slowly poisoned those who escaped and miraculously made it to Uganda. If really unlucky, they were sterilized. It sounded crazy but the commanders said some of the Banyankole officers did not want the Acholi to multiply.

Even if one small rumor was true, it was nothing to laugh at. He could not take the risk. He tried to convince himself that all the rumors were the result of the paranoia in the bush. The bush made people crazy, George knew, but he was not sure what to believe. He had been out of Uganda for more than two years; many things could have changed in that time. Or maybe he had just become paranoid and crazy, just like everybody else. "I need to find the other crazies," he decided.

He vowed to only take small amounts of foods from the luggage and try to find wild yams and berries to eat. That way if the owners of the bags appeared they would not punish him for stealing all of their food. He also thought he needed to stay in the forest a little longer so that he could rest and recover from the long journeys of the last few months. That night he started to think about his location and the quickest way to Obo. "I need to know where I am going if I leave this place," he thought.

He did not sleep all night and at dawn he did his usual patrol to position Bags to check if anyone had appeared or read his letter. He walked slowly not expecting to see anyone and was terrified when two men pushed him to the ground. "You are a dead man Yankee," they yelled. He recognized the voices of Abe and Trigger. They laughed, making fun of George's careless walking. George was happy to see them. "Good to see you Yankee," Trigger said. "You have grown too thin." "You finally look like a real guerrilla, Professor," Abe joked.

They told George they were part of a group led by Major Kibwola, a small-bodied, fierce fighter who had become one of Kony's most trusted men. Jon Bosco Kibwola rested in a small camp nearby with his men. They had arrived the previous evening, found the luggage and read George's letter. Kibwola had sent Abe and Trigger to bring him to camp. "Agweng has returned from Darfur," George thought, as the three walked to meet the others. He knew that Kibwola had gone to Darfur with Agweng. "If they made it back, surely this means we are going to Darfur, as Kony said."

Kibwola said he was happy to see him and said that he had returned from Darfur with Agweng who had already gone to meet Kony. Kibwola was staying behind to wait for another group, led by Colonel Abuchiu, before moving to Kony's base. Kibwola told George to join his group, which made George happy. George enjoyed talking to the other holies, recounting their stories of survival. It was the camaraderie he missed most when alone in the forest and he was glad he had waited to find it again. That evening, sitting near a small fire with Kiwbola's men, he told the story of the raid on Zangambaro and of the drunk man who was not afraid of the LRA but ended up burned alive. Everyone laughed.

Each morning Kibwola sent patrols to look for Abuchiu while George deployed as a camp guard. One of the patrols came back to report that a group of Mbororo was camped four miles to the north. In the afternoon Kibwola sent Abe, Trigger and three other men to ask the Mbororo for food. In the evening they returned loaded with cow meat and milk. "The Mbororo did not want to give us any, but we were really polite," joked Trigger, pointing to his gun.

One morning, one of the patrols reported seeing tracks they thought belonged to other holies. The entire group set off immediately. Kiwbola said it was probably Abuchiu and his people, which made him happy. He would find Abuchiu and bring him to Kony and then they would all go to Darfur. "You will all like it there," Kibwola said, "it is a nice, quiet area and the soldiers leave us alone." George was not thrilled to go on yet another difficult march but he could certainly live without the helicopter attacks and soldiers' ambushes in CAR.

Expecting to find Abuchiu and his men, George was surprised to see his old coy mates led by Obwoya, who had become chief bodyguard after Kony had dispatched Otika to find holies in Congo and bring them to CAR. George was pleased see to his old friends who told him they had made it to Kony's camp after the helicopter attack but the General sent them back to retrieve his belongings from position Bags. George immediately thought of the food he had taken and feared that Obwoya would find out and have him punished. Obwoya said that they would return to position Bags the next day and collect all of Kony's possessions. They were to wait for two groups coming from Congo before starting their march to Kony's new position in northwestern CAR and eventually to Darfur.

As soon as they reached position Bags the next day, Obwoya made straight for the luggage. The rest prepared their night quarters; leaves and dry grass on the ground served as a mattress and tree branches made up a roof that could be reinforced with tarpaulin when it rained. Some took out their torn mosquito nets and laid them next to their beds. As people went to fetch water from the stream so that they could prepare their evening meal, one of the bodyguards told George to see Obwoya.

George cursed under his breath knowing what was about to happen. "Deny everything," he told himself. "Who knows how many people went through the bags after I did, particularly Kibwola's guys?" Obwoya wasted no time. "Did you steal Ladit's food?" "No," George said emphatically. "You are lying," Obwoya yelled. "You are a liar and a thief." Then turning to Private Layibi he ordered, "Beat him." Before he could say a word, George found himself on the ground spread-eagled with his shirt and shoes off. He thought he preferred to be shot instead of this humiliation.

"Hit him on his back only, not even his ass, seventy times," Obwoya yelled to Layibi, who was quick to return with a few thick sticks and positioned himself on top of George while other bodyguards stared. A young man from Kibwola's group called Oryenya was also ordered to lie down with his shirt off, right next to George. He was to be beaten after George. Obwoya's men must have interrogated all of Kiwbola's group members while Obwoya questioned George. Oryenya must have taken sugar from

Kony's bags, George thought, remembering him and Abe drinking tea and wondering at that time where they had found the sugar. George wished he had eaten some of the sugar when he had had the chance.

George tried to turn his mind off the pain of the blows and felt a knot in his throat. His eyes became moist as the blows ended. He sank his face deeper in the dirt to shield his face and tried to hold back the tears. He did not want to be teased again, to be called a woman or a child. He took the beating in silence, slowly stood up and put on his shirt and shoes, lastly grabbing his gun, all under the watchful eyes of Obwoya's bodyguards. Layibi prepared new sticks, wiped the sweat off his brow and took his position on top of Oryenya.

George walked away, his back burning and aching. "There is no joy in the world," he thought. He despised Obwoya. He hated this group and this place. "I have to get out of here" he thought as he approached Abe and Trigger, who made fun of the way he walked. He wanted to say something terrible to them, curse them or call them "stupider than their mothers," but decided to turn around and walk to the little stream instead. He wanted to wash his bloodied body. He knew the pain would eventually subside but his wounds would become infected. He knew that because he had been beaten often, too often, during his time with the rebels. The realization made him sad and angry.

* * *

Agweng's group was making its way to Kafia Kingi in Sudan's South Darfur. Kafia Kingi is a relatively small area north of South Sudan's Western Bahr El Ghazal (WBEG) state. The enclave is disputed between the two Sudans but in 2009 Kafia Kingi remained under the control of (North) Sudan, as it does today. One of the southernmost barracks of the Sudanese Armed Forces (SAF) is situated near the small town of Dafak, approximately 35 miles from the CAR border and about 185 miles south of Nyala, the capital of South Darfur.

LRA envoys sent by Kony, most notably Odhiambo in 2007 and 2008, tried to reach Dafak from Garamba National Park but failed. Once Kony made it to southeastern CAR in the summer of 2009, he sent Agweng with a group of thirty to Dafak to ask for SAF protection. Kony knew there was no better place to hide and be shielded from attacks than in Sudan, where the Ugandan army was not allowed, and where LRA groups would be in close proximity to the SAF.

Agweng, one of Kony's most trusted men at the time, received detailed advice from Kony and another commander, both apparently in touch via satellite phones with elements in the SAF at least until early 2009. Kony instructed Agweng to ask SAF officers for protection in the name of the old alliance. Agweng was not to disclose to them that Kony intended to move to Dafak himself. "You cannot fully trust the Arabs," Kony said.

Agweng's group left in late August 2009 from southeastern CAR. They entered WBEG and moved north, toward Kafia Kingi. The group attacked a small village near Boro Medina in Raja County, abducting at least two people and looting food. In early October 2009 they made it to the SAF barracks in Dafak.

Agweng sent two envoys accompanied by two abductees from Raja who spoke Arabic and English and acted as translators. Kibwola was one of the envoys who went to the SAF base and asked to meet senior officers. As the group of four approached the barracks, armed soldiers poured out and arrested the envoys.

SAF soldiers shot at Agweng's group from their base, which caused the group to scatter and hide inside the bush. Two helicopters also strafed the LRA group. After the helicopters, a small white Antonov plane flew low over the bush to check on the armed men. Agweng said the Arabs were scared and were only warning them. He suggested they write a letter to explain that they were there to rekindle their relationship with the SAF. A young, unarmed fighter took the letter, written in English, and pinned it on a large tree opposite the barracks' main door. An SAF soldier ran to the tree, picked up the letter and disappeared inside the barracks. He reappeared soon after with a letter that he also pinned on the same tree. The young LRA fighter brought it to Agweng. "We want to meet with you," it said in English.

After a few letters had been exchanged agreeing on the time and place for the meeting, Agweng and a few other fighters met under a large tree with SAF soldiers including a colonel who flew in on a helicopter from a nearby town to meet the LRA members. There were also a lieutenant colonel, a captain, a lieutenant and many soldiers. The lieutenant said he was the commander of the Dafak barracks and that the lieutenant colonel and the captain were accompanying the colonel. Agweng and two other LRA members said they represented Kony. The meeting was held in English.

Agweng reiterated Kony's desire to rekindle the relationship with the SAF, noting that the LRA had always been loyal to Khartoum, including fighting the Dinkas. The SAF colonel said it was not possible for the old relationship to be reactivated because such a thing would be viewed unfavorably by the SPLA and the South Sudanese government, with which Khartoum had signed a peace treaty. The colonel promised to check with his superiors and requested a meeting in one year's time, at the same place, but with Kony present. Agweng agreed to pass on the message and inquired after his two men. The colonel said they had been taken to another town for a briefing with military intelligence but that they would be returned unharmed.

The group waited for a week until the two returned by helicopter. They emerged out of the barracks with a few bags of sugar, biscuits, flour and bread, while the Raja translators were kept in the barracks. The SAF lieutenant told Agweng, who went to receive the two men, that the group was no longer welcome and had to leave in the next twenty-four hours. Kibwola said they were not mistreated, had eaten well, and had had good discussions with the military intelligence officers. He also said they needed to leave. People in Khartoum did not want anyone to know that the LRA was in Darfur.

The group left for CAR, reaching the border in two days. It took Agweng three more weeks to find Kony near Djemah in CAR around mid-November 2009. Kibwola stayed north of Obo to wait for Abuchiu, where he found position Bags and the letter from George. Upon hearing the news from Agweng that the Arabs had refused to allow LRA groups in Dafak, Kony was furious. He cursed the Arabs and accused Agweng of being incompetent, as well as taking his time in returning, a delay *which caused many losses in his group. Agweng was demoted from colonel to captain and his escort cut in half.*

* * *

The night after the beating was long for George. He could not sleep because his back hurt. He could not reach the wounds and was unable to apply *moo ya* that might have helped allay the pain. George was surprised they had not taken his gun. That was the rule; you took the gun away from the man you beat, as he might try to take his revenge. George fantasized about shooting Obwoya. But he knew Obwoya was not responsible for his troubles. Obwoya was abducted, torn from his family and friends, just like everyone else, apart from George. "Why did I agree to join the rebels," he wondered. "If my mother had been alive, she would have never let me." He thought about escaping.

He feared the long distance, the soldiers on the way and the authorities. He did not want to end up in prison. He needed to find a way to leave the group and avoid being hunted by the other holies, who would come after him. He decided he would fall behind when deployed as a rearguard or if the group was attacked. He would disappear in the bush and take it from there. He felt slightly happier, momentarily forgetting the pain in his back.

In the morning, Obwoya, who took over control of the big group, talked about the day's plans. "We will stay here one more day to rest and prepare for the long journey to the Big Teacher. We will send out patrols today to continue to look for Abuchiu and others coming from

Congo but tomorrow we walk north." George hoped to be deployed as a scout for the day so that he could make his escape. He knew it would be easier to slip away as part of a team of two or three men. To his annoyance, Obwoya ordered him to stay at camp. "You need to rest after the beating," he said. "The first time he is being nice and it ruins my plans," thought George.

He walked to the stream to drink water and wash his body. After he was done, he rested on the shore as his clothes dried on top of shrubs. The sun was warm on his back and shoulders and he fell asleep, waking up a few hours later as the sun set. He took his supper – a few handfuls of peanuts and a bit of dry cassava – away from the main group and thought about his escape. George was certain that one or two scouts would be left behind to direct the Congo groups to Kony's location. If chosen as a scout, George would not need to abandon the group. He would have a legitimate reason to be alone or with another person. He was happy to find that even after a pleasant day, he remained determined to leave.

* * *

While waiting for Agweng to return from Dafak, Kony had started to feel the pressure from the Ugandan army and had decided to move further north into CAR, aiming to reach the Zemongo forest, a lush area northeast of Djemah and adjacent to the South Sudanese border. In early October 2009, on the way to Zemongo, Kony ordered an attack on Djemah to secure food and abductees. A standby of sixty led by Kony's half-brother,

Major Olanya, attacked the town on the night of 5 October, unaware that two Ugandan army companies had arrived in town the night before from Obo.

The standby planned to spend the night in Djemah, looting, eating and preparing to bring the loot in the morning to the main camp, three hours walk from Djemah, where Kony waited. Standby members shot in the air to scare the population into abandoning their homes, thus unknowingly alerting the Ugandan soldiers nearby. The soldiers turned up an hour after the looting had started. The holies, including women and children, ran into the forest dragging with them four young women and three boys from Djemah in addition to all the food they could carry.

The soldiers gave chase into the forest, killing many in the following couple of days, at least twenty-five by some accounts. A week after the attack Kony, who had run the entire time with only two bodyguards, joined the rest of the group inside the Zemongo forest. He was angry and ordered the immediate killing of the three boys from Djemah as retaliation. Kony took one of the young women from Djemah as his wife and gave the other three to his commanders. He ordered the commanders to immediately impregnate the women, "as revenge for the fallen Acholi fighters."

Kony and his group moved northeast of Djemah, waiting for Agweng and the Congo groups. The unexpected presence of the Ugandan army in Djemah unsettled the LRA leader and his plans changed once again. Rather than wait for the groups to join him at a prearranged rendezvous – a large white rock two days' walk north of Djemah – Kony moved deeper into the

Zemongo forest. The arrival of Agweng in mid-November 2009 at Kony's base in the forest and his report on the failed Dafak mission made the LRA leader move again, this time close to the CAR border with South Sudan's Western Bahr el Ghazal state.

Kony's constant changing of bases made it difficult for LRA commanders, as well as the Ugandan army, to find him. Many of the groups trying to reach Kony's position were lost, often falling into ambushes by Ugandan soldiers. In early November Otika, on the way from Congo to CAR to join Kony, lost more than fifty people – over half of his initial group – near Obo.

At the end of December 2009, Abudema, deputy to Odhiambo, was shot by Ugandan soldiers near Djemah. Abudema had walked for more than six months in the bush trying to find Kony. The slow unraveling of the LRA was in full effect. But north of Obo in late November 2009 Obwoya's and Kibwola's groups prepared to make their journey to Djemah, where they expected to find Kony and walk together to Darfur. In Darfur the peace would finally return, Kony had promised.

* * *

Two days after the beating, Obwoya summoned George. "I have decided you are no longer part of this team," Obwoya said, motioning to the group of bodyguards. "We will discuss your behavior with the General when we see him but for now you are to move with Kibwola." Both groups were to walk north but separately, to move fast and avoid detection from the gunships. "We leave tomorrow morning," he said, "and your group leaves tomorrow afternoon. Bring your stuff here. You are to make sure we leave without trouble before you report back to Kibwola."

Early in the morning Obwoya came to George's sleeping area. "Get up soldier," he said. "Give me your dry rations." George was surprised by Obwoya's behavior. He had not been treated this badly since his early days with the rebels. But fearing another beating, George took out all the food he had. Dry peanuts, some maize, a few wrinkled yam roots and a little bit of honey. Obwoya took everything and stuffed it in his backpack. "Go to your unit," he ordered.

George walked near the stream to Kibwola's group but found the place abandoned. It seemed as if the group had left a while ago. He was shocked. "Did Obwoya lie to me and intentionally leave me behind?" George would have loved to be alone but now he worried that if he did not join Kibwola, he could be in trouble for insubordination. Obwoya would report him to Kony as having disobeyed orders and tried to escape. "Obwoya is testing me," George thought, "trying to push me to escape so that I can be captured and executed."

"I have to find Kibwola," George thought and quickly found and followed the group's tracks. He spent the day running, trying to catch up, cursing Obwoya while contemplating the irony of the situation. He would have loved nothing more than to be alone, for a while at least, yet he tried his hardest to join people who did not want him either. On the second day he lost the tracks. He had gone to sleep the night before confident he was close, he even woke up earlier than usual to resume marching, convinced he would catch up before lunch. But by late afternoon he had no idea where the group had gone.

That night he felt uneasy. He worried Obwoya would turn up in the morning and kill him. What if Obwoya's group was following him, checking on him the whole time? He told himself to stop being paranoid. If Obwoya wanted to kill him he could have done it without needing an excuse. That thought calmed him and he slept soundly after a tiring day.

He found fresh tracks the morning after and followed them. He was sure they belonged to holies so he expected to find Kibwola and his men soon. And after midday saw the silhouette of a rearguard. He ran faster and whistled. The rearguard dropped to the ground and whistled back. George approached with his hands up, his gun on his shoulder pointing down. They met soon after but to George's surprise he did not recognize the rearguard, who introduced himself as Private Okello "Civilian." "Two others are ahead," he said.

One of the two other holies was a second lieutenant. He said his name was the Hidden One and that the other was called Kidega. "He does not talk much," said the Hidden One pointing at Kidega. "We are from Second Brigade," said the Hidden One before asking for a report. George said he was with Kibwola but was lost and looking for his group. "We were with Otika," said the Hidden One, "we came to CAR with him but got separated when the soldiers attacked us a few weeks back. We were to join the Big Teacher and go to Darfur."

* * *

George did not mind his new colleagues even if they were a little strange. But the problem of food remained the same; there was never enough. The four went on patrol daily trying to find other holies, and food, mostly wild roots and honey. Often they only ate berries all day. They spoke of looting food but they were too far from any villages or main roads. They were also too few in number to organize attacks on villages and they could easily end up dead. So they spent weeks eating little and waiting for other holies to appear. Before they knew it, Christmas came.

They would have not known it was Christmas had it not been for a small transistor radio the Hidden One took out of his bag once in a while and turned on, usually to UBC radio, the Ugandan national channel, on shortwave. He liked the Sunday religious programs that played sermons and religious songs in English. As Christmas approached, the religious songs and Christmas Carols were frequent, so the four spent many evenings listening to the radio for hours. The Hidden One had a good supply of batteries and George loved listening to the radio, even though he went to sleep hungry most nights.

Four days before Christmas the Hidden One decided that they should split in two groups and look for food as far as possible. "We need to celebrate the birth of our Lord Jesus with more than just wild berries," he said. "Come back here on Christmas Eve and we will eat whatever we bring back." He took off with Kidega in one direction while George and Civilian went the opposite way. George knew they were walking in the direction of Obo. He told

Civilian they should try to get as close to Obo as possible and try to find some cassava or bananas.

The first day they walked without stopping, crossing a small river and a few streams. They found old tracks, probably made by local hunters. But the morning after, the two came across footprints made by soldiers. "These are the boots of our Ugandan boys," said George smiling. Civilian was scared and said they should go back. George told him to walk west and see if he could find any abandoned homes or gardens while he would follow the track a little longer to see where it led. "Let's meet here this evening, "said George and took off without giving Civilian any time to object.

George knew the path led to Obo, he just wanted to know how far the town was exactly. He had learned throughout his time with the holies that knowing the territory was an advantage no worthy rebel could pass up. But he was also worried the soldiers could have put an ambush on the path or worse, mines. He continued to walk slowly, following the soldiers' tracks until he came to an area the soldiers must have used as their camp. There were the remnants of small fires and flat areas that must have been used for sleeping. He found two empty plastic bottles and put them in his bag. He could use them for water, cooking oil, *moo ya* or honey. He also found an unopened tin can with a note on it, held in place by a small rock.

George carefully picked up the can and read the note in English. It said, "Dear Ugandan brother. Eat this can of beans. I know you are hungry. We have plenty and don't need to carry a lot of it. It is not poisoned. Merry Christmas!"

George placed the tin and the note deep inside his bag. He returned to the rendezvous place where he found Civilian. He said he had found some moldy maize. George said he had found nothing. The two returned to their base picking up a few wild roots and edible plants on their way. Back at camp on Christmas Eve they found the Hidden One and Kidega, who were also empty-handed. They brought back some berries and other wild fruit and sat down to Christmas dinner. George felt guilty about the beans but he was sure they were hiding something for themselves too. George also worried that the Hidden One would make him throw away the beans, probably arguing they were poisoned.

The sight of grown men munching on wild berries was depressing but George took solace in listening to the Christmas carols on the radio and thinking about eating the canned beans when everyone slept. His own private Christmas feast. He had never had canned beans before and wondered how they tasted. "Softer than the ones we eat, probably better cooked also," he hoped. They were definitely not poisoned, he was sure. And if they were, so be it, he decided. He was too hungry. And it was Christmas.

The Hidden One said it was time to sleep and followed it with a quick "Merry Christmas." The other three followed suit, including Kidega, which made George smile. "A Christmas miracle," said Civilian. George waited for the rest to fall asleep, worrying they were probably trying to do the same – wait for the others to sleep so that they could have their own private celebration. With the can in his pocket and weapon in hand, George pretended he went to relieve himself in the bush. "Long call," he whispered to the three and walked into the bush. He dropped his pants, squatted and removed his bayonet from the gun. He pierced the can as quietly as he could, making a small hole.

He tipped the can over his mouth and felt a gooey delicious mass on his tongue. It was as if the beans were cooked in sugar even though they were soft and strangely salty. It was the best thing he had ever eaten. He pried the entire can top open with his bayonet and ate everything inside, scooping it all with his fingers.

He hid the can and took out the note. He tried to read it again but it was too dark and he could not make out the letters. He remembered the message well. "Eat it, it is not poisoned." "My Ugandan brother." "Merry Christmas." These were phrases he had thought about a lot since he had found the note. "We have plenty of it." The Ugandan soldiers had so much of this delicious food that they just threw it away. "While we eat berries and leaves," George thought.

"What am I doing here?" he said out loud, then quietly wondered, "What is the purpose of my stay and suffering in this place? Is there a purpose to this whole madness?" Right then, on Christmas Eve 2009, George Omona, nick-named Yankee, having consumed a can of baked beans while pretending to defecate in a dimly lit night, decided to leave the holies for good.

CHAPTER 16

DWOG PACO

George worried about even hinting at escape in front of the others, fearing the Hidden One. Kidega and Civilian would do whatever their commander said but the Hidden One was a typical holy, George was certain. Uneducated and in the LRA from a tender age, the Hidden One believed what his superiors had told him throughout the years. That he would be killed by soldiers or poisoned by government agents if he ever left. He even refused to listen to "*Dwog Paco.*"

Dwog Paco, which roughly means "Come Home" in Luo, was a popular program initially played on the Gulu-based Mega FM radio station. The program broadcast messages from people who had left the LRA to encourage others to leave. By late 2009 *Dwog Paco* began to play on radio stations in South Sudan and Congo, aimed at the LRA groups there. *Dwog Paco* was the reason Kony had forbidden non-officer ranks from owning radio sets. "The lies in the programs could corrupt their brains and trick them into trying to leave," he said. "But the officers knew better than to believe the lies of the Museveni regime, they would be killed by the soldiers if they ever left the rebellion."

The Hidden One acted exactly as George feared. He turned off the radio when the demobilization messages came on and refused to talk about life back home. George did not know how to bring up the issue of leaving, yet he was so anxious to go home that he worried he would lose patience and speak his mind. George did not want to escape alone. He believed that the odds of making it out alive were higher with others, there being definite strength in numbers if they came across hunters or diehards. George worried that they could not communicate with the locals, as all four in the group were Acholi and spoke none of the local languages.

George was convinced that the risks of trying to surrender in the battlefield were too high. Surrendering to

Two recently returned former LRA fighters in a rehabilitation center in Gulu, Uganda, April 2013.

a Ugandan army base, away from the chaos of the battle, was a safer bet. He decided doing it in Obo was best, even though he feared the wrath of the townspeople fed up with LRA violence. He only needed to find a way to reach the Ugandan army base unharmed. And to convince the Hidden One.

George could not find an appropriate way of broaching the subject of escaping. He tried first with Civilian, whom he liked and seemed reasonable. One day when they were alone and eating yet more wild yams George made a point of appearing annoyed and said loudly, "I am sick of these *obato*, I wish we could eat some real food, like *malakwang* as we do at home." He looked at Civilian who said nothing but kept on eating. George became afraid that he might report him to the Hidden One and quickly changed the topic. "Will the rains ever come back? It is so hard to dig out these roots from the dry earth."

George tried to talk to Kidega once, even though Kidega never spoke and was rarely separated from the Hidden One. "If he never talks to anyone, it might not matter what I say," George reasoned and asked him directly whether he missed his family. Kidega shrugged and walked away. George knew that the only chance of convincing the group to leave was to talk to the Hidden One. "I need to either convince him or have him kill me," he thought. He could no longer stand this way of life. There was no point in dying of hunger in the bush.

It was already the end of January 2010 when George mustered the courage to talk with the Hidden One. One morning he asked the Hidden One to go on patrol together while Kidega went with Civilian. George asked to walk south as he knew an old cassava patch in that direction, a lie to keep the Hidden One interested. George said he knew where Obo was and that there was a Ugandan army base there. "It would be a good place to go to when we have no hope left," he offered.

George was amazed at his courage and waited for the Hidden One's reaction. There was a long pause as they continued to walk. The Hidden One slowed down letting George walk ahead. "What if he shoots me?" he thought, feeling scared. He brought his AK close to his body and turned around to face him. "Relax Yankee," he said. "We have little hope left now." It was what George had hoped for this whole time, the small hint of how the Hidden One really felt. He knew he did not need to push the issue further but wait. So he said little else that day.

On Sunday the Hidden One said he wanted to find the *Dwog Paco* program. "Would be good to hear what they have to say," he said. He could not find a channel that night but it became clear to all that the plan to leave the bush was already made. The how was to be decided.

* * *

In late 2009, Kony, intent on reaching Kafia Kingi, divided his forces into a few groups and together with a small band of body-guards he walked from CAR's northern Zemongo forest into Western Bahr el Ghazal (WBEG) in South Sudan. Kony's advance unit was attacked in Boro Medina, in WBEG's Raja County, at the end of December 2009 by South Sudanese and Ugandan soldiers. Four men were killed, and the rest returned to report to Kony that the road was blocked by enemy troops. He attempted again using the same route in January 2010 but was attacked by a Ugandan army unit and was forced to return to CAR.

As Kony tried to reach Kafia Kingi, he sent word to Binany to perpetrate attacks in Congo. The main aim was to repeat the Christmas attacks of 2008 the LRA had carried out in retaliation for Operation Lightning Thunder. A second and equally important aim was to divert attention from Kony's attempts to enter Sudan. Operating from inside Garamba National Park, not far from the old LRA bases of Swahili and Gangboo, Binany set in motion a series of attacks on the villages of Gangala na Bodio, Kapili and Makombo that left more than 320 people dead during the week of 13 to 20 December 2009.

LRA violence in CAR was also significant. From early 2008, when Odhiambo first attacked inside CAR, until early 2010, there were more than 220 LRA killings of civilians. Over 500 people were abducted and 15,000 were displaced due to fear of LRA attacks. Entire villages, particularly around Obo in the southeast, were entirely empty of people, which caused a lot of hunger and misery as people could not farm and collect their crops. There was no help from the police or national army soldiers, who were too afraid to confront the LRA.

LRA groups also targeted Western Equatoria state (WES) of South Sudan. The UN reported that in 2009 the LRA killed more than 250 people. In the same year, more than 65,000 were displaced. A supreme chief of the Zande in WES said in November 2009 that the LRA seemed intent on exterminating *the Zande people. "This is the biggest threat to our people in my lifetime," he said.*

* * *

In their camp by the small stream, the Hidden One asked George how they should make their way out. "We walk to Obo," said George, "and find the Ugandan army base." The Hidden One came up with a long list of death-inducing problems: three or four days' walk with not enough food, lack of water, the hunters, the CAR army, Obo civilians and the Ugandan soldiers. "All these things could kill us," he said. George understood his task of convincing the Hidden One was much greater than he had initially envisioned.

George and the Hidden One went on patrol each morning and George addressed the Hidden One's concerns. The first day was occupied by talk of the logistics in reaching the Ugandan army barracks in Obo unseen and unharmed by civilians. George said they needed to find someone who could provide directions. The two spent days discussing how to find a civilian from Obo. Getting close to the town where all civilians lived – the surrounding villages had emptied after repeated LRA attacks – was dangerous; they could be attacked by the Ugandans, the diehards or the civilians if they saw the group was small and poorly armed. George said that they should throw away their guns before going to Obo. "No way," yelled the Hidden One. "I have had my gun for twenty years; there is no way I am letting go of 'my sweetheart.'"

Every evening around the fire Kidega and Civilian stared at George and the Hidden One with expectant eyes. George said little but the Hidden One made it plain every night that they were about to go home. "We will make a careful plan so that we don't end up dead," he would say each night reassuringly before he turned on the radio. He usually found the BBC World Service and kept it on for a while. But in early February 2009, the batteries died and the radio was never turned on again.

George took the end of the last contact with the outside world as a sign that he should try harder. Each morning George and the Hidden One set off in their daily mission with George presenting different ideas. One day they found a compromise. They would walk to the main road near Obo and wait for the Ugandan soldiers to appear and then surrender to them. They would hide their guns in the bushes at the last minute before facing the soldiers. The Hidden One seemed content that night; he even told Kidega and Civilian to prepare for an imminent departure.

But the next day the Hidden One had changed his mind. He had a bad dream and worried the soldiers would kill them on the road. He insisted that they were at risk by wearing their tattered military uniforms. If only they could find and wear civilian clothing, they could walk among the civilians undetected, they could even slip secretly back into Uganda. There would be no need to even deal with the army; just a long walk home and every-thing would be fine. "Not so," said George. "We will be spotted by the civilians. We speak no local languages and as civilians we will have to cross borders and need papers. It is too risky to cross into South Sudan. The Dinkas will kill us when they find us." The Hidden One nodded and they returned to camp once more with no clear plans.

Every day was the same. George thought they had agreed to a plan, with the Hidden One seeming optimistic at the end of the day, only for the next morning to arrive complete with renewed fears. One day George became frustrated after the Hidden One started to worry about being poisoned or castrated when back in Uganda. "Many years of being told the same thing has made you believe it, no matter how crazy," thought George. He told the Hidden One how he had never seen or heard of any cases of castration during his lifetime in Uganda. George knew that he was saying things that contradicted what Kony said – a blasphemy. It did not matter whether you did not like other fighters or even the commanders, but one did not criticize Kony. It was considered treason of the highest order. Kony was the father of the organization; he was the father of all holies. Who spoke badly of their own father?

But George could not hold back, he was already committed to leaving and he needed to do it soon. He feared the appearance of another group, especially one led by one of Kony's "loyal dogs." If another group turned up and found out about their plans – which would take little time after they were debriefed – George was certain the Hidden One would give him up instantly. There was no doubt in George's mind that at that moment, his so-called brothers posed the biggest threat to his life. He was prepared to do whatever it took to leave, including walking in broad daylight to the army base in the middle of Obo.

George spoke brazenly that night, deciding he needed the support of Civilian and Kidega. The least he could do was to make sure that all four spoke openly about leaving. Well, three, given Kidega's near-permanent state of silence. George told them that the chances of being killed at the hands of the Ugandan soldiers were small. Why kill us if we surrender? They will want to take us home, to show us off to the world, to prove that they are winning. We only have to make it to the army base. And if we do end up dead, then that is the will of God. But we should not wait for death to find us here, we should not wait for hunger to defeat us here, away from home. To his surprise he heard the Hidden One say, "Fine. We will do it tomorrow. We will walk to the main road and wait until the soldiers come, then we will come out without our guns. Prepare for the journey." George was stunned. He was happy to have rediscovered his old persuasive smart self. But he also worried that he was leading them to a terrible end. "What if we get killed?" he wondered.

* * *

In the morning the Hidden One said they should walk to the west, the road was closer, but George said they should go toward South Sudan. "There are soldiers coming and going from Sudan to CAR," he said. "I saw their tracks last year." But the Hidden One disagreed, saying they were safer walking away from South Sudan. "All those new soldiers coming in, eager to shoot holies. We should stay out of their way."

They walked for over three days, stopping late at night. On the fourth day they slowed down, worrying about soldiers or diehards who manned ambushes around the main towns. At the end of the fourth day they found small abandoned huts, some with overgrown vegetable gardens. They were happy to stop at one for the night and feasted on cassava and peanuts.

In the morning they reached the main road that connected Obo with other southern towns. Civilian hid under a large bush near the road while the three waited inside the forest. The plan was for everyone to take turns observing the road. All four took their turns but no soldiers showed that day. Only civilians walking or biking, and the occasional fast-moving car. At dusk, the four withdrew inside the forest and made camp hastily. "Maybe we should have gone east," George said.

The next day was the same; no soldiers of any color used the road. In the afternoon the Hidden One whistled for a meeting. "This is not working, we should walk to the abandoned hut to spend the night, before going back to our old position," he ordered. "Home sweet home," joked the Hidden One when they made it to the old camp, but no one laughed. They were exhausted by the long journey and annoyed that they had not made any progress. They resumed their old routine but the Hidden One went out on patrol with Kidega not George, who was paired with

Civilian. George spoke to Civilian about leaving with him only. "Let us try the other side of the road," he said, "I am sure there will be soldiers coming from South Sudan." Civilian said he was not leaving without the Hidden One.

That night at camp George asked the Hidden One to try and walk east, near South Sudan. He refused, saying it was not safe to try that route but maybe they ought to again think through the plan of going into Obo. "Yes," said George elated, "how do you think we should do it?" "We need good civilian clothes," he said "and a civilian from Obo to interrogate about the town and the whereabouts of the Ugandan troops." "But where do we get the civilian and what do we do after we get the information?" "Kill them," said the Hidden One.

"It does not make sense to get someone from Obo and kill them after they tell us what we need," said George. "What if they lie to us? Why can't we bring them along so they can show us how to get there and maybe help us in Obo?" "Too dangerous to keep a civilian with us, they will deliver us to the diehards," said the Hidden One. "And we need to find clothes. Perhaps we need to attack a small place near Obo and get clothes, food and information." "No," said George, "we cannot. We are too few."

Over the next few days George and the Hidden One rehashed the same conversation, which always ended with the Hidden One saying they needed clothes and an informant, with George having to nod and eventually be silent as the Hidden One was his superior. Everyone grew irritated by the lack of a resolution. One evening, amidst the tension, a cow walked into the middle of the camp, foraging for food amongst their stuff. The four, who sat idly by a small fire, were terrified by the animal's sudden appearance. They covered the fire with earth and looked around intently, worrying about people being nearby. But the cow was clearly lost, far from its owners. "Hallelujah," said the Hidden One, shooting the cow.

They spent most of the night preparing the meat. As most of it dried on top of small fires under the racks, they boiled and fried as much meat they could and ate till early in the morning. Joy returned to the little camp and with it the realization that they might have found a way to secure civilian clothing and information. All they needed to do was find the owners of the cow. The Mbororo would give them clothes and show them the best way to enter Obo. They decided to sleep all morning and find the Mbororo in the afternoon.

* * *

That afternoon they searched for cattle tracks and cow droppings. The mooing of the cows gave away their location and an hour later the four stood in front of a group of Mbororo men clad in black flowing pants and leather vests. George hoped they could communicate in English. "We want to talk to the sultan," he said to the Mbororo, who looked annoyed. "They must be sick of holies always hitting them up for milk and cows," George thought but continued undeterred.

"We come in peace and need your help."

The men, armed with handguns and one holding on to a shiny AK47, said little. Civilian twitched nervously and the Hidden One pointed his gun toward the Mbororo with the Kalashnikov. One of the Mbororo motioned to the four to wait. The sultan appeared alongside a young woman. She was dressed in bright flowery clothes, a true vision of colors that stood out in the dull dark green of the forest. The four stared at her as she walked toward them with her head slightly bowed down. Her skin was olive and she wore a necklace with three large gold squares. She glanced at them and stood quietly next to the sultan.

She listened to the sultan speak and turning to George, said in English, "What do you want?" Embarrassed he had been staring at her for too long, George quickly said, "we, friends." She translated it to the chief. "I mean we need help," George continued and, after a quick look at the other three. "We need your help to go home to our families." When the sultan and the Mbororo men heard what she said, they came closer and seemed to relax. "Let us sit down," said the sultan via the beautiful translator.

George explained the situation and asked for clothes and information on Obo. He made sure not to mention the cow or its remnants still drying on the racks back at camp. "We don't have much to give you," George said "but here is some money we have gathered," shoving in the chief's hands a few notes – mostly Central African francs they had found during lootings. George did not think the money was worth much but the Hidden One had specifically told him to give the Mbororo all the money they had. "They have to take us seriously."

The chief took the money and spoke to his men. George stared at the girl and wanted to ask her where she had learned English but worried the men would be annoyed and kept quiet. He noticed that a few young women and children had come out of the forest and were looking at them curiously from behind trees. He wondered why it was that these people lived like this. This gorgeous woman could easily have been a model or a television presenter. Instead she was here in the bush in the middle of nowhere. And these kids needed to go to school. They probably thought the same thing about him. What was he doing there?

The sultan said that his people agreed to help. They did not have a lot of clothes but would give them what they had. They would also explain how to walk to the Ugandan army barracks in Obo but could not provide a guide. "We are also foreigners in this country and the people accuse us of helping the rebels. We cannot be seen as bringing criminals into the villages even if your intentions are good."

George felt annoyed at the mention of "criminals" and wanted to explain to the translator that things were complicated and they were only trying to survive but he knew it would be no good and explained in Luo to the three what had been said. "We need a guide," cried the Hidden One but George, ignoring him, told the chief *Tamam*, "good" in Arabic, and smiled. "*Tamam, tamam*," the chief smiled back, and the rest of the Mbororo laughed.

That night the four returned to base with three large suits and a jacket as well as some milk and smoked meat. The Mbororo did not have trousers to go with the single jacket. The suits were much too large for the skinny men but George, Civilian and the Hidden One were quick to grab them, leaving only the jacket for Kidega. "I will be the one doing all the talking," said George sheepishly while the other two did not even bother to explain. "Sometimes it pays to talk," thought George as Kidega accepted his fate in total silence, once again.

They planned to follow the directions provided by the Mbororo, which George had noted down on a piece of paper. It had little space left to draw directions and a map, as the Hidden One had used it to keep the scores of all their card games for the last few months. "Why bother keeping the scores?" George wondered, noticing the Hidden One had won all the games.

The Mbororo told George how to walk to Obo using an old cattle path. "It will take you close to the barracks by the airstrip but you will have to walk through one of the *quartiers*, the 'neighborhoods.'" George hoped the distance to the barracks from the bush would be short and that the suits would help them blend in. The Hidden One agreed to hide the guns before they came out into the open. "God help us," he said and made the sign of the cross.

They packed all their food and filled their water bottles. Departure was planned for before dawn. They spoke excitedly that evening about the day ahead and what the morrow would bring and went to sleep. George was too excited to calm down. His heart raced as he thought about going home and then about the beautiful Mbororo girl. "I need a woman," he sighed.

* * *

They set off when it was still dark. Everything was packed, including a large amount of dried cow meat. The chief had told them to prepare for a week's walk but the Hidden One said it might take four days; they walked much faster than the Mbororo, who strolled behind their cattle. But when the sixth day dawned and they were still not near Obo, the Hidden One cursed the Mbororo chief and said he must have lied. He then yelled at George, "do you even know how to read the directions?" George said they were near Obo. He recognized the surroundings.

They were definitely about to reach the outskirts of the town, George could tell by the usual signs of civilian life; small vegetable gardens, broken tools and the odd stray chicken. That night they did not make fire in the camp, set up hurriedly in a small forest. "Eat your dry rations," said the Hidden One, who then gave orders to wake up early in the morning, clean up and change into their civilian uniforms. They hid their guns and all their possessions in the morning. "Best to have as little stuff with as us possible," the Hidden One said and then asked to talk to George separately. "We are doing this Yankee?" he asked with a slightly trembling voice, which surprised George. "Yes Sir," he answered, trying to sound confident.

George had never witnessed any of his superiors in such a state of open fear and weakness, devoid of all the pretend bravery and boasting. He felt sorry for the Hidden One. While George was eager to go back to a world he knew well and where he felt at ease, the Hidden One was about to enter a place he barely knew or remembered. A world in which he would have to renounce all the privilege he had accumulated through fighting and hard work during two decades in the bush. From now on he would have to give up all control and let George – who he tacitly agreed was the man to lead the group thereafter – be in charge.

In the morning they took off their military clothes and washed with a bit of water, trying to clean their hair as much as was possible without soap or a comb. They put on their suits, with Kidega donning the large jacket and his brown camouflage trousers. They laughed at the way he looked. The large jacket covered most of his body, reaching close to his knees. "Good thing," said the Hidden One, "it covers your Dinka parts," referring to the trousers, standard issue South Sudanese military uniform. They hid their guns and ammo and took a small path they hoped would lead straight to the Ugandan army base.

George thought they all looked ridiculous, oversize suits paired with gumboots, but stayed silent, as everyone was nervous already. They planned to walk slowly and not attract attention. George was to walk ahead together with Kidega while the Hidden One and Civilian would follow at a short distance.

Approaching the town they came across the first civilians, washing and brushing their teeth outside of their homes. George nodded here and there and people did not seem to mind the four men. After what seemed a long time of walking, and the sun feeling hotter under the thick suits, they finally entered what George imagined to be Obo town. The red dirt road widened and there were many more houses on both sides of the road. Young children ran around and men and women set off to their daily tasks, fishing, hunting or working in vegetable gardens.

They continued to walk until they reached a crossroads, whereupon they had no idea how to proceed. George had hoped they would see Ugandan soldiers in town but there weren't any. He stopped and the three soon joined him. "What now?" the Hidden One whispered. "I could ask for directions in English," George replied, "or we can sit somewhere and wait for the soldiers." "No way," said the Hidden One, "I am not sitting here, waiting for these people to kill me." "Ask someone, maybe a woman," he said, and continued a few paces ahead alongside Civilian. George saw a middle aged woman walking in the opposite direction and said in as gentle a voice as he could muster, "Excuse me madam, where is the base of the Ugandan army?" She looked at him in wonder, shrugged, said "No" and continued to walk.

George felt awkward standing in the middle of the road, not knowing which way to go in full view of everyone, and asked other people who walked by him. "Where are the soldiers?" he kept asking in English but people gave no answer or indication they understood him. He noticed a tall figure approaching him, initially slowly then increasingly faster until his features were clear for George to notice. The man seemed familiar. "Someone I know from back home?" George wondered with faint hope. "You," the man yelled menacingly in English, pointing his finger at George. "You, bastard."

The man's voice revealed his identity. Faustin, the *kurut*. He was abducted by Odhiambo's men from Obo in February 2008 and spent time in Kony's group. George's mind raced, trying to recall whether he had ever beaten Faustin, but he could not remember. No one was nice to the abductees. He had little doubt about Faustin's feelings when he saw his face, distorted in anger. George did not understand what he said but he knew they were in trouble. "Run," he yelled to the three and took off away from Faustin and a rapidly gathering crowd.

George was the first to run, followed by the Hidden One, Civilian and Kidega. Behind them followed a wild mob, people wielding sticks and machetes and throwing rocks. At first the four maintained a short distance between them and their pursuers but the yelling and loud noises attracted the attention of other inhabitants of Obo, who came out on all sides, often in front of the four, and hit them with anything they could; punches, rocks, pots and pans.

George was hit many times, mostly on his arms and shoulders and the Hidden One bled from his left ear. George turned his head without stopping and saw the crowd getting closer. They grabbed Kidega, who had fallen behind, first and then they got Civilian.

The Hidden One saw Kidega and Civilian on the ground, and screamed, "They are killing them." George saw his terrified blood covered face and yelled, "Keep running." But the Hidden One had already slowed down and three men jumped on him. They punched and kicked him as he lay on the ground trying to protect his head with his hands. George hesitated and thought about helping but more people ran toward him. He was about to reach the end of the road when he felt a sharp pain on the back of his head.

The blow made him stumble and fall. He thought the back of his head and shoulders became moist, probably from his own blood. He saw people gathering on top of him and tried to get away but they punched and kicked him in the body and face. He saw blood spurting from his nose and mouth and trickle in the red dirt beneath. He managed to get up and tried to run but his legs felt heavy. The tiredness and the blows knocked him on the ground again. "*Aol ki wot* (I am tired of walking)," he thought. "I will just lay here and rest, *ka yweyo.* This was God's will, there is nothing more to be done." He closed his eyes and thought of his mother.

* * *

He did not know where he was when he opened his eyes. He was stretched on a bed, a real bed, the kind he had not used in three years. He felt bandages around his neck and jaw and a needle stuck to his right arm connected via a tube to a white plastic bag that hung from a peg above his head. The bed stood inside a small room that had also a brown desk and a white plastic chair next to it. He tried to stand up but his whole body hurt. He put his head on the pillow and tried to remember. "How are you feeling?" a voice said in English. The man asking wore a white coat on top of an army uniform. "What is your name?" he asked.

George was in the Ugandan army base at Obo. He had made it. Somehow, he was spared and ended up in the army field hospital. The doctor patched him up and said he was fine. George could not believe it. He had been certain his end had come and yet he was fine. He walked out of the room soon after the doctor left, determined to find out what had happened to his three friends. He had a terrible feeling made worse by the fact they were not there.

The base was large and included a long flat piece of land where helicopters and airplanes landed. It was strange for George to see close up these beasts that had terrified him and the rest of the holies. There they lay silent and menacing. It was the same feeling with the Ugandan soldiers. Until recently they had been enemies; they could have taken his life, or he theirs. Now they looked at him, with curiosity and some contempt. But George did not care. He only wanted to know what had happened to his friends.

An officer who said he was a lieutenant summoned George for a preliminary debrief. George told him of how they made it to Obo. "What happened to my men?" he asked. "We sent two to Nzara to our hospital there," replied the lieutenant. "They needed a lot of patching up. They were not doing well when we picked them up. But the small one did not make it. He was badly beaten." George immediately knew but asked anyway, "Which one?"

"The one with the camouflage trousers," came the answer.

* * *

He stood up straight, looking around in the dense bush, the butt of his AK47 against his shoulder, the gun pointing forward. He was not comfortable in the brand new green army uniform. The black shiny boots felt tight but he knew they were at least two sizes too big for him. "I have gotten used to the stretchy gumboots," he thought. He turned around and saw his new colleagues from Bravo Company, as they were called. "I don't think they like me," he thought and heard the second lieutenant call to him, "Keep moving soldier."

It was the same officer who had gone with him to retrieve the guns they had hidden before walking to Obo. Everything was there, including Kidega's military jacket, all dirty and ripped. "Why did he save it?" George wondered. Kidega had so little in the world, he saved even the tattered jacket so that he could bring it home, the little he had to show for his years in the bush. George felt his throat tighten and his lower lip quiver.

The soldiers had questioned him for a long time. They asked about his background, his family and time in the

LRA. They asked about Kony and the other officers; what Kony ate, what Kony drank, Kony's wives, everything. He was exhausted. And then they asked him to fetch the guns. They assured him they would protect him.

When they returned to base with the guns, the soldiers seemed nicer. Maybe they finally believed what he said. He was assigned to a small low hut in the base, which he had to share with another soldier. It turned out the other man was a former holy but had left a long time ago when they were still in Uganda. The second lieutenant from Bravo appeared and said George was to join them. "You know how your people fight, you know their tactics, you have to fight for us now," he said. It sounded like an order.

"Don't worry," said the second lieutenant, "we will take care of you. A bank account has been opened in Uganda in your name and your money will be there when you go home." "I just want to go home," said George. "You need to help your country to get Kony," replied the second lieutenant. "It is your duty after we saved your life." The old holy in his hut told him not to believe anything about the bank account. "You will not be paid a cent. Only those who are trained and are formally enrolled get paid, you will get nothing. You don't have much choice. But you get to eat. Try not to be killed."

"Soon, much too soon," George thought. There he was, clad in green Ugandan army uniform with black boots and a Kalashnikov. He had lots of bullets and food in his backpack. Reaching the forest, he could not bring himself to take another step forward. It dawned on him that it was almost three years to the day since he joined the LRA. He had hoped never to see the bush again, never to hold a gun again, never to have to kill again, but despite his best efforts, he was once more in the bush holding a gun, ready to kill. To kill people, some of whom he had considered friends and brothers. Boys, taken by force from their families, and made to suffer, made to kill and die.

The faces of his fallen friends became vivid and he felt dizzy. His head felt heavy and his body started to shake. He lowered his gun to the ground and felt the tears come in violent spasms. His body and the gun in his hand trembled as he bowed, seeing his own tears fall on the thick grass. Through his loud crying he heard the soldiers laugh, then talk to each other in alarmed voices. He faintly heard the voice of the second lieutenant talking on the radio. Two men from his company came near; one took his gun and the other helped him walk away from the bush and to an open area. He heard the sound of a helicopter drawing near but he did not feel afraid. The beast from the sky that had come to hurt him came this time to save him. To take him home.

EPILOGUE

FAR FROM HOME

George was only able to return to Gulu six months after leaving CAR. His first stop in Uganda, after landing in Entebbe, was Kampala, where he spent six months in a so-called "safe house," effectively a detention center run by army intelligence. He was interrogated almost daily and not allowed to leave or speak to his family. The army officers had more questions about his family than Kony and the LRA. George answered the best he could. "Typical," he thought, that the Ugandan army was more interested in finding damning evidence about the political opposition rather than taking on Kony.

When he finally returned to Gulu, a free man, George was happy and relieved to make it out alive and physically unharmed. He even rejoiced to see Quinto, who was awkward and silent. He enjoyed walking the streets of Gulu and seeing old friends. It was strange to see former holies back at home. People who used to be powerful in the bush, now seemingly lost, with no money, homes or even families. Men who had beaten him in the bush now acted friendly, offering smiles and handshakes, and the occasional joke about how things differed in Kony's government.

George tried to resume reading books and fantasized about enrolling in university but found it difficult. He kept thinking instead of the life he had left behind. On more than one occasion he woke up alarmed his group had left him behind, that he was alone in the bush. Often he found himself awake in the middle of the night terrified that he was still in detention and could not leave. He was disturbed to find out that a woman who had come back from the bush a few weeks before still woke up each morning with her things packed, waiting for the whistle to start marching. He tried to avoid talking to former holies, worried that seeing them would continue to bring nightmares and bad memories. But he was terrified that his life was forever changed, forever marked by the LRA experience, forever stuck, waiting for the whistle to sound, waiting for his new life to start.

He tried to forget, he tried to leave it all behind but he was always reminded of the years with Kony. His old school friends avoided him; some even pretended not to recognize him. To them, George understood, he would be forever a violent rebel who could not see any logic beyond the gun. They even had a name for people like George, a *Kony*.

The initial excitement of returning home gave way to boredom and eventually frustration. With the way Quinto pretended the last three years had not happened, with the way his former friends shunned him and with the way his former LRA comrades looked up to him, as if he was now supposed to be in charge. George often told the holies he had nothing but bad memories from the bush and that he resented them for having mistreated him. Some just smiled and walked away, others ignored him but some offered apologies and at times sachets of gin. George noticed a few of them had turned to alcohol. He joined them and felt slightly better.

Before long George started to fight with Quinto, who wanted him out of the house. He was a bad influence on his kids, Quinto said. George knew that Quinto and the rest of the family were afraid of him. They thought George was violent so they always spoke to him carefully, even when arguing. It made George feel powerful at first but eventually he was saddened by the realization that his own family thought of him as dangerous. He wanted to blame Quinto, but decided not to tell him most of what he had done in the bush. "Why make him feel even guiltier than he already feels," George argued later. He eventually left Quinto's house and moved in with his maternal clan in a village far from Gulu.

* * *

In October 2011, about a year after George returned to Gulu, President Obama authorized a bill in support of the Ugandan army operations against the LRA. More than 100 US Army Special Forces, based in Uganda, South Sudan and CAR, acted as military advisers to the Ugandan army. The US government provided logistical support and intelligence to the Ugandan forces, often via US private contractors. The Pentagon had spent a reported $500 million by early 2015 on the counter-LRA

A printout, inside the headquarters of the African Union Mission to Counter
the LRA, Yambio, South Sudan, June 2015.

*operations and the US President authorized the mission
for another year, possibly the last one. The ever-dwindling
Ugandan troops on the ground in CAR appeared increasingly
fed up with the operation. "The President [Museveni] does not
even mention us in public addresses anymore," a Ugandan
commander said in July 2015, "we are orphans."*

*In December 2015 the LRA still existed, albeit at a signifi-
cantly lower capacity than at any point in its almost thirty-year
existence. Only about eighty Ugandan men remained, scattered in small groups in CAR and DRC. In early 2010 Kony
succeeded in making it to Sudan's Kafia Kingi and by early
2011 more than 100 people were based there, believed to be*

only about ten miles from the Sudanese army base of Dafak. The holies started to grow food and trade in the nearby market of Songo in South Darfur.

Many LRA commanders outside of Kafia Kingi were either killed or defected. In May 2012, Caesar Achellam surrendered to the Ugandan army in CAR. In early 2013, Binany was killed by the UPDF in CAR. Binany was returning from Kafia Kingi where he had delivered thirty-eight elephant tusks to Kony, who exchanged the ivory for food and ammunition in the Songo market. Clearly enraged by Binany's loss, Kony ordered the execution of Otto Agweng, his once loyal director general. Kony accused Agweng of having allowed Binany to die, since Agweng was tasked with escorting him unharmed to Congo where Binany's group poached elephants in Garamba Park.

Just weeks before Binany's death, in late 2012, Kony had also ordered the execution of three fighters from Binany's group who had moved the ivory on foot for hundreds of miles from Garamba to Kafia Kingi. Kony accused the three of having raped three young Congolese girls Kony wanted to keep as ting-ting. Fearing the spread of HIV and annoyed at the young men who had openly disobeyed his orders, Kony wanted to reestablish his waning authority. It did not work and combined with Agweng's death it created more discontent. Many defected, including Opiyo Sam, who left in 2014, and Dominic Ongwen, who surrendered in early 2015 and was eventually taken to The Hague to face charges at the International Criminal Court.

In May 2015, seven holies tried but failed to kill Kony before they escaped, later surrendering to the Ugandan army in Obo. It was the first time in the LRA's recent history that simple *fighters had tried to assassinate the Big Boss, signaling perhaps the beginning of the end for Kony and his nearly thirty-year-old organization.*

George's tormentors Otika, Justine, Obwoya and Omony died in the bush at different times after George's defection. It did not give George any pleasure to hear of their demise. He knew they had been forced to lead that life and would have chosen differently if they had a choice. George was upset to find out that Dog's Knee was killed in 2014, trampled by an elephant he had tried to kill in Garamba. "These fellows," George said in July 2015, "they had a very difficult life."

* * *

In July 2015, I met George for the last time. We had seen each other often since 2011 when I first met him. The man of 2015 was much different from that of 2011. His lower lip was no longer swollen and it no longer trembled. He spoke in a calm voice and smiled often. He did not want to talk about the bush or "those fellows" anymore and he never uttered the name Kony. Instead he wanted to talk about his new life in the village and his girlfriend he would like to marry at some point. "I need someone to take care of me," he said.

What had not changed was his desire to plan for the future, always thinking of new projects, which I tried to support as much as I could. In one of our first meetings he spoke of wanting to buy a bike so that he could transport goods between villages. At a later time, he discussed starting another business, this time making bricks for the booming construction business in the villages outside Gulu. If only he had saved the money I had given him and bought his bike, he could have had a way to transport all the bricks he would make, he lamented. In July 2015 his newest brainwave was planting and raising eucalyptus trees so that he could sell them when mature in five years. "There is plenty of money in timber," he told me, smiling.

When the subject of school came up, his mood changed and he became serious. With a hint of sadness he talked about his desire to graduate from high school. "I still want to finish high school and go to university," he said. "I will figure it out," he continued. "But for now I am working the land and making my own food. I don't think about the bush anymore. I am happy."

AUTHOR NOTE

Much has been written about the war between the government of Uganda and the LRA, but events post-Operation Lightning Thunder of December 2008 are less well-established. I hope this book contributes to a better understanding of the most recent chapter in the history of the conflict.

This book is the result of over 600 interviews I conducted between September 2009 and June 2015 in Uganda, South Sudan, the Democratic Republic of Congo and Central African Republic, including with military commanders and community leaders from all four countries and at least 500 people who either defected from or were abducted by the LRA. The vast majority of defectors left the LRA after December 2008.

Numerous former LRA members I spoke to largely corroborated George's version of different events that occurred inside the LRA in recent years. These include the turmoil leading to Vincent Otti's execution, Kony's various movements inside DRC, CAR and South Sudan since December 2008, Kony's plans including attempts to connect with Sudanese Armed Forces staff, and communication methods between dispersed LRA groups. For ease of reading, I narrate those events from George's perspective but in each case, I have gathered multiple eyewitness accounts from LRA combatants, members, and abductees.

Events that predate George joining the LRA and all other information unrelated to George's personal story come from extensive desk research and interviews with those affected by or experts in the long-running conflict.

Many people named in the book are real. In a few instances where I felt someone could potentially face reprisals from authorities or others, I have changed or otherwise obscured identities, especially low-level fighters, many of whom are attempting to rebuild their lives after leaving the LRA. Apart from certain facts I deliberately altered to protect George's identity, I tried to stay as close as possible to his version of events.

In some cases it was not possible to corroborate his account of certain events, particularly when George was alone or when the only other people present at the time are now dead. There might still remain disputable facts. All errors are mine.

SELECTED BIBLIOGRAPHY

Allen, Tim, *Trial Justice: The International Criminal Court and the Lord's Resistance Army*, London: Zed Books, 2006.

Allen, Tim and Vlassenroot, Koen (eds), *The Lord's Resistance Army: Myth and Reality*, London: Zed Books, 2010.

Amony, Evelyn, *I am Evelyn Amony: Reclaiming my Life from the Lord's Resistance Army*, Madison, WI: University of Wisconsin Press, 2015.

Atkinson, Ronald, *The Roots of Ethnicity: The Origins of the Acholi of Uganda*, Kampala: Fountain Publishers, 2001, 2010.

Behrend, Heike, *Alice Lakwena and the Holy Spirits: War in Northern Uganda 1986–97*, Oxford: James Currey, 1993, 1999.

Branch, Adam, *Displacing Human Rights: War and Intervention in Northern Uganda*, Oxford and New York: Oxford University Press, 2011.

Bussmann, Jane, *The Worst Date Ever, or How it Took a Comedy Writer to Expose Africa's Secret War*, London: Macmillan, 2009.

De Temmerman, Els, *Aboke Girls: Children Abducted in Northern Uganda*, Kampala: Fountain Publishers, 2001.

Dolan, Chris, *Social Torture: The Case of Northern Uganda*, Oxford: Berghahn Books, 2009.

Finnström, Sverker, *Living in Bad Surroundings: War, History and Everyday Moments in Northern Uganda*, Durham, NC: Duke University Press, 2008.

Green, Matthew, *The Wizard of the Nile: The Hunt for Africa's Most Wanted*, London: Portobello Books, 2008.

Human Rights Watch, *Trail of Death: LRA Atrocities in Northeast Congo*, 28 March 2010.

Human Rights Watch, *The Christmas Massacres: LRA Attacks on Civilians in Northern Congo*, February 2009.

Kobusingye, Olive, *The Correct Line? Uganda Under Museveni*, Bloomington, IN: Author House, 2010.

Mutibwa, Phares, *Uganda Since Independence: A Story of Unfulfilled Hopes*, Kampala: Fountain Publishers, 1992.

Soto, Carlos Rodriguez, *Tall Grass: Stories of Suffering and Peace in Northern Uganda*, Kampala: Fountain Publishers, 2009.

INDEX